The Worship of the American Puritans, 1629–1730

by

Horton Davies

Soli Deo Gloria Publications
. . . for instruction in righteousness . . .

Soli Deo Gloria Publications
P.O. Box 451, Morgan, PA 15064
(412) 221-1901/ FAX 221-1902

*

Printed in the United States of America.
Published by arrangement with
Peter Lang Publishing

*

Printed by Soli Deo Gloria in 1999

ISBN 1-57358-099-6

Acknowledgments

This work was prepared during the time I was a fortunate member of the Center of Theological Inquiry at Princeton. I am grateful for the friendships made there, and particularly for the encouragement of the Founder, and, until very recently, the Director, the late Dr. James I. McCord. I also wish to thank two admirable administrative assistants for their practical help: Kate Le Van and Patricia Grier. I am glad also to thank Michael Flamini, Senior Acquisitions Editor of Peter Lang Publishing, Inc., whose enthusiasm and warmth, as well as his illumination, reflect his name. The fine photographs illustrating the chapter on architecture are the products of my son Philip, and I thank him for them. Three friends have helped me in different ways: the Rev. Dr. John Booty of the University of the South; Professor John Fleming of Princeton University, and a self-denying publisher, Mr. Dikran Hadidian of Allison Park, Pennsylvania. Finally, I cannot hope to acknowledge adequately my continuing indebtedness to my wife, Helen, for affection and judgment in both academic and personal life.

Horton Davies
Center of Theological Inquiry
Princeton, NJ

Contents

Figures

Introduction

Why write a history of the first century of the worship of the American Puritans? Four reasons have determined the choice of this topic, three professional and the fourth entirely personal.

In the first place, while studies of the religion of the American Puritans abound, no full, detailed account of their worship has yet appeared. Certain aspects of the theme, however, have been thoroughly explored, and they have been of great value to me. Babette May Levy's *Preaching in the First Century of New England's Theology* (1945) drew primary attention to the climactic importance of the sermon in their worship, as well as to its structure and style, while Harry S. Stout's important *The New England Soul: Preaching and Religious Culture in Colonial New England* (1986) impressively argued that the regular Sabbath sermons had a paramount influence in "shaping cultural values, meanings, and a sense of corporate purpose" in New England. E. Brooks Holifield's significant *The Covenant Sealed: The Development of Puritan Sacramental Theology in Seventeenth Century New England, 1570-1720* (1974) expounded its theme as it applied to both England and New England with thoroughness and an enviable theological insight. Charles Hambrick-Stowe's *The Practice of Piety: Puritan Devotional Discipline in Seventeenth Century New England* (1982) fully and sensitively described the devotional discipline, familial and personal, of the American Puritans, but devoted only a single chapter to their public worship. Winton U. Solberg's *Redeem the Time: The Puritan Sabbath in Early America* (1977) is an excellent, exhaustive account of the major weekly red-letter day of the Puritan calendar, and William DeLoss Love's *Fast and Thanksgiving Days of New England* (1895) offers illumination about those special extra days. Zoltan Haraszti's introduction to his edition of *The Bay Psalm Book* (1956) is also a survey of early American Puritan praise.

Many books have also been written that elucidated Puritanism's faith and ways of life which incidentally refer to public worship. Such are the classical works of Samuel Eliot Morison, Perry Miller, and Edmund Morgan, to all of whom one is inevitably indebted when writing on any facet of American Puritanism. Furthermore, individual works of distinction have proved invaluable, such as David D. Hall's *The Faithful Shepherd: A History of the New England Ministry in the Seventeenth Century* (1972) and Robert Middlekauff's *The Mathers: Three Generations of Puritan Intellectuals* (1971). None of these, however, has addressed the public worship of the American Puritans in depth and detail. It is that lacuna that this book tries to fill.

My second reason for embarking on this enterprise is the conviction that the vision of Puritanism was normally communicated from one generation to another in the gathering of Puritan families on the Lord's Day in their meetinghouses at worship. There they heard the promises of the gospel, learned the obedience of faith, and responded with all the gratitude of the elect, as they received the sacraments of baptism for their children, and of the Lord's Supper for themselves, as the seals of the covenant in which God bound Himself to them and them to Him for time and for eternity. Above all, it was in their gathering for public worship that they heard the

Word of God in all its majesty as the minister, assisted by the Holy Spirit, conveyed the divine revelation in Scripture. This abased the proud and elevated the humble, and gave God's people their spiritual iron rations and their future marching orders.

Furthermore, the pioneering type of worship the Puritans developed in both England and New England, with its rigorously biblical basis, its extemporaneous prayers, its covenantal tie to God and each other, its expression of the priesthood of all believers, and its encouragement of a lay, uncloistered piety, while of historical interest, is also of current relevance. It is the parent of the Free Church tradition in worship, which has become the dominant mode in the Baptist, Congregational, Disciples of Christ, Methodist, Pentecostal, Presbyterian, and Reformed churches, as well as the Unitarian families of churches, which have thrived in the English-speaking parts of the world. Its impact, moreover, is far from spent because of the modern Charismatic movement, which employs supplementary extemporary prayers in the historic liturgies of the Roman Catholic and Anglican communions.

The third reason for this study is the importance that the founders of American Puritanism gave to a pure worship, unalloyed by merely human traditions without biblical mandate; this was a major reason for leaving England for New England, where in the wilderness they might adore God in the ways He desired without ecclesiastical and secular penalties, as was the case in Laudian England. This pious motive was discounted by James Truslow Adams in his *The Founding of New England* (1921); he argued that it was cod, not God, the first New Englanders sought. Even so, motives of the Puritan leaders certainly included the desire to practice a pure worship and a way to show their friends in England the worship of the future.

This was certainly the major motive of the primary theologian of New England, John Cotton. In his catechism, *Spiritual Milk for Babes in Either England*, published in London in 1646, and reissued in Boston in 1668, his answer to the question of the meaning of the Second Commandment was "that we should worship the true God with true worship, such as God hath ordained, not such as man hath invented."[1] This had been expanded in his important work, *The Way of the Churches of Christ in New England* (1645). There he insisted that, in the assembling for worship on every Lord's Day, "our principall care and desire is to administer and partake *in all*, and *no more then all*, the ordinances of Christ and in all those (so farre as the Lord has lent us light) in their *native puritie and simplicitie*, without any dressing or painting of humane inventions."[2]

Thomas Shepard's *Autobiography* (edited by Michael McGiffert under the title *God's Plot*, 1972) offers several reasons for his pilgrimage to New England, including the fact that Laud prevented him from exercising any ministry in England, the importunity of godly friends already in New England or intending to voyage there, and his dejection in seeing Puritan leaders such as Thomas Hooker and John Cotton leaving for America. A significant motive for him was the following: "My judgement was then convinced not only of the evil of ceremonies, but of mixed communion and joining with such in sacra-

---

[1] p. 2.
[2] p. 65.

ments." He added, "I saw it as my duty to desire the fruition of all God's ordinances which I could not enjoy in old England." With typical honesty he confessed, "Though my ends were mixed, and I looked much to my own quiet, yet the Lord let me see the glory of those liberties in New England and made me purpose, if ever I should come over, to live among God's people as one come out of the dead, to his praise."[3] These "liberties" included the opportunity to devote one whole day in seven, the Sabbath, to God, without sullying it with boisterous ales and games that *The Book of Sports* issued by James I and Charles I so strongly encouraged. Thus the Puritans dedicated the entire Sabbath to God with not only Sunday morning and afternoon sessions of worship, but with personal and family prayers in the morning and evening together with catechizing. In addition, the head of each family required the children and the servants to repeat the main points of the sermons they had heard that Lord's Day. Puritan devotional discipline was rigorous, and included the writing of diaries seen only by God, in which were detailed promises to serve Him and a list of sins committed and deeply regretted. It was this fully fledged religious discipline, aided by the Puritan calendar, with its special days of humiliation and days of thanksgiving correlated with the divine Providence, which could not be practiced in England without harassment, which made the wilderness of New England, for all its physical and cultural hardships, a veritable paradise for those men and women who aspired to be "visible saints."[4]

---

[3] *Op. cit.*, 56.
[4] For the important Puritan concept of "visible saints," see

John Allin, the earliest minister of the Dedham, Massachusetts church, insisted that "only the hope of enjoying Christ in his ordinances" was a sufficient motive to persuade the emigrants "to forsake dearest relations, parents, brethren, sisters, Christian friends and acquaintances, overlook the dangers and difficulties of the vast seas, the thought whereof was a terror to many . . . and go into a wilderness, where we could forecast nothing but care and temptation."[5]

While even the motives of the most earnest are mixed, Breen's study of the 273 migrants from East Anglia and Kent (on whom we have the fullest information as to age, origins, and occupations) comes to the conclusion that economic motives did not dominate religious considerations.[6] Skilled clothworkers, as many of them were, could have earned better livings in the Netherlands. It is likelier that they could no longer brook the harassment by High Church Bishop Wren's overzealous church officials, who drove out three thousand families from the diocese of Norwich between 1635 and 1638.[7] One of the victims, the master weaver, Michael Metcalfe, when

---

Edmund S. Morgan's *Visible Saints: The History of a Puritan Idea* (New York: New York University Press, 1963) and Geoffrey F. Nuttall's *Visible Saints, The Congregational Way, 1640–1660* (Oxford: Blackwell, 1957).

[5] *Defense of the Answer Made unto Nine Questions or Positions Sent from New England* (London, 1648), cited by Kenneth A. Lockridge, *A New England Town, The First Hundred Years: Dedham, Massachusetts* (New York: Norton, 1970), 23.

[6] See Chapter 3 of *Puritans and Adventurers: Change and Persistence in Early America* (New York: Oxford University Press, 1980).

[7] See R. W. Ketton-Cremer, *Norfolk in the Civil War: A Portrait of a Society in Conflict* (London: Faber, 1969), 70–79.

hauled into court for refusing to bow at the name of Jesus, defended himself with such pertinacity that the church official screamed at him, "Blockhead, old heretic, the devil made you, I will send you to the Devil."[8] It is significant that towns from which the East Anglians like Metcalfe emigrated to New England sent seven ministers there and two others to Holland.[9] It was common knowledge that the East coast towns made good tradesmen and good Puritans who loathed Laudian ceremonialism. Peter Heylin, subdean of Westminster Abbey, wrote: "It was not hard matter for those [suspended] Ministers and Lecturers to persuade them to remove their dwellings and transport their trades," for "New England was chiefly in their eye a Puritan plantation from the beginning and therefore fitter for the growth of the Zwinglian or Calvinian gospel than any country whatsoever." Significantly, Heylin insisted that these Puritans were "long discharged from the bond of ceremonies."[10]

Another inducement for lay Puritans to come to New England was that their own ministers were emigrating there, and this was a way of receiving Christ's unpolluted ordinances, but without harassment. In 1633, as Cotton Mather quipped, the people of the Bible Commonwealth had "*Cotton* for their *Clothing*, *Hooker* for their *Fishing*, and *Stone* for their *Building*."[11] There was a veritable apostolic succession of converting Puritan preachers, and two

---

[8] For his troubles, see "Michael Metcalfe," *The New England Historical and Genealogical Register*, XVI (1862), 280–88.

[9] Breen, *op. cit.*, 53.

[10] Cited in Browne, *A History of Congregationalism*, 101–2.

[11] *Magnalia Christi Americana* (London, 1702), III, 20.

of the most impressive were in New England. Darrett Rutman expresses their impact vividly:

> The generation of ministers of this sort approaches something of the quality of the opening chapter of *Chronicles:* "Richard Rogers begat [in a spiritual sense] Paul Baynes, who begat Richard Sibbes, who begat John Cotton, who begat John Preston, who begat Thomas Shepard."[12]

Moreover, the relationship of minister to congregation was much closer in New England than in Virginia. In 1650, there was a minister for every 415 people in Massachusetts, while in 1649 in Virginia there was a clergyman to serve 3,259 persons.

One of the pioneers, Captain Edward Johnson, published an enthusiastic account of New England in 1654 entitled *The Wonder-Working Providence of Sions Saviour in New-England.* He may very well have been a recruiter in Kent for Puritan emigrants to New England.[13] In his book, he insisted that all hardships and deprivations "in this howling desert" were cheerfully borne "that they might enjoy Christ and His Ordinances in their primitive Purity."[14] Johnson envisioned the spiritual life of New England as the furthest extension of the Reformation and the restoration of the true Church of Christ. He foretold the imminent ending of the sway of all officers of the traditional churches, as Christ's herald proclaims:

---

[12] *American Puritanism* (Philadelphia: Lippincott, 1970), 7.

[13] Breen, *op. cit.*, 67.

[14] *Wonder-Working Providence*, ed. W. L. Poole (Andover, Mass., 1867), Epistle to the Reader.

> Babylon is fallen, both her Doctrine & Lordly rabble
> of Popes, Cardinals, Lordly Bishops, Friers, Monks,
> Nuns, Seminary Priests, Jesuits, Ermites, Pilgrims,
> Deans, Prebends, Arch-Deacons, Commissaries,
> Officials, Proctors, Somners, Singing-men, Choris-
> ters, Organists, Bellows-blowers, Vergers, Porters,
> Sextons, Bends-men and Bel-ringers, and all others
> who never had name in the Word of God . . . .[15]

Johnson also claimed that in years of severe droughts the godly begged God's mercy, "urging this as a chiefe argument, that the malignant adversary would rejoyce in their destruction, and blaspheme the pure Ordinances of CHRIST, trampling down his Kingly Commands with Their owne inventions."[16]

The millennialism of Johnson probably exaggerated the purity of the motives of the settlers.[17] All in all, the motives must have been mixed, for these were men, women, and children, not angels. Along with religious enthusiasm, the desire for Christ's ordinances in their New Testament purity, and the ambition to be a saint in a church of saints, as well as a citizen of New or Newer Jerusalem, there were also those who sought the main chance, or who desired adventure, or wished to disengage themselves from unhappy situations, such as a spoiled marriage, domineering parents, or dictatorial employers. Nonetheless, the religious incentive was paramount for many and powerful for others.

---

[15] *Ibid.*, 23–24.

[16] *Ibid.*, 57.

[17] The most recent critical survey of the motives of those engaged in the "errand into the wilderness" is Andrew Delbanco's "The Puritan Errand Reviewed," *Journal of American Studies*, 18 (1984), 343–60.

The double concern of the new immigrants of 1638 for religious fidelity and liberty to worship in Christ's pure ordinances is powerfully expressed in Thomas Tillam's poem entitled *"Uppon the First Sight of New England."* It begins lyrically:

> Hayle holy land wherein our holy lord
> Hath planted his most true and holy word
> Hayle happy people who have dispossest
> Your selves of friends, and meanes, to find some rest
> For your poor wearied soules opprest of late
> For Jesus-sake, with Envy, Spite . . .

And he imagines that Christ fulfills His promise:

> Posses this country, free from all anoye
> Heare I'le bee with you, heare you shall enjoye
> My sabbathes, sacraments, my minestrye
> And ordinances in their puritye.[18]

The central importance of these pure ordinances of Christ in the life of New England, combined with a sense of God's smiling or frowning on the individual or the society in His providences, is plainly affirmed in Michael Wigglesworth's *Diary*, written from 1653 to 1657, as in the following entry: "prophaness [sic] of heart and spiritual slumber which is not savouring of the things of god, and a secret remissness in my spirituall watch, these frequently surprize me, though god be frequently jogging me by his ordinances and providences and will not suffer me to take any long and quiet sleep."[19] This reference is

---

[18] *Seventeenth Century American Poetry*, ed. Harrison T. Meserole (New York: Norton, 1972), 397–98.
[19] *The Diary of Michael Wigglesworth, 1653–1657: The Conscience of a*

significant, since it was never meant to be published, and least of all was it a theological advertisement as Edward Johnson's tribute was.

Fourthly and finally, as one who from 1940 to 1943 prepared an Oxford doctoral dissertation subsequently published as *The Worship of the English Puritans* (reprinted by Soli Deo Gloria in 1998), I have always intended to write this companion volume, to see exactly how Puritan worship developed in early America, freed of the constraints under which, then as today, Puritans labored in England. As a Congregational minister in England, one was made acutely aware of the so-called inferiority of the "chapel" compared to the superiority of the "church," and the very architecture of these Nonconformist chapels, described in Anglican derision as "squalid sluttery," emphasized that second-class status. It was a delight, in visiting New England in 1952, to contrast the size, situation, and style of historic Congregational churches in New England, where the famous Old South Church in Boston had almost the grandeur of a cathedral. Years later, I became familiar with the white-robed Congregational church in Brookfield, Connecticut, which was centrally located, and the elegant Congregational meetinghouse in Strafford, Vermont, which commanded the hill of the town. These examples were not atypical in their beautiful simplicity, their centrality, their purity of style, and their powerful historical impact on the spiritual and cultural life of their communities. The dissidence of Dissent was never a primary interest in

---

Puritan, ed. Edmund S. Morgan (Vol. #35 of the publications of the Colonial Society of Massachusetts, reissued as a Harper Torchbook, New York, 1965), 17.

classical Congregationalism. Its dissent was solely for the purpose of following Christ in His ordinances.

The number of these "pure ordinances" of public worship (note the implication of the word as being ordered by Christ for His Church), their character, their justification, and their historical development in early New England will be the theme of succeeding chapters. It will be interesting both to look out for innovations in New England's worship that distinguish it from English Puritan worship and to see the continuities that linked Puritanism on both sides of the Atlantic Ocean. The topic is, to use John Cotton's fine evaluation of Puritan ordinances, that "Adoration which is Christian worship."

1

The Beginnings

This chapter is meant to provide a general description of the earliest ordinances of worship in New England, using the accounts of Cotton and Lechford. Cotton was the outstanding spiritual authority who had himself been converted by the great Richard Sibbes, and in turn had converted Preston, the only Puritan to be chaplain to Charles I. Moreover, he was one of only three New Englanders appointed to the Westminster Assembly. His authority, therefore, is paramount as a reporter of the religious scene of New England, where he was minister of the First Church of Boston. Lechford, by contrast, was an Anglican layman who dissented strongly from the Puritan way and is interesting in providing alternative suggestions for the arrangement of worship.[1]

One is impressed by the novelty of the worship in several ways. First and foremost, one notes the determination to use all the ordinances in their pristine purity as Christ's commands in Scripture, and thus to avoid the

---

[1] The writings of John Cotton used in this chapter are *The Way of the Churches of Christ in New England* (London, 1645); *The True Constitution of a Particular Visible Church* (London, 1642); and *The Keyes of the Kingdom of Heaven* (London, 1644). Lechford's work used in this chapter is *Plaine Dealing: Or, Newes from New England* (London, 1642).

arrogance of human invention, which is idolatry
condemned by the Second Commandment. It is this that
accounts for the insistence on the biblical basis of all the
ordinances. This leads to the denial of any formal liturgy
and the demand for extemporaneous prayers, and it even
determines the correct order for the different types of
prayers. Cotton reports:

> First then when we come together in the Church,
> according to the Apostles direction, *I Tim. 2. 1.*, we
> make prayers and intercessions and thanksgivings
> for ourselves and for all men, not in any *prescribed*
> forme of prayer, or *studied Liturgie*, but in such a
> manner; as the Spirit of Grace and of Prayer (who
> teacheth all the people of God what and how to
> pray, *Rom. 8. 26, 27*) helpeth our infirmities; we
> having respect therein to the necessities of the
> people; the estate of the times and the worke of
> Christ in our hands.[2]

A similar biblical fidelity requires (as its sole justification) the use of two prayers of consecration in the
Lord's Supper, one for blessing the bread and the other
for blessing the wine. Cotton reports that the double consecration follows Christ's example in instituting the
Lord's Supper and that the elements are "not less *together*,
but either of them *apart*; the bread first by it selfe and
afterwards the wine by it selfe; for what reason the Lord
himself best knoweth."[3]

It is the absence of any biblical direction that accounts for the disuse of such ceremonies or customs used
in the Book of Common Prayer as the signing of the cross

---

[2] *The Way*, 66–67.
[3] *Ibid.*, 68.

in baptism and the insistence on fathers as sponsors rather than godparents. It also calls for the disuse of the kneeling gesture at Communion, and instead for the insistence on sitting for its symbolic value. Cotton says of kneeling that it is merely "an adoration devised by man but also a violation by man of the institution of Christ, diminishing part of the Counsell of God and of the honour and comfort of the Church held forth in it."[4] As for sitting, it is justified as the manner in which Christ administered the Last Supper, "who also made a Symbolicall use of it, to teach the Church their majoritie over their ministers in some cases, and their judiciall authoritie, as co-sessors with him at the Last Judgment."[5] Godparents are excluded because the divine covenant is offered to parents and their seed, and no substitution should be made: "The *Father* presenteth his only child to baptisme as being baptized by the right of *his Covenant*, and not of the Covenant unto God-fathers and God-mothers."[6] All these instances of citing a biblical basis for innovations are characteristic of Puritan worship; it gave it an authority even in its innovations and accounted for its strength.

Another impression one receives is the immense significance of the concept of visible sainthood, clearly insisted upon in the restriction of the sacraments to families of the church who are theologically instructed, who have had an experience of grace, and have solemnly covenanted to serve Christ. Cotton firmly establishes the preconditions:

---

[4] *Ibid.*, 68.
[5] *Ibid.*, 68.
[6] *Ibid.*, 68.

> Both the sacraments we dispence, according to the
> first institution [of] Baptisme to *Disciples* and (who
> are included in them) *their seed*. The Lords Supper
> [is given] to such as neither want *knowledge* nor
> *grace* to *examine and judge* themselves before the
> Lord. Such as lie under any offence publickly
> known, doe first remove the offence, before they
> present themselves to the Lords Table; according
> to *Mat.* 5.23, 24.[7]

The demand for visible sainthood is clarified in the
procedure for admission to church membership. This
takes place during the conclusion of the afternoon service
on the Lord's Day.[8]

Another radical innovation is found in the Puritan
calendar, so different from the Roman Catholic and
Anglican church year. The Puritan calendar is distinguished by its climactic red-letter Lord's Days and additional special days of thanksgiving and humiliation dependent upon their reading of the divine Providence.
Cotton reports as follows: "Besides the celebration of the
Lords Day, every weeke we sometimes upon extraordinary occasions, either of notable *judgements*, doe set apart
a day of *humiliation*, or upon speciall *mercies* wee set apart
a day of *thanksgiving*."[9]

The Puritan unwillingness to commemorate chief
events in the life of Christ, and the disuse of the sanctoral
cycle, are vehemently opposed by Lechford, who argues:

> And why not holy dayes as well as the fift of
> November, and the dayes of Purim among the

---

[7] *Ibid.*, 67–68.
[8] *Ibid.*, 70.
[9] *Ibid.*, 70.

> Jews? Besides, the commemoration of the blessed
> and heavenly mysteries of our ever blessed Savior,
> and the good examples and piety of the Saints?[10]

This worship also stresses the priesthood of all believers, since it requires a godly profession of faith from all church members, a hearty singing of psalms, and the equal vote of all the members in the decision to call and ordain a minister, and to admit or refuse new members into the church community. Moreover, the earliest simple churches, which were built by the hands of the flock worshipping in them, had no chancel separating priest and choir from the laity as in the Anglican or Roman Catholic manner. All suggested unity and equality under Christ. This all gave a powerful thrust toward democracy. The only exceptions were, of course, the minister and teacher, but even they, in the foundation of the earliest churches, had been elected and ordained by the people, instead of being set apart by a hierarchical representative such as a bishop, or by a group of ministers, as in Presbyterianism.

Larzer Ziff has rightly insisted on the centrality of the democracy of the community of the saints, because it was a case of "each man ultimately a priest in himself and the consequent view of the minister as a member of the community selected to be its leader because of his greater learning and discernment, but not because of what was indeed impossible, his superiority in grace."[11] However, with the restriction of church membership to the godly, and the further restriction of the vote in Mas-

---

10 *Plaine Dealing*, 20.
11 *Puritanism in America: New Culture in a New World* (New York: Viking Press, 1973), 279.

sachusetts to church members, the democracy of the "plebeian ordination" all too rapidly became an elite christocracy. But this was not foreseen at the beginning.

One is also impressed by the climactic role of preaching in the worship, symbolized by the elevated central pulpit, in front of which rested the Bible, emphasizing the minister's primary role as expositor of the oracles of God. One can imagine that when this part of the service was reached, members of the congregation would shuffle their chairs or benches to make themselves as comfortable as possible and settle down to concentrate on a holy oration. This would have been prepared by their minister after a week's reading of the Old and New Testament in the original languages, illuminated by the best commentaries. It would provide the congregation with a disquisition that pursued the triple structure of doctrine, reason, and use, combining intellectual illumination with appeal to the heart in order to nerve the will to Christian obedience. Children and servants would also listen to the sermon with rapt attention, because it was not a formal homily, nor a pedantic and witty utterance ("more of Plato than of Paul"), but the wisdom of God plainly delivered. In addition, the children and servants would be expected to recount the main points of the sermon when questioned that evening by the master of the house. Some of the more enthusiastic church members would summarize the sermon on notepads in their amateur shorthand. The Puritan sermon was a major intellectual exercise, and all Puritans honored a learned ministry. Why otherwise was Harvard College founded in the first decade after the arrival of the first settlers except to train an indigenous ministry? This is also why two sermons and a weekly lecture were required in all

Puritan churches.

As we have seen, the biblical mandate gave Puritan worship, despite its novelty, an awesome authority, yet, because of its novelty, an exciting and almost millenarian sense of the end of the days in which Christ's reign on earth was anticipated. The absolute insistence on reliance upon a God-initiated covenant, and the conviction that only a pure Church of visible saints was acceptable to Christ, nerved the Puritans, in dependence on grace, to heroic endeavors in the wilderness of New England. It also gave them coherence—a feeling of unity and interdependence—despite the independence of each local church. They were a consecrated theocracy, and were reminded of such in each diet of worship, and they could only survive through mutual aid under God in frontier conditions where the hostility of the Indians, the harshness of the winters, and the primitive nature of the earliest dwellings and horticulture created difficulties otherwise insurmountable. The need for absolute unity among the pioneers is perfectly expressed by Governor John Winthrop aboard the *Arabella*, on the Atlantic Ocean on his way to found the Massachusetts Bay Colony in 1630:

> For this end we must be knit together as one man. We must entertain each other in brotherly affection. We must be willing to abridge ourselves of our superfluities for the supply of others necessities. We must uphold a familiar converse with each other in all meekness, patience and liberality. We must delight in each other, rejoice together, mourn together, always having before our eye our community as one body. We must consider that we shall be as a city upon a hill. The eyes of all people are upon us.

Setting aside the explanatory material just considered, what then are the form and order of Puritan worship of the earliest years as certified by Cotton and Lechford with remarkable unanimity?

On each Lord's Day there were two services, one in the morning commencing about nine o'clock and the other in the afternoon beginning about two o'clock. Each service was arranged in the following order and we may assume that what was done in Boston was also done elsewhere in New England:

> Opening Prayer of Intercession and Thanksgiving
> Reading and exposition of a chapter of the Bible
> Psalm singing
> SERMON
> Psalm singing
> Prayer
> Blessing

The sole modification in morning worship was a monthly or bi-monthly celebration of the Lord's Supper. The only occasional changes in the afternoon service were baptism, a collection (called the "Contribution"), and, occasionally, the admission of new members.[12]

Lechford describes the collection vividly:

> One of the Deacons saying, Brethren of the Congregation, now there is time left for Contribution, wherefore as God hath prospered you, so freely offer. . . . The Magistrates and chiefe Gentlemen first, and then the Elders, and all the

---

12 The information is derived from Lechford's *Plaine Dealing*, 16–22, Cotton's *The Way*, 60–70, and Cotton's *The True Constitution*, 5–8.

> congregation of men, and most of them that are not of the Church, all single persons, widows, and women in absence of their husbands, come up one after another one way, and bring their offerings to the Deacon at his seate, and put it into a box of wood for the purpose. . . .[13]

Lechford adds that when meetinghouses are to be built or repaired, money or promissory notes may be offered, or even precious metals, and recalls, "I have seen a faire gilt cup with a cover, offered there by one, which is still used at the communion."[14]

The sacraments were celebrated with due care that they be unpolluted by unworthy Christians and attended only by "visible saints." Cotton emphasizes that the Lord's Supper is administered "to such as neither want *knowledge* nor *grace* to *examine* and *judge themselves* before the Lord."[15]

Such members as lie under any offense publicly known must remove it before attending Communion. Members of other churches will be admitted to the Lord's Supper only if they bring testimonial letters with them.[16] Similarly, an attempt is made to keep the Church pure by limiting baptism to "Disciples and (who are included in them) their *seed*."

The order for the Lord's Supper is as follows:

> In time of the *solemnization* of the Supper, the Minister having taken, blessed, and broken the bread, and commanded all the people to take and

---

13 *Plaine Dealing*, 18.
14 *Op. cit.*, 19.
15 *The Way*, 67.
16 *Ibid.*, 67-68. See also *The Keys of the Kingdom of Heaven*, 17.

> eate it, as the body of Christ broken for them, he taketh it himselfe and giveth it to all that sit at Table with him, and from the Table it is reached by the *Deacons* to the people sitting in the next seates about them, the Minister sitting in his place at the Table.
>
> After they have all partaked in the bread, hee taketh the cup in like manner, and *giveth thankes anew* (blesseth it) according to the *example* of Christ in the Evangelist who describes the institution. *Mat.* 26. 27. *Mark* 14. 23. *Luk.* 22.17. All of them together . . .
>
> After that celebration of the Supper, a Psalme of thanksgiving is sung, (according to *Mat.* 26. 30), and the Church dismissed with a blessing.[17]

Only ministers were allowed to administer the two sacraments. Repentance and faith were the conditions for admission. At the Communion, the sitting posture is strongly stressed. This is not only to avoid the idolatrous danger of kneeling, as implying a belief in transubstantiation, but positively and symbolically to emphasize the privilege of co-session with Christ in judgment at the Grand Assize at the end of history, and to remind Christians of the rest given by God to the faithful. As Stephen Mayor rightly observed of this gesture, "As always, symbolism expelled by the front door, reenters by the back."[18]

---

[17] *Ibid.*, 68–69.

[18] *The Lord's Supper in Early English Dissent* (London: Epworth Press, 1972), 67ff. Mayor provides an analysis of American conditions of admission to the Puritan Lord's Supper. He points out the paradox that ironically the demand by Cotton for restricting entry to the Church in order to avoid hypocrisy in its members finally endangered the sacrament by turning the Church into a small and

How long did the services last? The opening prayer took about a quarter of an hour, while the longer prayer after the sermon (which in some churches preceded it) could last an hour, indeed as long as the sermon itself. Thus, if we include the exposition of the lesson, the psalm-singing, the offertory, and the final blessing, each service must have lasted from three to three-and-a-half hours. Jasper Danckaerts, the Dutch Labadist, visited the Boston Church in 1680. He reported that "a minister made a prayer in the pulpit of full two hours in length" and that in the afternoon service "three or four hours were consumed with nothing except prayers, three ministers relieving each other alternately."[19]

Prolix prayers became even longer in the early eighteenth century, as can be seen from Peter Thacher's observation that he "stood about three hours in prayer and preaching." On another occasion he wrote: "God was graciously pleased to assist me beyond my expectation. Blessed be his holy name for it. I was near an hour and a half in my first prayer and my heart much drawne out in it, and an hour in the sermon."[20] The impression is given

---

self-satisfied elite. Edmund Morgan demonstrates in his *Visible Saints*, 64-113, that prerequisites to membership were tightened further by the requirement of a narrative of an experience of saving grace. The result was that it became necessary to liberalize the terms of admission to membership as both Baxter in England and Stoddard in New England saw. The latter even argued that Communion was a converting ordinance. For Stoddard's view, see *The Safety of Appearing at the Day of Judgement in the Righteousness of Christ* (Morgan, Pa.: Soli Deo Gloria, 1995).

[19] B. B. James and J. F. James, eds., *Journal of Jasper Danckaerts, 1679-1680* (New York: Scribner's, 1913), 261–62.

[20] Cited in Charles E. Hambrick-Stowe, *The Practice of Piety*, 104. Even in the 1640s, Thomas Shepard wanted to "stretch out" his

that the holier the minister, the longer his prayers, and ordination services in which several ministers prayed must have developed into spiritual marathons to the exhaustion of the congregation.

In any case, the six hours granted to the minister for preaching and prayer, to rehearse the mighty acts of God in salvation and the appropriate response of the people, made the Sabbath central to the existence of the people of New England, according to Sacvan Berkovitch.[21] The Sabbath was not only prepared for by the public weekday lectures and daily domestic prayers and Bible readings, but it was a completely holy day of rest with an eschatological reference to the destiny of human pilgrimage. This Thomas Shepard asserted in his *Theses Sabbaticae* (1649, reprinted by Soli Deo Gloria):

> And as the rest of the Day is the holinesse of it, so is all the labour of the week for this holy rest; that as the end of all the labour of our lives is for our rest with Christ in Heaven, so also of the six daies of every weeke for the holy rest of the Sabbath, the twilight and dawning of heaven.[22]

Thus the irksomeness a secular mind might sense in these services was not felt by these earnest Puritans, for the Sabbath was the climax of their week and the preparation for the anticipation of life with the saints in eternity.

---

prayers, arguing that brevity presumed formality and lack of affection. See his *Journal*, entry for August 29, 1642, in McGiffert, ed., *God's Plot*, 187.

[21] See *The American Jeremiad* (Madison: The University of Wisconsin Press, 1979).

[22] *Op. cit.*, 65.

Other services, according to Cotton, included lectures held upon a weekday, which he described as aiming "so that such whole hearts God maketh willing . . . (if they dwell in the heart of the Bay) may have opportunitie to heare the Word almost every day of the weeke in one Church or other, not farre distant from them."[23] These lectures were chiefly of a doctrinal character, supplementing the more evangelical and hortatory sermons preached on Sundays. Additional services were held on special occasions which Cotton specifies: "Besides the celebration of the Lords Day, every weeke we sometimes upon extraordinary occasions either of notable *judgements*, doe set apart a day of *humiliation*, or upon speciall *mercies* wee set apart a day of thanksgiving."

All special or occasional services, including weddings, funerals, and ordinations, will be treated in detail in subsequent chapters as we move from the seventeenth to the eighteenth century.

The chapter may appropriately end with the attempt to describe the spirit of an early American congregation at worship so that the bare bones of forms and orders will be fleshed out.

We must imagine the intensely expectant faces of the congregation, the older members of which have committed themselves firmly to the Christian way by the dangerous sea voyage that brought them from England to New England, the subsequent hardships of pioneers, and the solemn signing of the church covenant, by which they promised to follow Christ in all His ordinances and in return expected the felicity and rest of the saints in heaven.

---

[23] *The Way*, 70.

Their eyes are fixed on the minister, who wears the grave Genevan gown with the white neck bands, in the central, elevated pulpit. Below him the ruling elders sit, and below them the deacons. In the earliest days, there would be no pews, only seats and rough forms or benches. Later the towns would allow individuals to build pews in the meetinghouses at their own expense. Later still, it was customary for church officers to request that such pews be constructed "with wainscote worke and all of a kind."[24] The magistrate and the gentlemen would occupy the front seats and the men, women, and children would be separated according to sex on opposite sides.

They can see each other's eager faces as the sun streams through the plain glass windows, and this is in itself an encouragement. They take great pride in the meetinghouse built with their own hands. Cotton Mather, the first historian of New England, and a notable member of the third generation, declared that "every town, for the most part can say, We have a modest and a handsome house for the worship of God, not set off with gaudy, pompous, theatrical fineries, but suited unto the simplicity of Christian worship."[25]

The earliest meetinghouses were inevitably simple constructions of sawn planks with thatched roofs. In some cases they were protected by surrounding palisades, with a sentinel guarding the gate. Later the meetinghouses were more elaborate, larger and more elegant, being covered with boards and roofed with shingles,

---

[24] E. H. Byington, *The Puritan in England and New England* (4th ed., New York: Franklin, 1900), 143.
[25] *Ratio Disciplinae Fratrorum Nov-Anglorum* (Boston, 1726), 5.

often including a steeple with a bell.

The sun provided the only light in the meetinghouse and it must have been extremely cold in winter without stoves or any other means of heating. H. M. Dexter states that the first mention of a stove in a church was as late as 1773 in Boston's First Church.[26]

Points of interest would be provided by the simple visual drama and symbolism of the baptismal sprinkling of babies and the breaking of the bread on a pewter charger and the pouring of the wine in the gilt or pewter chalice at Communion, as well as in the procession of individuals placing their gifts in the deacons' box. There would also be interest in observing the men who went forward at the start of the service to give the minister the papers on which special petitions were written for him to include in his long prayer. Such were the major points of visual interest in a service that was dominantly aural.

The Puritans in their preparation for worship, in their solemnization of the Sabbath which began at sundown on Saturday evening,[27] in their regimen of daily prayers and introspective diaries, and in rehearsals of the sermon must have been inspired to worship with an intense ardor and expectancy. This all the records clearly indicate.

---

[26] Byington, *op. cit.*, 46, fn. 1.
[27] See Winton U. Solberg, *Redeem the Time: The Puritan Sabbath in Early America* (Cambridge, Mass.: Harvard University Press, 1977), 111.

2
The Theology of Worship

The theology of Puritan worship may be technically defined as scholastic Calvinism, or more precisely as federal or covenant theology. This had been further developed by such English theologians as William Perkins and his pupil William Ames, and the latter's pupil, John Cotton. Ames and Cotton, together with Bradshaw and Sibbes, were important members of the second Puritan generation. The conclusions of this system of theology were formulated in the Westminster Confession in 1643, which was modified only with reference to ecclesiology by the Independents in their Savoy Declaration of 1658. The liturgical compromise of Presbyterians and Independents in the Westminster Directory of Worship appeared in 1644. These formulae were prepared by English Puritans during the Commonwealth and Protectorate, while the first generation of settlers was established in the New England theocracy.

Puritanism, it should be recalled, was then almost three generations old since the Vestiarian Controversy at the start of Elizabeth's reign, which had been anticipated by Bishop Hooper in the days of Edward VI. Hence there was already available a detailed Puritan critique of the Book of Common Prayer backed by a vertebral theological defense.[1]

The Exclusive Authority of Scripture

This was essentially not a philosophical theology, but a biblical theology, and in this way it showed its Calvinian heritage. Luther had claimed that the Bible in general, and the New Testament in particular, was the authority for faith and ethics—to use his own word, it was a *Trostbuch*, eliciting faith. Luther allowed tradition to play a role in the church as long as it was not forbidden by Scripture. Calvin, by contrast, insisted that Scripture was to be dominant as God's law in church and state. His principle was, in reference to God, *Quod non jubet, vetat* (He forbids what He does not command). Thus Scripture was to be dominant not only in faith and ethics, but as God's law it must dictate church worship and polity. For Calvin the Bible was, in his own words, *"la saincte parole et loi de Dieu,"* the holy Word and law of God. The Puritans followed Calvin in their insistence that *sola Scriptura* (Scripture alone) was the paramount and exclusive liturgical criterion.

There were two reasons for this. One was that since Scripture was the divine law, God would disown human traditions and inventions oblivious of the scriptural mandates as sheer idolatry and disobedience.

A primary early authority for New England Puritans was William Ames, whose *Medulla Theologica* was translated as *The Marrow of Sacred Divinity* (London, 1638). He

---

[1] See my *Worship of the English Puritans* (Morgan, Pa.: Soli Deo Gloria, 1997) for a study of its theme from the time of Cranmer to Isaac Watts; and also my *Worship and Theology in England:* vol. I, *From Cranmer to Hooker,* and vol. II, *From Andrewes to Baxter and Fox* (Princeton, N.J.: Princeton University Press, 1970–1975).

affirms, "All things necessary to salvation are contained in the Scriptures, and also those things necessary for the instruction and edification of the Church." His conclusion is: "Therefore, Scripture is not a partial but a perfect rule of faith and morals. And no observance can be continually and everywhere necessary in the Church of God, on the basis of any tradition or other authority, unless it is contained in the Scriptures."[2] It should be recalled that the *Medulla* of Ames was the textbook in theology for all Harvard college students preparing for the bachelor's degree throughout the seventeenth century.

William Bradshaw, in his *English Puritanisme* (London, 1605), makes the same claim, affirming that the ways of worship "ought evidently to be prescribed by the Word, or else ought not to be done."[3] John Coolidge rightly asserted that "the Puritan understanding of the Scriptures is in terms of obedience."[4] In all Puritan justification of differences of worship from the Book of Common Prayer, this was the first authority cited and the last court of appeal.

The second reason proving the inadequacy of a dependence upon tradition or human invention in matters of faith was the *haereditas damnosa* since the Fall, or original sin. As St. Augustine had seen, man is hopelessly crippled, a moral hunchback, twisted in on himself. Perkins defined original sin "as nothing else but a disor-

---

[2] *Marrow*, 189. The best modern translation with a historical introduction is John Eusden, *The Marrow of Theology, William Ames, 1576–1633* (Austin, Tex.: Pilgrim Press, 1968). This work was reprinted by Baker Book House in 1998.
[3] *Op. cit.*, 4.
[4] *The Pauline Renaissance in England* (Oxford: Clarendon Press, 1970), 4.

der of evil disposition in all the faculties and inclinations
of men, whereby they are carried inordinately against the
law of God."[5] Puritans claimed that man was unable to
choose the good because his reason was blinded by pride,
and therefore he was incapable of the humility that repentance should bring. They would have argued against
the Anglicans, who valued tradition and human reason
alike, that the galleon of human nature, richly laden with
the treasures of antiquity and steered by man's natural
reason, was bound to shipwreck on the rock of human
perversity. God's law and direction in Holy Writ alone
could be trusted in matters of religion, however commendable reason and tradition were in secular life.

Thus the all-sufficiency of Scripture and the radical
inadequacy of man through original sin clarified the necessity for dependence upon the creative, providing, and
directing omnipotent adequacy of God the Father and
Creator, Christ the Savior and Exemplar, and the Holy
Spirit the Inspirer and Enabler, all revealed in Holy
Writ.

Justification by Faith and Predestination
These are the two central doctrines that preserve the
sole salvific mediatorship of Christ, and the divine omnipotence and direction of the world and mankind by
God. These were the breastplates of the Puritan theological armor. Predestination was the extension of justification by faith through grace. Predestination asserted that
salvation was wholly the work of God, and that Christ's
strong grip of the soul guaranteed salvation, despite the

---

5 *The Works of That Famous and Worthy Minister of Christ in the
University of Cambridge*, 3 vols. (Cambridge, England, 1613), I, 165.

soul's feeble grip on Christ. This assurance of belonging to the predestined elect offers great comfort to those who accept it, for it assures them that, however powerful temptation or suffering may be, they cannot lose their salvation, as God has willed it for His elect. The consolation is particularly strong when the faithful are part of a resistance movement such as that of the Huguenots in France (whose motto reminded them that the elect are an anvil that has worn out many hammers) or the persecuted Puritans in Restoration England, or their predecessors, the first New England Puritans fleeing Laudian persecution and enduring bitter hardships.

William Haller saw Puritanism's thrust as a vital form of English Calvinism centered on "the dynamic Pauline doctrine of faith, with its insistence on the overwhelming power of God, on the equality of men before God, and on the immanence of God in the individual soul."[6] The steel of the Puritan soul was the conviction of the truth of the doctrine of predestination with the ringing assurance of St. Paul's battle cry: "If God be for us, who can be against us?"[7]

The Puritan program was to purify or purge all elements of the worship and polity of the Church of England from false traditions and popish errors and to bring them into conformity with the Word of God, and to produce a holy commonwealth in New England. Although he was no friend of Puritanism, Heylyn knew its historical roots and the origin of its nickname, for under the caption "Anno Reg. 7" he wrote:

---

[6] *The Rise of Puritanism, 1570–1643* (New York: Columbia University Press, 1938), 8.
[7] See Romans 8:31 in the context of verses 28–35.

> This year the *Zwinglians* or *Calvinian* faction began
> to be first known by the name of *Puritans*, which
> name hath ever since been appropriate to them,
> because of their pretending to greater Purity in the
> Service of God, than was *held forth* unto them (as
> they gave it out) in the *Common-Prayer* Book; and to
> a greater opposition to the Rites and Usages of the
> Church of Rome, than was agreeable to the
> Constitution of the Church of England."[8]

Special Providence and the Covenant

Correlative to predestination was the strong belief in
special providence. This was the conviction of Puritans
that in the events of national, ecclesiastical, familial, and
individual life one must search for the hidden hand of
God. This would be found in teleological or dysteleolog-
ical events, indications of the divine favor or chastise-
ment. They were looking (to change the metaphor) for the
smiles or frowns of Providence in daily life. Milo
Kaufman makes the fascinating suggestion that the
Puritan's substitute for the guidance of churchly tradition
was the analysis of his own experience: "He made of his
past a surrogate for ecclesiastical tradition, and the surrogate was evaluated as a private tradition in which God
had disclosed His mind by the way in which He carried
out promises and threatenings in His Providence and
judgments."[9]

Hence life itself became a second scripture through
which the Written Word might be better understood.
Puritans took seriously the advice of Thomas Gouge: "In

---

[8] *Ecclesia Restaurata, A History of the Reformation of the Church of England* (London, 1661), 172.

[9] *The Pilgrim's Progress and Traditions in Puritan Meditation* (New Haven, Conn.: Yale University Press, 1966), 201.

reading the Promises and Threatenings, the Exhortations and Admonitions, and other parts of the Scripture: so apply them to thyself, as if God by name had delivered the same to thee."[10] Moreover, the Puritan treasured private providences as evidence of his election. There were, as will be seen later, two difficulties in the interpretation of providence and judgments: their ambiguity and the danger of dualism, positing God and Satan as the two ruling agencies.[11]

Nonetheless, this interpretation of the smiles and frowns of divine Providence became institutionalized in the Puritan calendar in special days of thanksgiving and humiliation. The idea was formulated within the context and structure of covenant or federal theology. It is clearly manifested in the instructions given in the Westminster Directory for the celebration of such days. The minister's task on a day of humiliation is:

> in his own and his people's names, to engage his and their hearts to be the Lord's, with professed purpose and resolution to reform whatever is amiss in them and more particularly such sins as they have been more remarkably guilty of; and to draw nearer unto God, and to walk more closely and faithfully with him in obedience, than ever before.[12]

---

[10] *Christian Directions* (London, 1661); the citation is from Gouge's *Works* (London, 1706), 199.

[11] This is discussed later in chapter 3.

[12] Note that the following citations from the English Puritan–Presbyterian *Westminster Directory of Public Worship* are contemporary with the first generation of Puritan immigrants to America, and certainly influenced their worship profoundly, especially considering that three of their number were invited as ministerial delegates to the Westminster Assembly. *Op. cit.*, "Concerning Solemn

Such duties were incumbent on individuals as well as nations. According to the Directory, the minister may instruct the individuals:

> out of scripture that diseases come not by chance or by distempers of the body only, but by the wise and orderly guidance of the good hand of God to every particular person smitten by them . . . and whether this is intended as Divine displeasure against sin for its correction or for trial and exercise of his graces, it will work for good if a sanctified use is made of God's chastening.[13]

Furthermore:

> when some great and notable judgements are either inflicted upon a people or are apparently imminent, or by some extraordinary provocations notoriously deserved; as also when some special blessing is to be sought and obtained, public solemn fasting . . . is a duty that God expects from that nation or people.[14]

The prayer on such a national occasion, the main topics of which are listed in the Directory, demands an acknowledgment of God's majestic sovereignty, a recognition of His righteousness and of human sinfulness; implores His mercy on church and nation; refers to the divine promises; and reaffirms the covenantal commitment.[15]

Special providence in the life of the individual, the nation, and the church all presupposed a covenant rela-

---

Public Fasting," 76–77.
[13] *Op. cit.*, 66–67.
[14] *Op. cit.*, 73–74.
[15] *Op. cit.*, 75.

tionship between God and His people. The Puritans emphasized the difference between the Old and the New
Covenants. The Old was a covenant of works, the New a
covenant of grace. The Old demanded perfection and led
to despair, while the New, through the mediatorship of
Christ, imputes righteousness to the believer, engages
him to serve God cheerfully, and gives him the grace to
perform this religious life. A new church was gathered
and founded on the basis of a minimum of seven men
uniting in a solemn covenant to serve Christ. Members
were added to a church by signing a covenant. The very
sacraments of the gospel—baptism and the Lord's
Supper—were seals of the covenant, through which God
performed His promises for His people. When the third
generation of American Puritans was apparently growing
slack, as in its religious duties, and the ministers
preached jeremiads, the backsliders were encouraged to
renew their church covenant by the indefatigable
Increase Mather.[16]

Covenants provided two advantages in the religious
life. In making them one was committed to serve God
with heart, mind, and will. This was more than a top-of-
the-mind religion, or making a historical assertion as in a
creed; it was a solemn engagement in depth for time and
eternity. Second, it gave great encouragement. Puritan
scrupulosity often caused the individual to wonder
whether he or she was one of the elect, but the taking and
keeping of the covenant helped to diminish anxiety be-

---

[16] John Quick, *The Young Man's Claim to the Holy Sacrament of the
Lord's Supper* (London, 1691; Boston, 5th ed. 1728), 8-9, the Boston
edition. For a full account of the spiritual significance of the
covenant, see Peter Bulkley, *The Gospel-Covenant; or the Covenant of
Grace Opened* (2nd ed. London, 1651).

cause God kept His promises. Furthermore, it was "a reaction against a mechanistic version of Calvinistic deter-
minism."[17] It is not, as Perry Miller had argued,[18] that a
bargain had been struck after haggling which obligated a
reluctant deity to keep His promises, but, as Norman
Pettit insists,[19] that if the individual exhibits faith and
obedience, God will do His part.

Ecclesiology

The simplicity, solemnity, and thoroughness of
commitment in making a church covenant can best be illustrated by citing in full the covenant of the Church at
Salem, founded in 1629. The covenant was elaborated
about a decade later. It reads as follows:

> 1. First we avowe the Lord to be our God, and our-
> selves his people in the truth and simplicitie of our
> Spirits.
>
> 2. Wee give ourselves to the Lord Jesus Christ, and
> the word of his grace, fore the teaching, ruleing and
> sanctifyeing of us in matters of worship, and con-
> versation, resolveing to cleave to him alone for life
> and glorie; and oppose all contraire wayes, canons
> and constitutions of men in his worship.
>
> 3. Wee promise to walk with our brethren and sis-
> ters in the Congregation with all watchfullness, and
> tendernis, avoyding all jelousies, suspitions, back-

---

17 H. Richard Niebuhr, "The Idea of the Covenant and American
Democracy," in *Church History*, XXIII (June, 1954), 129-35.

18 *The New England Mind: From Colony to Province* (Cambridge,
Mass.: Harvard University Press, 1937), 2, 19, 55.

19 *The Heart Prepared: Grace and Conversion in Puritan Spiritual Life*
(New Haven, Conn.: Yale University Press, 1966), 120, 219f.

byteings, conjurings, provoakings, secrete riseings
of spirit against them, but in all offences to follow
the rule of the Lord Jesus, and to beare and for-
beare, give and forgive as he hath taught us.

4. In publick or private, we will willingly doe nothing to the offence of the Church, but will be willing to take advise for ourselves and ours as ocasion
shall be presented.

5. Wee will not in the Congregation be forward
eyther to show our owne gifts or parts in speaking
or scrupuling or there discover the fayling of our
brethren or sisters butt attend an orderly cale there
unto; knowing how much the Lord may be dishon-
oured, and his Gospell in the profession of it,
sleighted by our distempers, and weakness in pub-
lyck.

6. Wee bynd ourselves to studdy the advancement
of the Gospell in all truth and peace, both in regard
of those that are within, or without, noe waye
sleighting our sister Churches, but useing theire
Counsell as need shall be; nor laying a stumbling,
before any, noe not the Indians, whose good we desire to promote, and soe to converse, as wee may
avoyd the verrye appearance of evill.

7. Wee hearby promise to carrye ourselves in all
lawfull obedience, to those that are over us in
Church and Common weale, knowing how well
pleasing it wil be to the Lord, that they should have
incouragement in theire places, by our not greive-
ing theyre spirites through our iregulareties.

8. Wee resolve to prove our selves to the Lord in
our particular calings, shunning ydlenes as the bane
of any state, nor will we deale hardly, or opressingly
with Any, wherein we are the Lords stewards: also

9. Promyseing to our best abilitie to teach our children and servants, the knowledge of God and his
will, that they may serve him alsoe and all this, not
be any strength of our owne, but by the Lord
Christ, whose bloud we desire may sprinckle this
our Covenant made in his name.[20]

Other striking characteristics of the Salem covenant,
beside the depth of the commitment involved, are its
realism in anticipating communal difficulties, and its
mutual concern for, as well as dependence upon, grace.
The same characteristics are true of almost all ecclesiastical covenants.[21] The essence of taking a church covenant
is concisely described by Samuel Sewall, the future
judge, in a diary entry for March 30, 1677: "I, together
with Gilbert Cole, was admitted into Mr. Thacher's
Church, making a solemn covenant to take the L. Jehovah
for our God, and to walk in Brotherly Love and
watchfulness to Edification. Goodm. Cole first spake,
then I, then the Relations of the Women were read: as we
spake, so were we admitted, then alltogether covenanted.
Prayed before, and after."[22]

If the covenant conception is one pointer to the
Puritan definition of the church, the other is the concern
for visible sainthood. The two concepts are interrelated,
as is made clear in John Cotton's definition of the
Church. His catechism in reply to the question, "What is

---

[20] *The Records of the First Church in Salem, Massachusetts, 1629–1736*
(Salem, Mass.: Essex Institute, 1974).
[21] See Champlin Burrage, *The Church Covenant Idea* (Philadelphia,
1904).
[22] *The Diary of Samuel Sewall*, ed. M. Halsey Thomas, 2 vols. (New
York: Farrar, Straus & Giroux, 1973).

the Church?" answers, "It is a Congregation of Saints joyned together in the bond of the Covenant, to worship the Lord, and to edify one another, in all his Holy Ordinances."[23] Calvin had defined the Church as existing where the gospel was preached and where the sacraments of baptism and the Lord's Supper were administered, and where a godly discipline was maintained. The Puritans went one rigorous step further by insisting that the Church must consist of *visible saints*. Previous theologians had claimed that the Church was invisible because only God knew the human heart. The Puritans, however, delved into motives. As Edmund S. Morgan has so convincingly shown, the demand for a test of saving faith in all candidates for church membership originated among the nonseparating Puritans in Massachusetts and spread thence to the communities of Plymouth, Connecticut, and New Haven and then back to England.[24] Sainthood had to be made *visible*.

Narrations of Saving Faith

A careful procedure was established whereby the candidate was interviewed by the elders as to his knowledge of the fundamentals of Christian doctrine, and as to his appropriate behavior. Then one of the ruling elders at the church meeting would ask members to check by inquiring as to the future member's behavior. Any infractions of Christian behavior required either explanation or repentance. The latter could be private or public. Finally, the candidated was required to give an account of

---

[23] *Spiritual Milk for Babes* (Boston edition of 1668, originally London, 1646), 11.
[24] *Visible Saints*, 66.

the work of grace in his soul, which took about a quarter of an hour, and a statement of his beliefs. If these conditions were fulfilled as confirmed by the vote of the church members, he accepted the covenant and thus became a full member of the local church.[25]

Thomas Shepard prescribes the ideal type of narration of saving grace in *The Parable of the Ten Virgins*, which, although published in London in 1660, was based on sermons preached between 1636 and 1649 [and has been reprinted by Soli Deo Gloria]. The best relations include "such things as tend to shew, Thus I was humbled, then thus I was called, then thus I have walked, though with many weaknesses since, and such special providences of God have seen, temptations gone through, and thus the Lord hath delivered me, blessed be his Name, &c."[26]

Shepard's abstract account, however, needs to be supplemented by the vivid reality of these "relations" or narrations as told by prospective church members. Several of them were recorded by Shepard himself, and the most detailed and extensive narrative (it is rather a religious autobiography) is the work of Captain Roger Clap. Finally, it will be worth comparing these relations with those recorded by the Reverend John Rogers, Puritan pastor in Dublin.

Shepard recorded the confessions of the route to salvation offered by fifty-one persons applying for member-

---

[25] The paragraph is a summary of Cotton's *The Way*, 6–10, 54–58; Lechford's *Plaine Dealing*, 12–29; Edward Johnson's *Wonder-Working Providence*, 214–17; and Edmund S. Morgan's *Visible Saints*, 88*f.*
[26] *Op. cit.*, II, 200, cited by Morgan, *Visible Saints*, 92.

ship in the Cambridge Church between 1638 and 1645.
Unlike Saul's dramatic conversion on the road to
Damascus, these conversions were the result of an extensive period of agonizing introspection, and of considerable doubts and fears that any sense of assurance was
prompted only by hypocrisy. Recurring temptations
followed by renewed repentance and debilitating uncertainty marked the preparatory path to salvation, always
leaving the soul afraid of unworthiness and frequently
seesawing between fear and hope. Brother Crackbone's
wife, for example, reported: "and so [I] thought of seeking
after the ordinances, but I knew not whether I was fit.
Yet heard I was under the wings of Christ, one of them,
yet not under both."[27] The intensity of the hunt for
saving grace is illustrated by the relation of a seaman,
William Andrews:

> And at sea I got books, searching between a true be-
> liever and a temporary, as Dike [probably Daniel
> Dyke's *The Mystery of Self-Deceiving*, London, 1615]
> and Rogers's *Seven Treatises*. And I sought God to
> give peace and searched after promises that He
> would take away [a] stony heart.[28]

Some earnest souls, such as Barbary Cutter, sought a
positive value in the negative experience of doubting:
"And since, [the] Lord hath let me see more of Himself
as in doubtings. That Lord did leave saints doubting as to
remove lightness and frothiness, hence doubtings, and to

---

[27] *Thomas Shepard's Confessions*, eds. George Selement and Bruce C.
Woolley (Boston: Collections of the Colonial Society of Massachusetts, vol. VII, 1981), 140.
[28] *Ibid.*, 119.

cause for fresh evidence, and by this means kept them from falling."[29] The second generation, as in the case of Will Ames, son of the famous theologian, feared that advantages might become disadvantages: "But when encouragements came in that I was born of good parents in covenant yet I could not but see I might be Esau and hence I resolved and renewed resolution to seek after God."[30] These testimonies indicated the deep seriousness of the strenuous self-analysis included in the preparatory discipline prior to receiving the gift of grace.

Roger Clap, a captain of militia, came across to New England in 1630 at the age of twenty-one, and became Captain of the Castle, or chief fortress of the province. Grateful for the guidance of Providence, he wished to direct his seven surviving children to follow God as he had done, though in easier circumstances than the first Dorchester settlers. Despite the early difficulties ("Bread was so very scarce, that sometimes I tho't the very Crusts of my Father's Table would have been very sweet to me"[31]), the consolations were richly spiritual. The gospel was preached with fidelity, and the fruit of the preaching was conversion: "The Discourse, not only of the Aged, but of the Youth also, was not, *How shall we go to England . . . ?*, but *How shall we go to Heaven? Have I true Grace wrought in my Heart? Have I Christ or no?*"[32] Clap asserts that many reports of saving grace helped others to see "whether any work of God's Spirit were

---

[29] *Ibid.*, 92.
[30] *Ibid.*, 211.
[31] *Memoirs of Roger Clap, 1630* (Boston: Collections of the Dorchester Antiquarian and Historical Society, 1844), 20.
[32] *Ibid.*, 20–21.

wrought in their own Hearts or no?"[33] He adds that these
relations indicate

> that God doth work diverse ways upon the Hearts of
> Men, even as it pleases him; upon some more sen-
> sibly, and upon others more insensibly, verifying
> the text in the 3d Chapter of John 8th Verse, "The
> wind bloweth where it listeth, and thou hearest the
> sound thereof, but canst not tell whence it cometh
> and whither it goeth. So is every one that is born of
> the Spirit."[34]

Unhappily, Captain Clap had to confess, "If ever
there were the Work of Grace wrought savingly in my
Heart, the Time when, the Place where, the Manner
how, was never so apparent unto me, as some in their relations say it hath been unto them."[35] He tells of his
early Sabbath-breaking, of his doubts, of John Cotton's assurance that "a little constant stream of Godly Sorrow, is
greater than great Horrour."[36] Finally, during one exhausting night, he tested himself by asking and answering
the following question: *"Whether if God would assure me
that I should be saved, although I should commit such a sin, my
heart were willing to omit it or no?* And my Heart and Soul
answered, *No, I would not sin against God, though I should
not be damned for sinning, because God has forbidden it."*[37]
This experience assured him that he was indeed a child
of God. The sense of assurance was so powerful "that it

---

[33] *Ibid.*, 21.
[34] *Ibid.*, 21.
[35] *Ibid.*, 22.
[36] *Ibid.*, 24.
[37] *Ibid.*, 25.

did so transport me as to make me cry out upon my bed with a loud voice, *He is come, He is come*: And God did melt my heart at that time, so that I could and did mourn and shed more tears for Sin, than at other times: Yea, the Love of God, that He should elect me and save such a worthless one as I was, did break my very Heart."[38] The struggle of Clap's soul against sin, fear, temptation, and uncertainty can be measured by the relief that came with the assurance that he was, indeed and at last, one of God's elect, though undeserving.

The forty narrations of grace reported by Rogers seem to establish a firm pattern. Most begin with a profound sense of sin as a divine call. Sometimes this is accompanied by the fear of hell, which leads to a desire to follow an improved life. This legalistic sorrow and the attempt to gain salvation by good works are discovered in time to be formalistic and futile. The recognition of the impossibility of earning grace leads to the acceptance of Christ's full forgiveness, an inner peace in the heart, and the sense of the Holy Spirit enabling one to live a sanctified life. These intending church members seem to experience less fear of hypocrisy and less desperate searching for assurance than the souls in Thomas Shepard's keeping. Also, while several are called to God in vivid dreams or trances, many others experience quiet and undramatic conversions.

Captain John Jecock, for example, heard the call of God in a troubled conscience, so afflicted that he acknowledged, "I was afraid of every bush and tree that I met with in the darke," but was helped by prayer, and by the unusual experience of the coruscating blinding of

---

[38] *Ibid.*, 25–26.

God's light—"The sweet manifestation of love."[39]

The experience of Humphry Mills was less miraculous. His father was High Sheriff and he was one of eleven sons. Upon the death of his father, the family broke up, and Humphry was in sorrow for his sins for three whole years, although he attended sermons regularly. During this time he was a formalist and a precisian, delighting to censure reprobates. He finally found grace in a "precious" Christian wife and in the ministry of Dr. Sibbes—"that sweet saint"—and he is careful to add that, although he lost fourteen hundred pounds sterling in trade, "I found God to deal very graciously with me."[40]

Frances Curtis had a harsher but not atypical experience. She was called by afflictions outward and inward. She reported, "In these I was stripped by the Rebels," heard that her husband had been killed by the Rebels, and was later turned out of doors with her child in her arms. Nevertheless, God saved her life and her husband's: "In hearing my prayers and tears and now in satisfying my soul with himself, I have received much sweet satisfaction by Mr. R[ogers]."[41]

One wonders if the unity discerned in the Rogers narrations is partly due to editorial work. Several thank Mr. Rogers or other Puritan ministers for their help. Many claim to have been formalistic and precisians. Two intriguingly use the Puritan vernacular, claiming to "roll

---

[39] The relations reported by John Rogers are included in his treatise, *Ohel or Beth-Shemesh, A Tabernacle for the Sun or Irenicum Evangelicum* (London, 1653). Jecock's narration, the sixth, is on pp. 389–90.

[40] *Ibid.*, 410. This is the twelfth narration.

[41] *Ibid.*, 423. This the twenty-seventh narration.

on Christ."[42] Even allowing for editorial adaptation, the Rogers narrations show their authors had a smoother path to salvation than the rockier road and slippery path in New England.

Another characteristic of Puritan ecclesiology was the democratic and unhierarchical nature of the early Independent religious communities. The first American churches expressed the priesthood of all believers strikingly in that they were often founded by laymen, who then ordained their ministers even if they had previously ministered to other congregations. Nothing could more strikingly demonstrate their unity as equal servants of Christ. The ligature of the ecclesial community is the covenant.

But, as the seventeenth century wore on, partly through Presbyterian criticism (chiefly that of Samuel Rutherford and Charles Herle) embarrassing American Puritans, and partly through the growing educational advancement of ministers, and the increasing number of Anglican priests, so-called "plebeian ordinations" (as Cotton Mather termed them) ceased. The first exclusively clerical ordinations took place in 1681 at Milton, in the case of Peter Thacher, where, according to his diary:

> Mr. [Increase] Mather called the Votes [for Thacher's election], Old Mr. Eliot, Mr. Torry, Mr. Willard laid on Hands. Mr. Torry gave the Charge, Mr. Willard gave the right hand of fellowshipe. We sung the 24ps[alm]. Then I gave the blessing.

---

[42] "Rolling on Christ" is a phrase employed by the thirteenth and thirty-fifth narrators, respectively Ruth Emerson and Jeremy Heyward.

Apart from their votes in the election, the lay officers of the local church took no other part in the ordination. But the democratic nature of the local churches gave each member in good standing an equal vote and the right to full expression of his or her views.[43]

Paradoxes of Puritan Theology

The manifold and profound anxieties manifested in the New England relations of the work of saving grace exhibit the paradoxes in Puritan preparationist theology, and the circularity of some Puritan arguments that made the path to salvation a razor's-edge climb up a high mountain with steep precipices on either side. One has only to examine Thomas Shepard's *Journal* to see how hard it was to find assurance unparalyzed by the fear of hypocrisy and the scrupulous anxiety that defeated the confidence in one's election. As Michael McGiffert defines the problem, "Often a perpetuation of the ill was included, as Shepard's experience suggests, in the prescription of the cure."[44]

There were many factors that rendered a sense of assurance extremely problematical. Firstly, it was an unpenetrable mystery: only God knew who were saved and who were damned. Secondly, it was commonly assumed that the number of those elected was small—Shepard had declared that only one in every thousand damned was saved.[45] Thirdly, salvation implied an unlikely victory

---

[43] Thacher's "Diary," MS I, 212 (typescript in the Massachusetts Historical Society, Boston).

[44] *God's Plot: The Paradoxes of Puritan Piety, Being the Autobiography & Journal of Thomas Shepard* (Amherst: University of Massachusetts Press, 1972), 4.

[45] *The Sincere Convert*, 4th edition, corrected (London, 1646), 98,

over the power of original sin, total depravity, and a limited atonement—a formidable set of hurdles. Fourthly, the search for faith (since it was by faith and not by works that souls are saved) was a radically inward investigation subject to the many dangers of subjectivity. Fifthly, the fear of hypocrisy could confuse the individual believer and render assurance uncertain. Sixthly, the Puritan road to salvation ran between the opposing snares of Antinomianism and Arminianism. And, finally, if one felt pleased at the thought of being elect, that probably meant that one was relying on feelings, not faith, for salvation. The ambiguities created by all these negative factors are clearly expressed in Shepard's journal entry for December 7, 1642:

> On lecture morning this came into my thoughts, that the greatest part of a Christian's grace lies in mourning for the want of it. I say the greatest part because there is some life and feeling withal. And hence (1) I saw that he who hath his grace lying and appearing chiefly in feeling of it is a pharisee and proud, if there be high-flown expressions and the least part is mourning for want or equally mourning for want; (2) that a poor Christian lamenting his wants is the most sincere; (3) that the Lord when he shows mercy to any of his, it is in withholding much spiritual life and letting them feel corruption.[46]

In what David Levin has described as "the dizzy world of circular argument" of the Puritans, it was essential to accept the central paradox that one's claim to

---

reprinted by Soli Deo Gloria in 1991.
[46] *God's Plot*, 198.

election depended upon one's conviction that one does
not deserve election, nor can one earn it. As a consequence, Levin rightly insists that for many of them "the
drama of guilt, self-doubt, and self-accusation was a terrible reality. . . . The penitent sinner who wanted to join
the Church might be crushed (in Edward Taylor's
phrase) between desire and fear—between a longing to
profess his conversion and a fear that it is delusory."[47]

Another Puritan paradox is illuminated by Peter
Benes. He argues that the New England Puritans, as
Calvinists, believed in total depravity, the irresistible
work of grace, and the ultimate salvation of a handful of
saints. Yet, as covenanting Calvinists, binding themselves
to live exemplary lives, they acted as if the converse
were true—that good works were an essential condition
of salvation. Even if this expression of their views is corrected by the more accurate concept that sanctification
follows justification, this meant that an individual's disposition to behave like a saint was a consequence of his
having been elected by God, yet it was entirely beyond
the individual's control. Benes therefore concludes,
"The Puritan thus placed himself in the unenviable position of striving to receive a spontaneous and God-given
assurance of grace, without being able to do anything to
bring it about."[48] This further accentuates the problem
of Puritan belief. All this, in fact, makes it more difficult
to understand the conviction of the true Calvinist that
election is a most comfortable doctrine, since God's

---

[47] *The American Puritan Imagination*, ed. Sacvan Bercovitch, 148.
[48] *The Masks of Orthodoxy: Folk Gravestone Carving in Plymouth
County, Masssachusetts*, 1689–1805 (Amherst: University of Massachusetts Press, 1972), 4.

promises never fail, and salvation is the act of God, not man.

This custom of requiring accounts of saving grace was probably begun in 1633 and fully established by 1640. As early as 1631, under the leadership of Governor John Winthrop, the General Court had opened freemanship to all church members, when the tests were not as stiff as they became in 1636. It was the Puritan zeal for holiness that lay behind this demand for purity in church members.

Fitness for Admission to the Sacraments

As we shall see in considering the two gospel sacraments of baptism and the Lord's Supper, great controversies arose in New England regarding how to prevent their profanation by lax conditions, on the one hand, while, on the other, to avoid church membership dwindling away by rigorous conditions of admission. Over-rigorous tests, which required evangelical narrations of conversions, meant that if the situation continued, the majority of the congregations would have unbaptized children. Thus it was that in 1662, the famous or infamous "Half-Way Covenant" was devised and approved. This allowed the children of baptized parents in good standing to be baptized, and affirmed that "Church-members who were admitted in minority, understanding the Doctrine of Faith, and publickly professing their assent thereto; not scandalous in life, and solemnly owning the Covenant before the Church . . . their Children are to be Baptized."[49]

---

[49] Williston Walker, *The Creeds and Platforms of Congregationalism* (Boston: Pilgrim Press, 1960), 325–28.

It was inevitable in time that there should be not only a liberalizing of the terms of admission to baptism but also of admission to the Lord's Supper. It was Solomon Stoddard, Northampton pastor, who in 1677 relaxed the conditions of entry to Communion by not requiring any narration of saving grace, and who came to believe that the Lord's Supper was itself a converting ordinance. This led to a prolonged theological battle between the Mathers and Stoddard, but the latter's view did not become dominant among the ministers of New England.[50]

There were, of course, difficulties in deciding whether one had in fact received saving grace or not. God dealt severely with some, and gently with others. Thomas Hooker said that the Holy Spirit enters the hearts of some with a pin and others with a sword.[51] Not everyone had the gift of public utterance, so in time intending members were allowed to provide written attestations. But the rigorous insistence upon evidence of conversion seemed to the first and second generation of American Puritans the only way to secure the purity of the church, and to distinguish the elect sheep from the reprobate goats.

It is clear that the insistence upon the exclusive authority of Holy Writ, the demand for a covenant, and the

---

[50] See Increase Mather's veiled reference to Stoddard's views in 1677: "I wish there be not Teachers found in our Israel, that have espoused loose, large Principles here, designing to bring all persons to the Lord's Supper, who have a Historical Faith, and are not scandalous in life, although they never had Experience of a work of Regeneration in their Souls." (In *A Discourse Concerning the Danger of Apostacy*, an election day sermon of 1667, reprinted in *A Call from Heaven, 84.*)

[51] Cited by David Hall, *The Faithful Shepherd*, 61.

restriction of membership to the covenanted pure in
heart, as well as the importance of preaching for conversions, the significance of days of thanksgiving and humiliation, and the need for souls to climb the steep Puritan
road to salvation through the approved Pauline stages of
election, vocation, justification, sanctification, and glorification,[52] all involved significant innovations in Puritan
worship, which deviated radically from the Anglican
worship formulated in the Book of Common Prayer.

The Impact of Theology on Worship
    In using the biblical criterion rigorously for worship,
the Puritans took a hatchet to liturgical tradition. First,
the very idea of a set liturgy was excised, in conformity
with Romans 8:26, and in the conviction that the Lord's
Prayer was a model for the Christian's original prayer,
rather than a prescribed prayer to be repeated word for
word. Furthermore, it was decided on the authority of
I Corinthians 14:14 that responsive prayers were unac-
ceptable since, apart from the approving "Amen," only
the minister's voice was to be heard in public prayer. As
early as 1642, John Cotton had written a treatise affirming
the necessity of free or extemporary prayers against a defense of liturgies. His opening definition read, "Lawfull
prayer is a lifting up (or pouring out) of the desires of the
heart unto God, for Divine blessings, according to his
will, in the name of Jesus Christ, by the helpe of the

---

[52] William Haller remarked about these stages of the soul's
progress, "Here was the perfect formula explaining what happens
to every human soul born to be saved." See *The Rise of Puritanism*,
93.

Spirit of Grace."[53] It was characteristic in its double emphasis on natural simplicity and the dependence on the Holy Spirit. Cotton insists that God commands His people to prayer in the Spirit, according to Ephesians 6:18, "which implies not onely with such affections as his Spirit kindleth and stirreth up, but also with such matter and words as his Spirit helpeth us unto."[54] A later and fuller defense of free prayers would also urge not only the Pauline strictures against set prayers, but that they lacked the flexibility to meet changing needs, deprived ministers of the gift of moving prayers, brought persecution in their train, and led to formality on the part of congregations and laziness on the part of ministers.[55] But the primary reason was the divine demand in Scripture which Cotton stated clearly: "Wee conceive it also to be unlawful to bring in ordinarily any other Bookes into the publique worship of God, in the Church, besides the Book of God."[56]

Enemies of the Puritans might accuse them of having a dervish's idea of praying, but they were affirming the sovereign freedom of the Creator Spirit whom liturgists try to trap and tame into formulae. They were afraid of the formality and dullness engendered by repetition and the staleness that breeds indifference. They had learned in the love of Christ to speak to God as Father, and it seemed to them as if the Anglicans wished only to ap-

---

[53] *A Modest and Cleare Answer to Mr. Balls Discourse of Set Formes of Prayer* (London, 1642), 1.
[54] *Op. cit*, 14.
[55] This later critique of liturgies is described in my *Worship and Theology in England, II,* 191–94.
[56] *A Modest and Cleare Answer,* 5.

proach a distant and dignified deity with the words,
"Your Majesty"; while Puritans would prefer to say,
"Abba, Father." The simple spontaneity of such extemporary prayers was matched with assurance, naturalness,
intimacy, and a moving directness.

A further consequence of using the biblical pruning
knife on centuries of tradition was the excision of many
ceremonies from worship. The Second Commandment,
with its prohibition of idolatry, was the authority cited
for eliminating not only the High Church custom of
bowing in the name of Jesus (for which a biblical authority could be found),[57] but also kneeling for the reception
of the Communion (implying a belief in the miracle of
transubstantiation), as well as the signing of the cross in
baptism and the use of the ring in marriage. Because of
their association with Roman Catholicism, the priestly
garments such as the alb, the stole, and the surplice were
all rejected in favor of the grave Genevan gown and white
neck bands of the Puritan pastor.

The Puritan Calendar

Another striking departure from ecclesiastical tradition was the excision of the Christian Year and of the
sanctoral cycle. Here, again, the authority was the Bible.
Instead of the traditional christological calendar from
Advent to Easter, with its meditative retrospective gaze,
and the sanctoral cycle which stresses the significance of
saints as imitators of Christ, the Puritans emphasized the
climactic importance of the Sabbath, consecrating one
day totally to God in every seven, imitating God's own
rest on the seventh day, looking forward to their own ul-

---

[57] See Philippians 2:10.

timate rest with the saints in God's unveiled presence in eternity, and recognizing in the immediacy of events His providential presence. Puritans rejected the Christian Year because of its plethora of saint's days, which obscured the supreme and solitary splendor of the King of saints, Christ. They purified Sunday from the beery buffoonery that had characterized its celebration in early Stuart England. The center of Puritan interest was not the Incarnation, and the incidents recorded in the Gospels, but in the Acts of the Apostles and the Epistles of St. Paul, for Puritans were absorbed in trying to live in the Spirit.

The point of departure for Puritans was not the Nativity, the Passion, nor the Resurrection, but their consequences in the glorification of Christ at His Ascension and the fulfillment of His promise in the descent of the Holy Spirit at Pentecost. Their interest was not in the historic drama of the past, but in the spiritual civil war of the present, in which Christ fought against Satan for the possession of souls. Puritans, in their type of spirituality, did not, like Roman Catholics or Anglicans, aim directly at the imitation of Christ. Rather they recapitulated in themselves the story of Everyman Adam, from temptation and fall, through reconciliation, restoration, and renewal. They moved carefully through the Pauline stages of the soul, going successively through election, vocation, justification, sanctification, toward glorification. Though not oblivious of the major events in the life of Christ, Puritans concentrated on the rebirth of their own souls, on the crucifixion of the old Adam by the power of the new Adam. For the Puritans, life was an unending war against the forces of the Evil One under the orders of Christ, the Captain of salvation, as His elect troops. There was no armistice in this lifelong struggle, but the tired warriors were encouraged by the assurance that the victory of Christ and His saints on earth was sure and would be the prelude to the return of Christ with all His saints to heaven. For Anglicans, life was a pilgrimage toward the shining towers of the heavenly city glimpsed mystically as the clouds part, while for Puritans, life was fighting the good fight of faith, with the courage of obedience, using the sword of the Spirit.

Another set of changes was concerned with the sacraments, with the intention of making them correspond more accurately with the records of their biblical institution. Godparents were rejected in baptism because the covenant of God was made with parents and their seed rather than with godparents. Moreover, this sacrament was to be no hole-in-the-corner affair, celebrated in emergency by a midwife, or in the home, or even when in the church only in the presence of the family. It was always celebrated by the minister as part of a regular service in the presence of the members of the local church, who would share with the parents the responsibility for the spiritual upbringing of the child.

In the case of the Lord's Supper, this was not reserved, as in the custom of the Church of England, and used for the communicating of the sick. It was always celebrated by a minister before the congregation of church members. A peculiarity of Independent administration of the Lord's Supper was the double consecration separately of the bread and the wine, since this was the custom reported in the synoptic gospels, in their accounts of its origin. Moreover, neither sacrament could be received unless parents of children to be baptized had accepted the covenant of the local church, and the signing of the covenant was an essential condition for admission to the Lord's Supper. Both sacraments were carefully hedged in to prevent their pollution by the unworthy, since early on in New England membership was reserved for visible saints who could give a narration of the experience of saving grace.

A further consequence was that the admission of new church members by the signing of the covenant became an important part of the regular Sabbath afternoon service, since it also reminded existing members of the importance of the vows they had taken to follow Christ, which, by implication, they were renewing. And at the end of the second generation of Puritans in New England, when jeremiads were preached against a supposedly backsliding generation, it was customary to require a formal act of covenant renewal.

Hence the sacraments were celebrated with intense seriousness and careful spiritual preparation. Yet even so, they were not the highest and most climactic points of worship for the Puritans. That was the sermon, for in it the minister expounded the very oracles of God by the illumination of the Holy Spirit, who also evoked the response of faith in the hearts of the believers.

Music

Further, in the realm of music the Puritans refused to use organs or strings or wind instruments in worship because there was no New Testament authority for their liturgical use.[58] On the other hand, psalms were sung,

---

[58] If the Puritans seemed to banish music from their meetinghouses, they welcomed music in their homes, as Percy Scholes amply documents in *The Puritans and Music in England and New*

since the Book of Psalms was part of Holy Writ, and because they had been strongly recommended by Calvin in the form of metrical psalmody,[59] and set to the majestic music of Bourgeois. For a while the American Puritans seemed to have used the shambling Pegasus of the Stern and Hopkins version, and occasionally that of the plodding Hebraist and Separatist, Ainsworth. By 1640, however, they produced their own version of the metrical psalms, namely, *The Bay Psalm Book*.[60]

Cotton, whom Haraszti believes to have composed the *Bay Psalm Book* version of the 23rd Psalm, wrote proudly in *The Way of the Churches of Christ in New England* (1645) that they sang psalms in their own version:

> Before Sermon, and many times after we sing a Psalme, and because the former translation of the Psalmes, doth in many things vary from the original . . . we have endeavoured a new translation into English meetre, as neere the originall as wee could express it in our English tongue . . . and those Psalmes wee sing, both in our publicke Churches, and in private.[61]

England (London, 1934; 2nd ed. New York: Oxford University Press, 1966).

[59] Calvin had recommended metrical psalms thus: "We cannot find better or more appropriate songs for this purpose than the psalms of David, which the Holy Spirit himself has dictated and composed." Cited in R. E. Prothero, *The Psalms in Human Life* (London, 1903), 140–41.

[60] See *The Bay Psalm Book*, by Zoltan Haraszti, 2 vols. (Chicago: University of Chicago Press, 1956). Vol. I is a facsimile of *The Bay Psalm Book* of 1640; Vol. II is an interpretative companion volume, *The Enigma of the Bay Psalm Book*.

[61] *Op. cit.*, 67.

Apart from the congregation's loud "Amens" at the end of prayers, their only vocal part in worship was the singing of metrical psalms in which they expressed the priesthood of all believers. Lutherans sang oratorios and hymns, Anglicans in cathedrals and collegiate churches sang anthems and chants, but Puritans refused all four in favor of metrical psalmody. When these were "lined out," this must have strained the concentration of the literate among the congregation, but even this awkwardness was accepted because these were the words of the Word of God. No more august authority existed. They became the battle songs of a great spiritual resistance movement, whether on the lips of the Huguenots or the Roundheads.

Finally, as plainness and purity became the watchwords of the Puritan sermon and worship, so they characterized the architecture of the Puritan meetinghouse. The light of God's sun shone through the windows of plain glass, as the light of God's eternal Son shone through the exposition of His Word in the lection and the sermon. The central high pulpit on which the sacred Scripture rested, from which the black-gowned preacher applied the message to the condition of the minds and hearts of his listeners, was appropriate for the seriousness and high sincerity with which they came to worship God. Any aesthetic aids, such as stained-glass windows, richly embroidered vestments, and altar frontals or banners, would have seemed otiose and as out of place as gilding the lily or varnishing the sunlight. For here were gathered extraordinary, committed men and women, whole congregations of God's visible saints adoring their Creator, Redeemer, and Sanctifier, the one mysterious Triune God.

3

The Calendar

As an act of iconoclasm, the rejection of the Anglican calendar was second only to the abolition of the liturgy of the Book of Common Prayer. The striking character of the Puritan calendar was its almost total rejection of the past tense for those of the present and future. While the Christian year kept by the Church of England was dominantly retrospective as it meditated on the Incarnation from Advent through Lent to Trinity Sunday, the Puritan year featured weekly red-letter days on their Sabbaths, where the authority was God's rest after Creation, but the emphasis was on the anticipation of the everlasting rest of God's saints in eternity, and the preparation for it during a day of rigorous devotional discipline in the meetinghouse and in the home. Furthermore, the Anglican calendar was repetitive, cyclical, and static, whereas the Puritan calendar recognized in energetic manner the present and continuing activity of God in providence and history. The dynamic sense of God's presence in contemporary events was institutionalized in fast days and days of thanksgiving in which, respectively, penitence for divine displeasure and gratitude for divine mercy were expressed. An additional constituent of the Puritan calendar was the representation of civil religion on election and artillery days, which were appointed during the

second generation when the society had become sufficiently stabilized to warrant them.[1]

The negative novelty of the Puritan calendar must at
first have seemed nothing less than blasphemous. How,
for example, could the abolition of Christmas Day—the
celebration of the Incarnation—be otherwise interpreted? The abolition of May Day was, because of its
abuse by rowdiness and bawdiness in England, understandable. Yet there was a logic in the Puritan profanation
of Christmas Day, as J. P. Walsh observed: "The Puritans
rested on the Sabbath in order to keep it holy; they
worked on December 25 in order to strip it of its sanctity."[2] Samuel Eliot Morison has further maintained that
the first Puritans wisely substituted Thanksgiving for
Christmas Day, and instead of May Day there were two
holidays in spring and early summer: Election Day and
the Harvard College commencement.[3] It would occasion
no surprise, however, that these committed Protestants
and patriots kept Guy Fawkes Day, with its commemoration of the overthrow of the Gunpowder Plot,
most religiously. Despite it being fifty years after the
larger body of Puritans arrived, Sewall reports that on
November 5, 1685, "although it rained hard, yet there

---

[1] While the first general day of thanksgiving in New England took
place in 1637, election and artillery sermons were only regularly delivered from 1659, and they were required to be printed only from
1672. Samuel G. Drake, *The History and Antiquities of Boston* (Boston:
Luther Stephens, 1856), 236).

[2] "Holy Time and Sacred Space in Puritan New England," *The
American Quarterly*, 32, 1 (Spring 1980), 81.

[3] *The Puritan Pronaos; Studies in the Intellectual Life of New England
in the Seventeenth Century* (New York: New York University Press,
1936), 23.

was a Bonfire made on the [Boston] Common, about 50 attended it."[4] This commemoration lost its popularity only when tolerated Episcopalians made much of it in their services, and preached sermons against Dissenters.[5]

Sabbaths

Sabbaths were the regular red-letter days of the Puritan calendar. They could claim the authority of God Himself for their institution, while the origin of Christmas Day and Easter Day and the other days of the Anglican calendar could only claim ecclesiastical authority. Keeping the Sabbath day holy was not only scripturally mandated in the Decalogue; it was an essential part of the cosmic scheme. For had not God, according to Genesis, created the world in six days and rested on the seventh? So must man labor for six days, and on the Sabbath rest from daily labor and honor God in worship, as well as in all the exercises prescribed for the edification of the elect. Richard Byfield explodes with Puritan horror at the thought that holy days are only matters of state (and therefore of human) appointment: "Then also the Feast of Christ's Nativity, of Easter, of Witsontide, etc. are all of equall authority with the Lord's Day, which thing what eares can heare with patience?"[6] The Puritan Sabbath also looked forward to the rest and delight of eternity, which would be the reward of the godly

---

[4] *The Diary of Samuel Sewall*, ed. M. Halsey Thomas (New York: Farrar, Straus & Giroux, 1973), I, 82.
[5] William DeLoss Love, *The Fast and Thanksgiving Days of New England* (Boston: Houghton Mifflin, 1895), 228–229.
[6] *The Doctrine of the Sabbath Vindicated* (London, 1637), 134.

at the end of history and the justification of all their toil
and sacrifice.

The regularity of the six days of labor and the seventh
day of rest also had profound economic consequences, as
Christopher Hill has pointed out.[7] It was the pre-
dictability and regularity of their holy days (compared
with the irregular intervals and frequency of the holy
days in the Roman Catholic and Anglican calendars),
combined with the acute Puritan dislike of idleness, that
made rational planning possible for merchants and masters of crafts. Puritans were especially critical of the lax
Anglican mode of spending their Sundays, marked more
by distractions than by devotions. For example, Nicholas
Bownde complains of Anglicans that "when they would
seeme to be most devoutly keeping the remembrance of
. . . the *birth and incarnation of Christ* . . . they doe celebrate the feast of the drunken God Bacchus."[8] Indeed,
the serious keeping of the Sabbath became an early distinguishing mark of Puritan behavior, as Richard Baxter
attests in his autobiography, where the following classical
cameo warrants citation:

> In the village where I lived the reader read the
> Common Prayer briefly, and the rest of the day
> even till dark almost, except eating-time, was spent
> in dancing under a may-pole and a great tree not far
> from my father's door, where all of the men of the
> town did eat together. And though one of my fa-
> ther's own tenants was the piper, he could not re-

---

[7] See the masterly chapter titled "The Uses of Sabbatarianism" in
his *Society and Puritanism in Pre-Revolutionary England*, 2nd ed.
(New York, 1967).

[8] *The Doctrine of the Sabbath, plainely layde forth, and sundly proved*
(London 1595), 133-134.

strain him or break the sport. So that we could not
read the Scripture in our family without the distur-
bance of the tabor and pipe and noise in the street.
Many times my mind was inclined to be among
them, and sometimes I broke loose from conscience
and joined with them; and the more I did the more
I was inclined to it. But when I heard them call my
father Puritan it did much to cure me and alienate
me from them; for I considered that my father's
exercise of reading the Scripture was better than
theirs, and would surely be better thought on by all
men at the last.[9]

The Westminster Directory gives the fullest instructions on how the Lord's Day or Christian Sabbath should
be spent. It was to be carefully prepared for, so that "all
worldly business or our ordinary callings may be so ordered, and so timely and seasonably laid aside, as they
may not be impediments to the due sanctifying of the day
when it comes." Next, the entire day was to be sanctified, both publicly and privately, with "a holy cessation,
or resting all that day, from all necessary labours; and in
abstaining, not only from all sports and pastimes, but also
from all worldly words and thoughts." The family diet
for the Sabbath is so to be arranged "as that neither servants be unnecessarily detained" from public worship,
"nor any other person hindered from the sanctifying of
that day." Furthermore, every person and each family
must prepare for the Sabbath by prayer for themselves
and the divine assistance for the minister, and for a

---

[9] The substance of the original *Reliquiae Baxterianae*, ed. M.
Sylvester (1696), has been re-edited by J. M. Lloyd Thomas in an
Everyman edition titled *The Autobiography of Richard Baxter* (London,
1925). The citation is from p. 6.

blessing of his ministry, "and by such other holy exercises as may further dispose them to a more comfortable communion with God in his public ordinances." Worship is to be so organized that the entire congregation is to be in time for the beginning and is to stay to the end of the service, and "with one heart solemnly to join together in all parts of the public worship." Thus it is clear that the climax of the climactic day of the week was the worship of the living God in obedience to His ordinances. The time before and after worship is to "be spent in reading, meditation, repetition of sermons; especially by calling their families to an account of what they have heard, and catechising of them, holy conferences, singing of psalms, visiting the sick, relieving the poor, and such like duties of piety, charity, and mercy accounting the Sabbath a delight."[10]

To understand what the Sabbath meant to New Englanders of the first generation, it is essential to realize that to serve God with unidolatrous ceremonies and an unprofaned Sabbath were two of the hallmarks of Puritanism in New England. Edward Johnson is explicit in accounting these major motives for the founding of the new theocracy:

> When England began to decline in Religion, like lukewarme Laodicea, and instead of purging out Popery, a further compliance was sought not onely in vaine Idolatrous Ceremonies, but also in prophaning the Sabbath, and by Proclamation through-

---

10 All the citations in this paragraph come from the Directory's section headed "Of the Sanctification of the Lord's Day." *Reliquiae Liturgicae*, ed. Peter Hall, vol. III: *The Parliamentary Directory* (Bath: Binns and Goodwin, 1847), 58–60.

out their Parish Churches, exasperating lewd and prophane persons to celebrate a Sabbath like the Heathen to Venus, Baccus and Ceres; in so much that the multitude of irreligious lascivious and popish affected persons spred the whole land like Grasshoppers, in this very time, Christ the glorious King of his Churches, raises an Army out of our English Nation, for freeing his people from their long servitude under usurping Prelacy; and because every corner of England was filled with the fury of malignant adversaries, Christ creates a New England to muster up the first of his Forces in.[11]

The fullest treatment of sabbatarianism by an American in the sevēnteenth century is Thomas Shepard's *Theses Sabbaticae; Or, The Doctrine of the Sabbath* (1649).[12] In the preface he admits that Charles I and his bishops regarded sabbatarianism as a judaizing novelty, maintaining instead that it was an ecclesiastical appointment conveniently arranged to provide for divine worship and human recreation. For Anglicans in authority, sabbatarianism, says Shepard, was "a superstitious seething over of the hot or whining simplicity of an over-rigid, crabbed, precise, crack-brain'd, Puritanicall party."[13] For Shepard it was not the lord bishops but the

---

[11] Johnson's book was published in 1654 as *A History of New England,, from the English Planting in the Yeere 1628 untill the Yeere 1652*. It was republished in 1910 and edited by J. Franklin Jameson, and titled Johnson's *Wonder-Working Providence* (New York: Scribner's).

[12] First published in London, it was reissued in 1650 and 1655, and again in *The Works of Thomas Shepard*, 3 vols., ed. John A. Albro (Boston, 1853), 3:7–271. All citations are from the Albro edition, which was reprinted by Soli Deo Gloria from 1990–1992.

[13] *Ibid.*, 3:4.

Lord Jesus who was the supreme authority. As Winton U. Solberg rightly insists, "There is momentous theological confusion in identifying the Christian holy day with the Sabbath of the Decalogue," yet the Puritans "found in the Fourth Commandment the only explicit warrant for keeping the holy day."[14] Shepard's book was published in 1649, but it comprised sermons that had been delivered to Harvard undergraduates late in the fourth or early in the fifth decade of the century.

Shepard argues that it is appropriate to give God a day in which to honor Him, as a "magnificent day of state," and for the public recognition of religion, but its chief purpose is to worship Him in obedience in ordinances He has prescribed:

> Is it comely and good to have God to be our God in the first commandment, to worship him after his own mind in the second, to give him his worship with all the highest respect and reverence of his name in the third; and is it not as comely, good, and suitable that this great God and King should have some magnificent day of state to be attended on by his poor servants and creatures, both publicly and privately, with special respect and service, as oft as himself sees meet, and which we can not but see and confess to be most equal and just, according to the fourth commandment?[15]

Shepard also insists that the Gospel requires a new

---

[14] *Redeem the Time: The Puritan Sabbath in Early America* (Cambridge, Mass.: Harvard University Press, 1977), 34. This book, to which I am greatly indebted, is a comprehensive study of the Sabbath in England and New England.

[15] *Op. cit.*, 3:46.

seventh day. The main cause is the will of God, but the Resurrection of Christ is the moral cause for the change.[16] In addition, it was important that the whole day should be consecrated to God, for "such is the overflowing and extrinsic love of a blessed God, that it cannot contain itself, (as it were), so long a time from special fellowship with his people here in a strange land . . . and therefore will have some special times of special fellowship and sweetest mutual embracings; and this time . . . a whole day, that there may be time enough to have their fill of love in each other's bosom before they part."[17] Shepard can hardly control his excitement at the thought of the privilege of Christians at worship renewing their spiritual strength as they stand before their God and King on "this day of state and royal majesty, when all his saints compass his throne and presence with our most beautiful garments."[18] Each Sabbath Christ descends in His ordinances, leaving heaven for His elect.[19] Each Sabbath is a foretaste of eternity:

> Look therefore, as when man hath run his race, finished his course, and passed through the bigger and larger circle of his life, he then returns unto his eternal rest, so it is contrived and ordered by divine wisdom, as that he shall in a special manner return unto and into his rest once at least within the lesser and smaller circle of every week, that so his perfect blessedness to come might be foretasted every Sabbath day.[20]

---

[16] *Ibid.*, 3:191.
[17] *Ibid.*, 3:265.
[18] *Ibid.*, 3:261.
[19] *Ibid.*, 3:260.
[20] *Ibid.*, 3:26.

Shepard also reminds his readers how the Sabbath should be spent. It must include rest from all servile works as well as from worldly sports and pastimes. However, such essential duties as getting food ready or preserving life (as rescuing an animal, putting out a destructive fire, and steering a ship) are permitted. Activities that could be done as well before as after the Sabbath, such as bringing in the harvest, sweeping the house, washing clothes, or buying at a shop, are prohibited. Such necessary tasks as watering animals, preparing hot food, putting on comely garments, and washing the hands and face are allowed.[21]

It is of special interest to note that the Puritans were the only Christian sabbatarians to insist that the day ran from Saturday evening to Sunday evening, and concluded at the sacred hour of 3:00 p.m., which was the hour of Christ's death. Shepard argues, "If, therefore the Sabbath began at evening from Adam's time in innocency till Nehemiah's time, and from Nehemiah's time till Christ's time, why should any think but that where the Jewish Sabbath, the last day of the week, doth end, there the Christian Sabbath, the first day of the week, begins?"[22]

Shepard asserted that the holiness required on Sabbaths differed from that required on weekdays in five ways. It was more immediate, since in God's ordinances "the Lord comes down from heaven to us in his ordinances, and thereby makes himself as near to us as he can in this frail life."[23] Sunday holiness should be marked with greater intensity, since "in the week time we are

---

21 *Ibid.*, 3:257f.
22 *Ibid.*, 3:252–253.
23 *Ibid.*, 3:260.

sinfully drowned in the cares of this world and affections
thereto."[24] Holiness on Sundays is constant and to be
continued for the whole day.[25] It must also be "a sweet
and quieting rest," anticipating the time when we shall
appear before the face of God, "whom at the last we shall
find when our short day's work here is done, and our long
looked-for Sabbath of glory shall begin to dawn."[26]
Finally, Christians are to do their utmost to see to it regarding others "under us, or that have relation to us, that
they sanctify the Sabbath also." This requirement applies to children, servants, and guests or strangers in the
house; the magistrates also have a similar responsibility,
since they are, as it were, fathers of great families.[27]
Jasper Danckaerts visited Boston in 1680 and found sabbatarianism rigorously practiced there. He observed:
"All their religion consists in observing Sunday, by not
working or going into taverns that day; but the houses are
worse than the taverns. No stranger or traveller can
therefore be entertained on a Sunday."[28] Solberg's comment is both more charitable and more understanding:
"The Sabbath was New England's glory. Its observances
required duty, but the day of rest and worship brought
physical and spiritual refreshment and was an occasion of
great joy."[29]

Sabbatarianism in New England, with its compulsory
attendance at Sunday worship, encouraged both piety and

---

[24] *Ibid.*, 3:260.
[25] *Ibid.*, 3:261.
[26] *Ibid.*, 3:261–262.
[27] *Ibid.*, 3:262–263.
[28] *Journal of Jasper Danckaerts* (1679–1680), 294.
[29] *Redeem the Time*, 265.

civilization, each of which might otherwise have perished in a primitive wilderness context. While it may also have encouraged the growth of capitalistic industrialism, its ethical component prevented it from losing compassion. It may also, as Solberg insists, have "instilled into the American character a strength and simplicity dependent upon the severity of an unwavering religious discipline."[30] Cotton Mather believed this to be true when he wrote, "It hath been truly and justly observed, that our whole Religion fares according to our Sabbaths, that poor Sabbaths make poor Christians, and that a strictness in our Sabbaths inspires a Vigour into all our other duties."[31]

Fast Days or Days of Humiliation
    These contrasted days, in which fasts recognized the displeasure of God and thanksgivings His benevolence toward His covenanted people, were modeled on Old Testament parallels and expressed a profound sense of divine Providence. The interpretation of Providence, as we shall see, could be exceedingly ambiguous. It could also change quite rapidly. In one celebrated case, a congregation preparing for a day of humiliation gathered for a day of thanksgiving. It appears that the Reverend John Wilson, renowned teacher of the Boston Church, had returned to England to bring back his wife, but when the return was delayed, according to Edward Johnson, in 1633, the disappointed congregation was to meet for a day

---

[30] *Ibid.*, 301.
[31] *Magnalia Christi Americana*, 2 vols. (London, 1702; rpt. Hartford, Conn., 1820), Book III, p. 178 (This work has been reprinted by the Banner of Truth Trust).

of humiliation, "wholly to be spent in seeking the pleasing Face of God in Christ, purposing the Lord assisting to
afflict their soules, and give him the honour of his All-
seeingness, by a downe right acknowledgement of their
sinnes, but the Lord, whose Grace is alwayes unde-
served, heard them before they cried, and the afternoone
before the day appointed brought him . . . in safety to
shore."[32] In 1630 a similar transformation of an intended
fast into an occasion of thanksgiving had taken place. In
that autumn the newly arrived colonists lived in
ramshackle huts, and many of them were sick. They had
not had the time to plant seed so late in the year.
Governor Winthrop, expecting an acute shortage of food,
had arranged for Captain William Peirce to sail to the
nearest Irish port for provisions. The captain was delayed by towing a dismasted ship at sea to her home port
of Bristol. So desperate was the state of the colonists in
winter that their fare was only acorns, groundnuts, mus-
sels and clams. In the situation a day of fasting and prayer
was appointed, probably for February 5, 1630 (Old
Style), but the arrival a few days before of the *Lyon*, with
its cargo of wheat, meal, peas, oatmeal, beef and pork,
with lemon juice for curing scurvy, caused the governor
and council to order a day of thanksgiving on February
22.[33] These two incidents make it plain that the scowl of
God's judgment was seen in threatening events and the

---

[32] *Wonder-Working Providence of Sion's Saviour in New-England*
(London, 1654); ed. W. F. Poole rpt. (Andover, Mass., 1867), 56.
[33] Cited in William DeLoss Love, *The Fast and Thanksgiving Days of
New England* (Boston: Houghton Mifflin, 1895), 104–5, from a
Memoir of Roger Clap in *Collections of the Dorchester Antiquarian
and Historical Society* (with an unpaginated and unnumbered
reference).

smile of His approval in benevolent occasions.

Days of humiliation, in which penitent Puritans sought God's forgiveness, were occasioned by severe droughts, seriously depleted harvests, incursions of destructive insects, the spread of diseases, losses at sea, the presence of prodigies, and defeats in warfare. Those were all group calamities, but Puritans also regarded individual illnesses, fire or storm damage to homes, and deaths in the family as divine judgments calling for private days of humiliation. Whatever the secondary causes of events might be, these were traced back to their initiator and controller, Almighty God. These abstractions will become concrete only by illustration.

Many days of humiliation were called for in New England during the ill fortune of the Roundheads in the English Civil War.[34] Droughts were the commonest cause of fasts in Massachusetts, as on June 13, 1639, July 3, 1644, June 5, 1662, and June 21, 1662. The blasting of the wheat crop required fast days in Massachusetts on September 1, 1664, and in Connecticut on May 29, 1668. Caterpillars destroyed the corn in the summer of 1646, causing the churches to keep a day of humiliation in the Bay Colony, and a fast day on June 22, 1665, was called because of the cankerworms that were ravaging the apple trees. Many threatening diseases called for days of humiliation (or also for days of thanksgiving if averted), especially between 1644 and 1649, and also between 1658 and 1666. Comets seen on the deaths of leaders such as John Cotton or Governor Endicott called for fasts. A surfeit of such experiences, culminating in the drought of 1662, led Michael Wigglesworth to write a jeremiad in

---

[34] *Ibid.*, 177–191, summarized.

verse, the melancholy *God's Controversy with New England*. Its conclusion is orthodoxly Puritan:

> The clouds are often gathered
> As if we should have rain:
> But for our great unworthiness
> Are scattered again.
> We pray & fast, & make fair shewes,
> As if we meant to turn:
> But whilst we turn not, God goes on
> Our field & fruits to burn.

The numerous fast days called by the General Court of Massachusetts from 1632 to 1686 are also significant, and they have been analyzed by Richard P. Gildrie according to their major themes.[35] In these fifty-five years, twenty-nine fast days were held because of troubles in the order of nature, comprising threats to harvest, disease, losses at sea, and others. By contrast, over the same half-century fifty-eight fast days were held because of troubles in the social order, comprising heresy, contention, death of or lack of leaders, neglect of public or family order, the younger generation, threats from England or other nations, and weighty occasions. Other troubles in Christendom accounted for forty fast days, comprising difficulties in England, Europe, and the New World. Finally, sins, both unspecified and private (the latter including vanity, luxury, oppression, uncleanness, drunkenness, pride, and sensuality), required twenty-three fast days, and another twenty-two fast days were

---

[35] "The Ceremonial Puritan Days of Humiliation and Thanksgiving," *The New England Historical and Genealogical Register*, CXXXVI (January, 1982), 14.

held for unspecified purposes and unspecified troubles. Altogether in these fifty-five years, 172 fast days were held, a fast day occurring approximately once every four months. It should also be observed that fast days were called for far more frequently when the political horizon was darkened, just after the Restoration and when New England's liberties and privileges were reduced, and when jeremiads required the renewal of church covenants. Thus from 1660 to 1668 there were forty-seven fast days, and forty between 1678 and 1686.

As for more personal "providences," these can be discovered in the diaries of Judge Samuel Sewall and of Dr. Cotton Mather, and in the autobiography of the Reverend Thomas Shepard of Cambridge. The latter shows the divine hand as manifested mainly in unexpected deliverances from life-threatening dangers, including saving the rider even when the horse falls on a flooded bridge, or when the ship driven by a fierce gale seems certain to founder but God averts the apparently inevitable wreck.[36] Sewall's diary entry for July 15, 1685, reads:

> One Humphry Tiffiny and Frances Low, Daughter of Antony Low, are slain with the Lightening and Thunder about a mile or half a mile beyond Billinges Farm, the Horse also slain, they that rode on, and another Horse in Company slain, and his Rider who held the Garment on the Maid to steady it at the time of the Stroke, a coat, or cloak, stounded but not killed. Were coming to Boston. Antony Low being in Town the sad Bill was put up

[36] See Michael McGiffert, ed. *God's Plot: The Paradoxes of Puritan Piety, Being the Autobiography and Journal of Thomas Shepard* (Amherst: University of Massachusetts Press, 1972), 5.

with [regard] of that Solemn judgment of God: Fast-
day Forenoon.[37]

Dr. Cotton Mather found it necessary to discipline
himself spiritually by a private day of humiliation and
fasting from time to time. On one such occasion, which
proved to be a deep psychological self-examination, he
"made a Recapitulation of the humbling Things that had
befallen me; and I confessed and bewayled the Special
Miscarriages, by which I had rendered myself most
worthy to be Humbled with such Dispensations of
Heaven."[38]

In the earliest days of New England, the minister or
elder of a church could call for a stated day of fasting (or
thanksgiving) by giving the reasons for it. This would
then be sustained by the votes of the church members,
and then enacted. As churches increased in number, it
became customary for groups of ministers to prepare a
proclamation and to present it before the General Court
or the governor and council for ratification. The secular
authorities, so the theory went, acted at the desire of the
churches. Thus the fast day's character of holiness was
legally sanctioned and attendance at its services of worship was compulsory throughout New England. Further,
as we have seen, an individual might put up a bill for a
prayer of confession or thanksgiving which the minister
would include in his petitionary prayer in the Sabbath
service.[39] Thus divine Providence ruled the private as

---

[37] *Diary* (ed. M. Halsey Thomas), I, 71.

[38] Cotton Mather, *Diary* (New York: Frederick Ungar, 1911).
Sewall also wrote (*Diary*, 102): "I kept a Fast to pray that God would
not take away but uphold me by his free spirit" (April 20, 1691).

[39] Love, *op. cit.*, 220–221.

well as the public life of the Puritans.

It was important to know how to prepare for such fast days. *The Westminster Directory for Public Worship* was specific in its recommendations. These included that each family was required to prepare their hearts, to arrive early at the congregation, and to be dressed in simple, unostentatious garments without ornaments. The major part of such a day was to be spent in listening to the preaching of the Word, in the singing of psalms, and, particularly, in prayer. The purpose of the day was to afflict the soul, with the minister instructed to engage the hearts of the people to be the Lord's with the determined resolution to reform whatever was amiss with them.

The most important sermon ever delivered in New England on the meaning of a fast was preached in 1674, printed in 1678, and strongly recommended in Cotton Mather's *Magnalia Christi Americana*. It was Thomas Thacher's *A Fast of Gods chusing, Plainly opened . . .* , and Increase Mather gave it his blessing in a preface. Thacher defined a fast as "an extraordinary part or act of Gospel worship wherein for a convenient Season we abstain from the comforts of this life, and upon due examination of our wayes towards God, and consideration of Gods wayes towards us, we make a solemn and real profession that we justifie God and judge ourselves."[40] God is justified for the evil of the affliction that is either felt or feared, godly repentance and sorrow is expressed for the sin, God's forgiveness is sought, and, lastly, the people "bind ourselves to reform the evil of our wayes, and to walk before God in new obedience according to his

---

[40] *Op. cit.*, 3.

Word for the time to come."[41]

Thacher lists the special occasions when public fasts
are appropriately kept. These include: public danger;
when a notable but hazardous duty must be undertaken;
in time of great sickness; when a notable blessing is
lacking or a great transgression has been committed; and
when a calamity threatens.[42] In each case Thacher gives
an Old Testament example of a fast as his authority.
Thacher insists that proper preparation includes an examination of our ways and the ways of God, as well as a
genuine confession, sincere contrition, asking God's forgiveness, and forgiving all others who have wronged us.
Finally, and significantly, he adds that the people of God
bind themselves to reform what is wrong, an act that is
"an implicit making and renewing of Covenant with
God."[43]

It is interesting to compare another sermon on the
same text, Isaiah 58:5, with a similar title, *The Fast which
GOD hath chosen*, which Benjamin Colman preached in
Boston sixty years later, on March 21, 1734. The phrasing
is more elegant and the ethical requirements are more
stringent. The elegance is seen in such an approach as
"We are indigent Beggars at the Gate of Heaven, and
there we lay in our Sores as well as Rags, unworthy of a
Crumb, but Supplicants for the Riches of Grace, Bounty
and Mercy."[44] The ethical emphasis is seen in the
charity with which we feed the poor and respect our

---

[41] *Ibid.*, 3.
[42] *Ibid.*, 4.
[43] *Ibid.*, 6–7.
[44] *Op. cit.*, 4–5.

neighbor whom we are to love as ourselves.[45] It is worth recalling that at every public fast there was a collection for the needy.[46] Colman's conclusion sums up the whole intention of a public fast:

> But if God see us more sincere and fervent in secret worship, more careful in Sabbath-Sanctification, more just and righteous in our Dealings, more kind and good, charitable and merciful, more sober, chaste and temperate, and all from true Humiliation for Sin and Faith in our LORD JESUS CHRIST, then he will accept our Persons and Prayers, and make good all the great and precious Promises in our Context to his repenting and reformed People.[47]

Thanksgiving Days

Equally interpreted in the light of the divine Providence, thanksgiving days were more cheerful occasions than fasts or days of humiliation. The chief occasions for New England thanksgivings were three: harvests saved in the early years of the settlements, the arrival of ships when famine was predicted, or the arrival of friends.[48] Thanksgiving days for the first cause were held in Massachusetts on November 11, 1631, June 13, 1632, September 27, 1632, June 19, 1633, and August 20, 1634.[49]

The first Thanksgiving Day in New England was held in the fall of 1621, as recorded in William Bradford's *Of*

---

[45] *Ibid.*, 9.
[46] Love, *op. cit.*, 51.
[47] Colman, *op. cit.*, 21.
[48] Love, *op. cit.*, 109.
[49] *Ibid.*, 110.

Plymouth Plantation, although the exact day is not listed.[50] It was in gratitude for the very first harvest of the Pilgrims. It was an extended celebration lasting three days. However, the first generally celebrated Day of Thanksgiving in New England was held in 1637 on October 12. This celebrated the victory of the colonial soldiers over the Pequot Indians.[51]

Thanksgiving days were celebrated for wider as well as for narrower concerns. For example, the colonists celebrated the victories of Gustavus Adolphus, whose Protestant armies were advancing southward against the Catholic forces of Europe, in the Thirty Years War. As Love reports, "The King of Sweden and the Emperor of Austria played unwittingly the parts of David and Saul in the dramatic language of their supplications."[52] These were a parallel to New Haven's system of monthly fasts, which the Connecticut Colony adopted beginning on January 10, 1643 (O.S.), which met the popular demand for linking the Puritans with their opposite numbers fighting in the Parliamentary forces in England against the Cavaliers. Cotton Mather reported a general Day of Thanksgiving on January 24, 1705, in the following words: "There was a Day of *Thanksgiving* celebrated, thro' the Province, for the Smile of Heaven on the Arms of the Allies against France in the year past."[53]

---

[50] *Op. cit.*, 90. For a modern annotated edition, see *Pilgrims: Of Plymouth Plantation* by William Bradford, with notes and introduction by Samuel Eliot Morison (New York: Knopf, 1952).

[51] Love, *op. cit.*, 136, based on Hammond Trumbull's manuscript on the Wolcott Notebook in Connecticut Historical Society Collections, I, 19.

[52] Love, *ibid.*, 112.

[53] *Diary*, 530.

The fullest analysis of Thanksgiving Days called by the Massachusetts General Court between 1632 and 1686 with their major themes is provided by Richard P. Gildrie.[54] For the acknowledgment of mercies in the natural order, twenty days were called for improved harvests and better health. Thirty-one days were required to express gratitude for blessings in the social order, which included peace and unity, civil and sacred liberties, good leaders, victory in war, peace with others, and improved relations with England. On five occasions there were Thanksgiving Days for the well-being of England and for peace in Europe. Finally, there were five days when the mercies were unspecified. Thus altogether, there were sixty-one Days of Thanksgiving in fifty-five years, or approximately one in every year. It is significant that in periods of acute political difficulty (the Restoration of the monarchy in England and the loss of privileges for the Puritans), Thanksgiving Days were held far more frequently; for example, there were sixteen such days between 1660 and 1668, and fourteen such days between 1669 and 1677, which argues that the New England Puritans were grateful that matters were not as bad as they had feared.

Narrower concerns were also expressed in wholly personal and private days of thanksgiving. For example, Sewall noted a particular "providence" in the fact that he found a lost horse and saddle.[55] If this seems rather trivial to modern eyes, what is one to think of Cotton

---

[54] "The Ceremonial Puritan Days of Humiliation and Thanksgiving," *The New England Historical and Genealogical Register*, CXXXVI (January, 1982), 15.

[55] *Diary* (ed. M. Halsey Thomas), I, 27–28.

Mather recording his gratitude to God for his having parted with one watch only to receive a superior one in return? His account displays considerable naiveté:

> I was the owner of a Watch, whereof I was very fond, for the Varietie of Motions in it. My Father was desirous of this Watch, and I, in a manner, gave it him, with such Thoughts, *I owe him a great deal more than this; and the Observation of the fifth Commandment, never wants a Recompense.* Quickly after this, there came to me a Gentlewoman, from whom I had no Reason to expect so much as a Visit, but in her Visit, she to my surprise pray'd mee to accept, as a present from her, a *Watch*; which, was indeed preferrible [sic] unto that which I had before parted with.[56]

There were inevitably difficulties in the readings of divine Providence in temporal events, compounded when they seemed relatively unimportant to common sense, and piety tended to exaggerate them. Many of the events were highly ambiguous in nature. For example, Sewall's diary provides two telltale instances of extraordinary obscurity. In one case, he tells of the greatest fire that up to that time had broken out in Boston on November 27, 1676, and adds "N.B. The House of the Man of God, Mr. [Increase] Mather, and Gods House were burnt with fire. Yet God mingled mercy, and sent a considerable rain, which gave check in great measure to the (otherwise) masterless flames; lasted all the time of the fire, though fair before and after. Mr. Mather saved his Books, and other Goods."[57] He seems to be afraid to

---

[56] *Diary*, May 14, 1683. 63.
[57] *Diary* (ed. M. Halsey Thomas), I, 131.

read the event as a judgment on minister and people and
in relief records the rain that limited the damage and
even prevented the minister's books from burning. But
there is clear hesitation and perplexity in the writing.
Another puzzling phenomenon is referred to in the same
diary ten years later, which also caused problems of interpretation. This time it was a prodigy in the heavens—
no less than an inverted rainbow. An upright rainbow
was, of course, the sign of salvation to Noah and his crew,
a covenant promise. But an inverted rainbow could be
interpreted as a sign of divine disapprobation. Its appearance clearly worried the colonists who saw it on the afternoon of Tuesday, January 18, 1686 (O.S.). At the lecture on the following Thursday, the preacher, Lee, ex-
horted to quietness under God's hand, and referring to
the ambiguous rainbow, stated, according to Sewall, that
it meant "God shooting at somebody. And that our Times
[were] better than the former, and expected better still."
A third case of ambiguity occurred when Dr. Cotton
Mather was dining in Judge Sewall's home and referred
to a severe storm that later damaged the Judge's house:

> [Mather] had just mentioned that more Ministers
> Houses than others proportionably had been smit-
> ten with Lightening; enquiring what the meaning
> of God should be in it . . . I got Mr. Mather to pray
> with us after this awfull Providence; He told God he
> had broken the brittle part of our house, and pray'd
> that we might be ready for the time when our Clay-
> Tabernacles should be broken.[58]

U. Milo Kaufman rightly sees that the difficulties of

---

[58] *Diary*, I, 122.

interpreting "providences" are due both to ambiguity and to dualism.[59] If destiny proved increasingly malevolent, it was natural to attribute it to Satan, but with that admission the omnipotence and benevolence of God were severely compromised. Cotton Mather, as his diary indicates, solemnly resolved in March, 1680, "To bee diligent in *observing* and *recording* of *illustrious Providences*,"[60] yet had to confess on the 14th of May, 1683, "I am extremely defective in recording particular Providences, that appear in the conduct of my Life. But indeed I am so shallow, that I cannot easily avoid the Fault of being, either *negligent* on one side, or *superstitious* on the other."[61] That again is a pointer to the ambiguity in interpretation. Indeed, with the increasing emphasis of the natural sciences on secondary causes, to say nothing of the excessive attribution of ill to supernatural causes in the Salem witchcraft debacle, providential interpretation became less confident as the eighteenth century came in view. Increase Mather's *Essay for the Recording of Illustrious Providences* of 1684 was a rather unconvincing rearguard action, even though it encouraged his son, Cotton Mather, in the *Magnalia Christi Americana* to give examples of remarkable providences, of which one example may be given:

> An honest carpenter being at work upon an house, where eight children were sitting in a ring at some childish play on the floor below, he let fall accidentally, from an upper story, a bulky piece of timber just over these little children. The good man, with

---

[59] *The Pilgrim's Progress and Traditions in Puritan Meditation*, 204–12.
[60] *Diary*, 5.
[61] *Diary*, 63.

> inexpressible agony, cried out, "O Lord, direct it!"
> and the Lord did so direct it, that it fell out on end
> in the midst of the little children and then canted
> along on the floor between two of the children,
> without even touching one of them all.[62]

One difficulty the Mathers both faced was that they were apparently reintroducing the concept of miracle into Christian apologetics at a time when Protestant orthodoxy believed miracles had ceased. As Robert Middlekauff interprets Cotton Mather, "He continued to make distinctions between special providences—divine interference that remained within natural law—and miracles—divine interference that occurred above natural law, distinctions which most men of his day no longer respected."[63] Furthermore, science in the day of Newton was removing miracle to the realm of mystery, the as-yet inexplicable in terms of natural laws. The latter would increasingly be viewed as primary, not secondary causes.

Days of Civil Religion

The term "days of civil religion" is meant to denote the regular days associated with elections and militia training (the latter occasionally termed artillery days), which continued to have a religious character in the New England theocracy because they were celebrated in a context of prayer and preaching and were proclaimed by the magistrate. As Charles Hambrick-Stowe rightly observes, "Every inhabitant of New England was by definition a member of the social covenant and hence took

---

[62] *Op. cit.*, II, 356.

[63] *The Mathers: Three Generations of Puritan Intellectuals* (New York: Oxford University Press, 1971), 292.

part in a number of devotional acts that attended the civil year."64

Each year on election day in the capitols of the New England colonies a minister was invited to preach a sermon extolling the godly society and the complementary duties of magistrate and citizens, and most sermons were printed. The covenant relationship was not only presupposed, it was stressed, as in a famous election-day sermon preached by Jonathan Mitchel in 1667. This was titled *Nehemiah on the Wall in Troublous times* and was published in Cambridge, Massachusetts, in 1671. Mitchel reminded his civic congregation of their historical origins and their religious significance as "a part of Gods *Israel* but a part, yet no inconsiderable part of the people of God at this day in the world: such a part of Gods people as are retired to these Ends of the Earth for known ends of Religion and Reformation." He even reminded his audience of the very words of the founders of New England: "The eyes of the whole Christian World are upon you; yea, which is more, the eyes of God and his holy Angels are upon you."65 Clearly there was a covenant relationship between God and New England where His chosen people lived. In fact, the election of the magistrates depended upon the election of this people by God. Election-day sermons were a vigorous and long-lived tradition in New England. Beginning in 1634 in the Massachusetts Bay Colony, they were discontinued only

---

64 *The Practice of Piety: Puritan Devotional Disciplines in Seventeenth-Century New England* (Chapel Hill: University of North Carolina Press, 1982), 18.

65 *Op. cit.*, 18–19; cited by Hambrick-Stowe, *op. cit.*, 133.

after 1884.[66]

Another civil religious occasion to which crowds flocked was a public execution, at which a sermon was preached. In November of 1698, Cotton Mather preached on a lecture day to a crowd of between four and five thousand, which had gathered to see the execution of a woman. He records his excitement in his diary, mentioning that "the greatest Assembly, ever in this Countrey preach'd unto, was now come together." He had to climb over the pews and heads of the people to get into the pulpit. When there, he adds, "I preached with a more than ordinary Assistence, and enlarged, and uttered the most awakening Things, for near two Hours together." He handed the sermon to a bookseller for printing and annexed a history of criminals executed in New England, hoping in this way " to warn others against Vice."[67]

Another civil religious occasion that endured throughout the seventeenth century was the militia sermon, when militia companies invited local ministers to pray with and preach to their members. When the annual election of officers took place, a sermon was requested, and often these were printed. According to Hambrick-Stowe, these were of two kinds. One made a sermonic image of the calling of a soldier to battle with Satan and sin, hoping that every soldier was a true believer, as Urian Oakes did in his sermon, *The Unconquerable All-Conquering, and More-Then Conquering Souldier* (1674). The other type of sermon affirmed that the task of the militia of New England was, under God's direction, to preserve the colony's way of life. This is what S. N.

---

[66] See Mason Lowance, *Increase Mather* (New York, 1974), 114.
[67] Cotton Mather's *Diary*, 279.

(Samuel Nowell) did in his sermon, *Abraham in Arms*, printed in Boston in 1678. This pugnacious sermon implied that the training of the militia was a preparation for Armageddon.[68]

It remains only to point out that the apparent declension of religion in New England, which produced sermons known as jeremiads, also led to a renewal of the taking of covenants. Hambrick-Stowe points out that this was no invention of the second generation, as a result of the Reforming Synod of 1679–1680, as is commonly supposed, but that the Boston Church renewed its covenant at the start of the Antinomian troubles, while the Reverend John Fiske used the same custom to expand the doctrinal content of the original covenant. Increase Mather was the major influence in requiring a public renewal of the church covenant, as a proof of a penitent people's contrition and resolve to live a better Christian life. Such, too, was the aim of jeremiads, so called because they originated with the prophet Jeremiah, famous for his Lamentations, and aimed at a communal purgation and renewal of consecration. A notable example of such sermons is Increase Mather's *The Day of Trouble Is Near* (1674), which comprises two sermons, each with the same lesson. The theme is that God is afflicting His people, but aims at their correction, and leaves the door open for repentance. He is clearly concerned to measure contemporary New England in terms of its glorious past, but also to show how the lost faith can be recovered that would ensure salvation. The conclusion is, "It concerns us in this day of trouble to be a Reforming People. Let us amend our wayes and our doings, and the Lord will cause

---

[68] This information was derived from *The Practice of Piety*, 135.

us to dwell in this place."[69]

This entire chapter on the Puritan concept of sacred time, from its treatment of the Sabbath as a day of total consecration to God, followed by considering days when the smiles or frowns of divine Providence are recognized in days of thanksgiving or of humiliation, and even in the more secular occasions of election and militia days and public execution sermons, all presuppose a covenanted people in New England, an elect and holy nation, a new Israel. This covenant conception provided the transforming myth by which successive generations felt their country to be unique, their spiritual future assured, their way of life hallowed, and their values approved by God. If it lacked flexibility, this firm conviction was the strength and support of the Puritan soul.

---

[69] *Op. cit.*, 29.

4

Sermons

The sermon was the climax of Puritan worship, as the exposition of the Word of God in both condemnation and consolation, expressing the divine anger and the divine mercy. Puritan ministers believed that every faithful preacher had to be a Boanerges, or son of thunder, before he became a Barnabas or son of consolation. The importance of the sermon in New England is evident in myriad ways. It is visible in the profusion of printed sermons, which were the major genre of the earliest New England literature in both quality and quantity.[1] The enthronement of the sermon in worship is seen in the dominance of the central pulpit on the long wall of practically every Puritan meetinghouse, as well as in the symbolism of the open Bible resting on a velvet cushion on the pulpit's edge. It is also seen in the ample provision of sermons for each individual congregation: two on the Sabbath, and a third, a lecture with a biblical basis, on a weekday.

---

[1] Samuel Eliot Morison, *The Puritan Pronaos: Studies in the Intellectual Life of New England in the Seventeenth Century* (New York: New York University Press, 1936), 159, in which the author refers to the notes of John Cotton's sermons (written by Robert Keane and now in the archives of the Massachusetts Historical Society), and the shorthand notebooks of Thomas Hooker's sermons (in the keeping of the Connecticut Historical Society).

Special occasions of an apparently civil character—such as election days, artillery days, and the execution of criminals—also required sermons. Their significance is additionally indicated by the expectation that heads of households would test their children and servants by questioning them on the content of the sermons they had heard at worship when they retired to their homes.[2] Moreover, several persons brought paper and inkhorns to church with which to record their shorthand accounts or summaries of the sermons.[3]

Nor should the extraordinary length of sermons, varying from an hour to two hours or more, be forgotten as a further index of their presumed value, as is the self-denying stress on "plain" and "painful" preaching, so that the most simple could understand, for sermons took the place of our modern newspapers, magazines, lending libraries, radios and television sets, and adult education programs.[4] Harry S. Stout's important study of the American Puritan sermon claims in its title that regular Sunday preaching was "the soul of New England." A single paragraph substantiates the claim:

> New England's unique social structure of interlock-
> ing institutions governed by a single nucleus of
> covenanted saints gave congregations the coercive
> powers necessary to impose their brand of piety on
> society, and it also endowed the sermon with un-

---

[2] See the example of Charles Chauncey, president of Harvard College, as reported by Cotton Mather in *Magnalia Christi Americana* (London, 1702), I, Bk. iii, 423.

[3] Morison, *The Puritan Pronaos*, 163.

[4] Ola E. Winslow, *Meetinghouse Hill*, 1630–1783 (New York: Macmillan, 1952), 92.

precedented range and influence. Although spoken
exclusively by the ordained ministers, the sermon's
source was not ministerial wisdom but Scripture,
and its powers were the common possession of
ministers, magistrates, and congregations. Besides
dominating the Sunday worship services, sermons
were delivered at every significant event in the life
of communities. They were authority incarnate.[5]

The primary function of the sermon was to proclaim
the gospel of the mighty acts of God culminating in the
redemption accomplished in the atoning crucifixion and
resurrection of Christ, which guaranteed absolution to
the penitent and promised eternal life for men and
women of faith and sanctity. This conviction was attested
by the New Testament record of how Jesus preached the
imminent arrival of the Kingdom of God, established in
His person as Messiah, and demanding repentance. Thus
to imitate Jesus required a primary personal commitment
on the part of the Puritan ministers to make preaching
their main duty, and engagement on the part of the members of each church to listen ardently in faith to the
proclamation of the gospel. Furthermore, no one since
the time of Jesus had insisted on this joint responsibility
more ardently than Paul, the great apostle to the Gen-
tiles,[6] and all the apostles made preaching their major
activity.[7]

Preaching, Paul averred, might seem the most arrant

---

[5] *The New England Soul: Preaching and Religious Culture in New
England* (New York: Oxford University Press, 1986), 23.
[6] See, *inter alia*, Rom. 10:14 ("How shall they hear without a
preacher?"); 1 Cor. 1:23; 9:16 ("Woe is me if I preach not the
gospel"); 2 Tim. 4:2 ("Preach the Word, be instant in season").
[7] See, *inter alia*, Acts 8:4; 11:19–20; 15:35; 28:31.

stupidity to the natural man, "for the word of the cross is foolishness to those who are perishing, but to us who are being saved, it is the power of God," and he added that "the foolishness of God is wiser than men."[8] Puritan ministers offered sermons that had been prepared in their studies after careful analysis of the Hebrew and Greek originals in which the will of God, Creator, Redeemer, and Sanctifier, had been finally declared, hoping for the assistance of the Holy Spirit to move the stubborn, sin-encrusted hearts of their listeners to melt in gratitude and love, and thus be transformed from sinners into saints.

The urgent solemnity of the Puritan preacher's task is admirably expressed in Richard Baxter's renowned couplet:

> I preach't as never sure to preach again,
> And as a dying man to dying men![9]

The Plain Style

Baxter was an exponent of the favored Puritan "plain style." This famous Puritan preacher in Commonwealth and Restoration days also provided a more elaborate definition of the preacher's task and its difficulties in his influential volume, *The Reformed Pastor*, which emphasized that the Puritan preaching aimed at salvation by instruction in Christian doctrine, by reaching the religious affections, and by silencing the critic who keeps God at a distance. It reads: "It is no small matter to stand up in the face of a congregation, and deliver a message of salvation

---

[8] 1 Cor. 1:18, 25.
[9] *Love Breathing Thanks and Praise*, part II.

or damnation, as from the living God in the name of our Redeemer. It is no easy matter to speak so plain, that the ignorant may understand us; and so seriously, that the deadest hearts may feel us; and so convincingly, that contradictory cavillers may be silenced."[10]

An initial understanding of the distinctive character of the Puritan sermon may be attained by comparing Puritan and Anglican homiletics from 1625 to 1645, when the metaphysical preaching style was at its peak of popularity in the Church of England. Puritan critics during the Commonwealth, and Anglican critics during the Restoration, virtually sank the ornate and overweighted galleon, witty and erudite though it was, by the following series of salvoes of fire against the popular metaphysical style in poetry and in the pulpit. They criticized it for unnecessary complexity in sermon structure; obscurity and pedantry in development and citations; the use of fantastic conceits and images; the employment of pert and facetious wit which in its levity gloried in puns, paronomasia, and quibbles and riddles, a playing with and crumbling of the text; a preference for paradoxes that seemed more like contradictions; a fondness for allegorical interpretation that departed too readily from the primary literal and historical sense of the Scriptures; an offensive obseqiousness to royalty; applications to the congregations which were either nonexistent or too brief to be effective; and for much of the content of the sermons supposedly being speculative and unscriptural. The sum total of the charges implied that the metaphysical preachers exemplified artificial eloquence designed to advertise the ingenuity, the wit, and the wide learning of the

---

[10] *Op. cit.* (London edition of 1860), 128.

preachers, rather than being proclamations by humble servants of the Word of God.[11]

The Puritans were also learned men in their studies, but were convinced that pedantry and affected phraseology did not belong in the pulpit and that, in Shakespeare's words, "taffeta phrases, silken terms precise, three-pil'd hyperboles, spruce affectation, figures pedantical"[12] would darken the understanding of the men and women in their pews; hence, their own preference for the plain style. The high style would not lead to the desirable humility that preceded conversion. Giles Firmin, minister and physician in both Englands, insisted that "Silken Language sutes not those who are cloathed in Sackcloth."[13] As for the display of learning, Puritans would have agreed with Samuel Rutherford that learning was needed in the study but should not be advertised in the pulpit. "The pot may be used in the lithing, but not brought in with the porridge"[14] was the summary view of this Church of Scotland commissioner to the Westminster Assembly. Wit was only a distraction in a sermon which should be serious. Similarly, speculation was out of place in sermons, as Cotton Mather made plain in his encomium on the sermon style of John Eliot, New England's famous missionary to the Indians, when he ob-

---

[11] See my "*Like Angels on a Cloud*": *The English Metaphysical Preachers*, 1588–1645 (San Marino, Calif.: The Henry E. Huntington Library, 1986), Chapter XI, for documentation of the series of criticisms.

[12] *Love's Labour's Lost*, Act V, Scene i, lines 407f.

[13] *The Real Christian*, or *A Treatise of Effectual Calling* (Boston, 1742), xxxi. A posthumous publication, since Firmin died in 1691.

[14] *The Book of Common Order*, eds. G. W. Sprott and T. Leishman (Edinburgh, 1901), 338.

served, "It was food and not *froth*, which in his publick
sermons he entertained the souls of his people with, he
did not starve them with empty and windy specula-
tions."[15] In the same encomium on the plain style that
was inconsistently expressed in florid English, Cotton
Mather commended Eliot because "His way of *preaching*
was very *plain*, so that the very *lambs* might wade into his
discourses on those themes wherein *elephants* might
swim."[16] The aim of the New England preachers was
perfectly expressed by Thomas Hooker: "I have accounted it the chiefest part of judicious learning to make a
hard point easy and familiar in explication."[17]

The Puritans wanted their sermons to be plain and
persuasive to all. Thus they appealed to both the reason
and the emotions of their listeners, and they aimed to
make the extensive applications at the close of their sermons climactic and convincing. In short, the Puritans did
not cultivate pulpit oratory, but the exegesis and application of Scripture. Their aim was not primarily to delight
and amuse, but to instruct the congregation, and they believed that true art hides art. Their own genius as
preachers lay in combining fidelity to the biblical record,
with relevant and illuminating imagery, and a psychological penetration that would force the evasive soul, am-
bushed in its own dark excuses and illusions, out into a
coruscating exposure to the Light of the World.

A historian of preaching might well wonder if this
subjection to the Word (and perhaps often also to the

---

[15] Cotton Mather, *Magnalia*, I, Bk. iii, 495.

[16] *Ibid.*

[17] Preface to *A Summe of the Survey of Church Discipline* (London,
1648).

letter of Scripture) would allow for any variety on the part of the Puritan preacher. The answer might be that room for variety could be found in the selection of texts and expository passages, and especially in the important applications of them to the needs of differing listeners (as a result of pastoral visitation and the diagnosis of spiritual illnesses), as well as in the analogies and illustrations of sermons drawing on a wide swath of human experience. Furthermore, occasional sermons differed from the regular Sunday preaching in their distinctive cultural and ethical demands. Indeed, the very length of sermons demanded variety so as not to bore or exhaust the congregation. Cotton Mather's *Magnalia Christi Americana* clearly records the contributions of a variety of pulpiteers in New England while also emphasizing the unity of the Puritan brotherhood in preferring the plain style in sermons, although he also notes the exceptions. The exceptions were the Reverends Nathanael Rogers, pastor at Ipswich, and John Sherman of Watertown. Cotton Mather reports of the former that he was "a lively, curious, florid preacher . . . a fisher of men, who came with a silken line and a golden hook, and God prospered him also. . . . He knew not only how to build the temple, but also how to carve it." Mather wrote of Sherman's preaching style that he had a "natural and not affected loftiness of stile; which with an easy fluencie bespangled his discourses with such glittering figures of oratory, as caused his ablest hearers, to call him a second Isaiah, the honey-dropping and golden-mouthed preacher."[18] It should be remembered that the plain style was refracted through the prisms of differing personalities, aptitudes,

---

[18] *Magnalia*, I, Bk. iii, 377 and 465.

and variegated life experiences, changing from the first to subsequent generations of preachers.

Structure

There was a definite triadic structure for the Puritan sermon consisting of Doctrine, Reason, and Use. This is carefully described in what is perhaps one of the dullest, if most accurate, passages in the writings of Perry Miller:

> The Puritan sermon quotes the text and "opens" it as briefly as possible, expounding the circumstances and context, explaining its grammatical meanings, reducing its tropes and schemata to prose, and setting forth its logical implications; the sermon then proclaims in a flat, indicative sentence the "doctrine" contained in the text or logically deduced from it, and proceeds to the first reason or proof. Reason follows reason, with no other transition than a period or a number; after the last proof is stated there follow the uses or applications also in numbered sequence, and the sermon ends when there is nothing more to be said.[19]

The compilers of the Westminster Directory give the following instructions for composing sermons according to this method:

> In raising doctrines from the text his [the minister's] care ought to be, First, that the matter be the truth of God. Secondly, that it be a truth contained in, or grounded on, that text that the hearers may discern how God teacheth it from thence. Thirdly, that he chiefly insist upon those doctrines which

---

[19] *The New England Mind: The Seventeenth Century* (Cambridge, Mass.: Harvard University Press, 1954), 332–333.

> are principally intended, and make most for the ed-
> ification of his hearers.[20]

Evangelical teaching ("edification" means building up in the Christian faith) was the primary aim of the sermon, so it had to be solidly grounded on Scripture, then explained to the congregation, and this involved the reconciliation of apparent contradictions. The Directory urges: "The arguments or reasons are to be solid; and, as much as may be, convincing. The illustrations, of what kind soever, ought to be full of light, and such as may convey the truth into the hearer's heart with spiritual light."[21] Thus Doctrine, Reason, and Use may not unfairly be defined as the Declaration, the Explanation, and the Application of the biblical basis of the Christian faith. The first two parts of the sermon sought to convince the reason, whereas the third part aimed at warming the affections into an acceptance of the doctrine by its relevance to eschatological hope and fear and present fortification for living.

The threefold structure of the Puritan sermon may be illuminated by its exposition in the important, early, and much used homiletical textbook of William Perkins, *The Arte of Prophesying*. According to Perkins, the preacher's task was: (1) "to read the Text distinctly out of the Canonicall Scriptures"; (2) "to give the sense and understanding of it being read, by the Scripture itselfe"; (3) "to collect a few and profitable points of doctrine out of the naturall sense"; (4) "to apply (if he have the gifte)

---

20 Hall, *Reliquiae Liturgicae* (Bath: Binns and Goodwin, 1847), III, 37.
21 *Ibid.*

these doctrines rightly collected to the life and manners of men in a simple and plaine speech."[22] The most illuminating section is the one dealing with the application. He distinguishes seven ways or applications dependent upon the state of religious health of the persons as follows:

1. "Unbelievers who are both ignorant and unteachable,"
2. "Some who are teachable but yet ignorant,"
3. "Some have knowledge but are not humbled,"
4. "Some are humbled,"
5. "Some believers,"
6. "Some are fallen,"
7. "There is a mingled people."

Further, he describes two major kinds of application. One is mental, which comprises both doctrine or right teaching, and refutation (against errors); the other is concerned with practical matters, and comprises instruction for either consolation or exhortation and correction and admonition.[23]

William Ames, who was ready to join the New England community if death had not prevented him, stressed the importance of applications even more strongly than Perkins, insisting that every doctrine must be explained in terms of its use, while expanding the various desirable uses. In his influential *Medulla Theologica*,

---

[22] First written in Latin, then translated into English, Perkins's *The Arte of Prophesying* appeared thereafter posthumously in the second of the three-volume *Workes of That Famous and Worthy Minister of Christ in the University of Cambridge* (Cambridge, England, 1613). The references are to II, 673 ff. This work has been published in a modern format by the Banner of Truth Trust.

[23] *Op. cit.* (London, 1643 edition), a summary of pp. 158–160.

which was translated as *The Marrow of Sacred Divinity* (1638), he listed the types of applications as follows: information in proving a truth, refutation in confuting error, instruction in demonstrating a life to be followed, correction in condemning a life to be shunned, consolation to remove or mitigate grief or fear, exhortation to start or strengthen an inward virtue, and admonition to correct a vice. This structure was clearly followed by Charles Chauncey, the early and erudite president of Harvard College, in emphasizing the significance of the five Uses and advising his students, "But be most in *application*; which is spent in *five uses*, *refutation* of error, *information* of the truth, *correction* of manners, *exhortation* and instruction in righteousness. All of which you find in 2 Tim. iii, 16, 17. And there is a *fifth* use, viz. of comfort. I Cor. xiv. 3."[24]

Although his own style in the early eighteenth century showed a concern for fashionable elegance, nonetheless Cotton Mather delights to tell how his famous grandfather, John Cotton, the patriarch of New England, was in his years as a Cambridge don in England converted to the plain Puritan style of preaching through the influence of William Perkins, its leading exponent in Cambridge, and of Richard Sibbes, another famous Puritan theologian and preacher, who under God was responsible for his regeneration. When it came Cotton's turn to preach in the university church, St. Mary's, "an high expectation was raised, through the *whole university*, that they should have a sermon, flourishing indeed, with all the *learning* of the *whole university*." Cotton was worried that "if he should preach with a scriptural and

---

[24] *Magnalia*, I, Bk. iii, 425.

christian *plainness*, he should not only wound his own *fame* exceedingly, but also tempt carnal men to revive an old cavil, *that religion made scholars turn dunces*, whereby the name of God might suffer not a little. On the other side, he considered, that it was his duty to preach with such a *plainness*, as became the *oracles* of God, which are intended for the conduct of men in the *paths of life*, and not for *theatrical* ostentations and entertainments, and the Lord needed not any *sin* of ours to maintain his own glory." The result was that he resolved "that he would preach a plain sermon, even such a sermon, as in his own conscience he thought would be most pleasing unto the Lord Jesus Christ; and he discoursed practically and powerfully, but very solidly on the plain doctrine of repentance."[25] The university wits who expressed their delight in a sermon refrained pointedly on this occasion from showing their displeasure, but the sermon won a notable recruit for Puritanism, namely, John Preston, later master of Emmanuel College and chaplain to King Charles I. With this example before them of one in the Puritan apostolic succession from Perkins and Sibbes to Preston, who had thrown in his lot with the wilderness of New England, the plain style of sermon would flourish vigorously in Cotton's adopted land until the end of the century. In his encomium of Cotton, the grandson emphasizes that "though he were a great scholar, yet he did conscientiously forbear making to the *common people* an ostentation of it. He had the *art of concealing his art.*"[26]

The Puritan critique of ornamental elocution and the

---

[25] *Ibid.*, 234–235. Mather's narrative is summarized with interspersed citations.
[26] *Op. cit.*, I, Bk. iii, 250.

display of learning and wit are derived in part from St. Paul's declaration (in 1 Corinthians 2:4), "And my speech and my preaching were not with enticing words of wisdom, but in demonstration of the Spirit and power." These words were interpreted by William Perkins as an instruction to observe "an admirable plainness and an admirable powerfulness."[27] Facetious conceits in sermons were excoriated by John Collinges, who declared that "Wit is the soul's worst carver."[28]

Plainness, however, was not to be interpreted as unsophisticated and uncouth rusticity. Greenham makes this clear in holding up St. Paul as a model for the Christian preacher, since the apostle was "read in Aratus, Epimenides, Menander, made Felix to tremble with his eloquence, was thought Mercury for his eloquence at Lycaonia, by the notable course and vein of all his epistles, not inferior to the writings of any of the heathen."[29] Moreover, as will be seen, Puritan preachers in New England illuminated their discourses with illustrations and images drawn from life and literature.

One of New England's most esteemed preachers, expert in diagnosing the ills of the soul and prescribing to

---

[27] *Of the Calling of the Ministerie* (London, 1618), 430. For a full discussion of the origin, aim, and use of the plain style, see William Haller, *The Rise of Puritanism* (New York: Columbia University Press, 1938), 129–134: Perry Miller, *The New England Mind*, 331–62: and Lawrence A. Sasek, *The Literary Temper of the English Puritans* (Baton Rouge: Louisiana State University, 1961), *passim* and especially Chapters I and V.

[28] *The Spouse under the Apple-Tree* (London, 1649), dedicatory epistle.

[29] From the *Works* of Richard Greenham, 399-400, cited by Sasek, *op. cit.*, 48. St. Paul cites Aratus in Acts 17:28, Menander in 1 Cor. 15:33, and Epimenides in Titus 1:2.

prepare for its reception of the divine grace that heals, was Thomas Hooker, the patriarch of Hartford, who gave great attention to applications of doctrines. A renowned sermon of his is *The Soules Ingraffing into Christ* (1637),[30] and it will illustrate the attention to uses. The text is Malachi 3:1: "And the Lord whom ye seeke shall suddenly come into His Temple." He begins by defining engrafting in Christ, which has three characteristics: the sinner is humbled and broken-hearted, is made partaker of all the good things that are in Christ, and all this is the work of the Holy Spirit. Then he turns to his text, which he explains as a prophecy of John the Baptist, who was the harbinger of Christ, and the temple is explained physically as the Jerusalem temple and spiritually as the Church of Christ in the number of the faithful, each of whose hearts is a temple in which the Spirit dwells. The prepared temple "is nothing but the heart truly broken and humbled." Christ as King takes possession of the soul when the heart is empty—to make full provision for it.

The Doctrine thus explained has three Uses: firstly, it is a comfort to every humbled soul; secondly, it serves for examination and trial; and thirdly, it is a ground of instruction whereby we learn wisely to choose our companions. After speaking of the means of getting a humble heart, Hooker suggests motives to provoke his hearers to brokenheartedness: "First, consider what an unreasonable thing it is that thou shouldest rather keep out the

---

[30] This sermon has been reprinted with two others by Thomas Hooker with notes and an introduction by Everett H. Emerson as *Redemption: Three Sermons (1637–1656) by Thomas Hooker* (Gainesville, Fl.: Scholars' Facsimiles & Reprints, 1956).

Lord Jesus Christ, than cast out a company of base lusts,"
and also, "As it is unreasonable, so in the second place,
what an uncomfortable thing will it be! Ah think of it in
time: for the time will come, at the great day of account,
when we shall need a Saviour, and crave his presence,
and be forced to desire Christ to come to us."[31] While
Hooker does not dangle the souls of the congregation over
the pit of hell, he does suggest that only one in a thousand
shall be saved. He then anticipates objections, which he
answers, and goes on to indicate how God hides
Himself—refusing His approval for sins—with a simple
but serviceable illustration.

Illustrations and Imagery

This vivid domestic image, which deserves full quo-
tation, leads us into a consideration of the importance and
variety of illustrations, metaphors, and similes which
brightened the New England sermons. If illustrations are
like windows, then the New England illustrations are as
transparent as their church windows, avoiding the or-
nateness of Anglican stained glass. Here is Hooker's first
extended image in the same significant sermon:

> I have seene the father deale so with the child;
> when the father is going on in his journey, if the
> child will not goe on, but stands gaping upon vanity,
> and when the father calls, he comes not, the onely
> way is this, the father steps aside behind a bush, and
> then the child runs and cries, and if he gets his fa-
> ther againe, he forsakes all his trifles, and walkes on
> more faster and more cheerefully with his father
> than ever. So when the Lord Jesus Christ some-

---

[31] *Op. cit.*, 96–97.

> times makes knowne himselfe to us, and would carry
> us on in a Christian course cheerefully, we are
> playing with trifles, and grow carelesse, and cold,
> and worldly, and remisse in prayer, and dead hearted;
> the onely way to quicken us up is to hide himselfe,
> and to make us give ourselves for lost; & then they
> that could scarcely pray once a weeke, now will pray
> three or foure times a day.[32]

Later in the sermon, Hooker indicates that he has
more to teach his congregation, but they are not yet ready
for this instruction, and he drives home the point by another illustration equally simple, in monosyllables
whenever possible, so that all may understand:

> As it is with a little barke, if it should have a great
> maine mast, and broad sail cloathes, then instead of
> carrying it, it would be overthrown by them: there-
> fore men proportion their mast according to their
> ship or bark . . . the sense of God's love and mercy
> is like the saile that carries us on in a Christian
> course: and if we get but a little saile of mercy and
> favour we goe on sweetly and comfortably but if
> God gives us abundance of assurance, our cursed rot-
> ten hearts would overturne, and instead of quickning
> of us, it would overthrow us.[33]

For those who despair of divine consolation, he also
has an illustration, equally effective because equally
simple and drawn from everyday life. He reports a minister saying to such a person who finally received consolation, "The Lord will not always give his children a
cordiall, but he hath it ready for them when they are

---

[32] *Op. cit.*, 118.
[33] *Op. cit.*, 132–33.

fainting."[34] By the practicality of his applications and the
simple relevance of his illustrations, Hooker shows the
value of the plain style in the hands of a master preacher.
And he was not unusual in this respect, except perhaps in
range and profundity, among the earliest New England
divines.

Another preacher with a great gift for simple illustrations was the compassionate and lovable Thomas
Shepard, whom Cotton Mather calls, in a pun, *Pastor
Evangelicus*, "shepherd of the church in Cambridge." His
images come from three major sources: the sea (from
which he was delivered when shipwreck seemed certain),[35] the observation of bees, and everyday domestic
life. Maritime imagery includes the landlocked landlub-
ber satisfied by his limited horizon compared with the
mariner seeking for the coast: "Men that live on land and
love the smoke of their own chimneys, never look out to
other coasts and countries, or to a strange land; but sea-
men that are bound for a voyage, and have a pilot with
them that has seen the coast, that is it they look for," just
as "the church and people of God . . . now are no more of
this world, but look out of it, and verily expect the second coming, and glorious appearing of Christ."[36] Shepard
thinks that when all is peaceful, the temptation to forsake
Christ is powerful: "like sailors that in a storm at sea,

---

[34] *Op. cit.*, 134.

[35] For his fascinating autobiography, see *God's Plot: The Paradoxes of
Puritan Piety, Being—The Autobiography and Journal of Thomas Shepard*
(1605–1649), ed. Michael McGiffert (Amherst: University of
Massachusetts, 1972).

[36] *The Parable of the Ten Virgins* in John A. Albro, ed., *Works*
(Boston: Doctrinal Book and Tract Society, 1853), II, 143-144. (This
work has been reprinted by Soli Deo Gloria.)

every man is ready, and will be pulling his rope; but
when a calm, go to their cabins, and there fall asleep
. . ."[37] Shepard's congregation was familiar with bee-
keeping, so it was natural for him to advise them to gather
grace in good times, as the bees then make honey: "and
therefore, as bees, gather in your honey in summer-
time."[38] Another minister, William Hubbard, the pastor
of Ipswich, produced an extended illustration that contrasted the industrious bee with the idle butterfly:

> The prudent husband man uses more to be de-
> lighted in the busie, active yet stable bee, than in
> the gaudy Butterfly, which it may be ranges all over
> the field to get only fine colours wherewith to paint
> her wings, from those flowers whence the other
> diligent creatures fetch both wax and honey,
> wherewith they both build their houses and furnish
> them with provision to feed themselves and refresh
> their owners, while the other are but the object of
> children's sport.[39]

Shepard's images are never ponderous like
Hubbard's, and he excels in figures drawn from domestic
life, especially the relations between husband and wife
(not surprisingly, since he was married three times). He
contrasts the mutuality of husband and wife with the de-
pendency of servants on masters and mistresses in an extended image: "Servants give work for their wages, and
masters give wages for their work, but husbands and
wives give themselves one unto another . . . so servants
in the church they do for God in hope of wages . . . but

---

[37] *Op. cit.*, II, 65.
[38] *The Sound Believer, Works*, I, 215.
[39] *The Happiness of a People* (Boston, 1676), 56.

he that is espoused to Christ gives himself."[40] Another delightful image of happy domesticity illustrates how one can be too busy for God: "It is with most professors, commonly, as it is with a woman that loves her husband, and begins to dress herself, but so much business to do, that she doth it but by starts; hence, call her never so late, she will say she is not yet ready, she has so much to do she can not: so it is here. . . . O betimes, do this work; set things to right in your souls."[41]

Shepard is equally effective in using medical images. It is, he argues, only troubled persons that seek a physician, or the physician of souls, Christ: "Whole men have no heart or desire after physicians; when all limbs are whole and strong, no desire after plasters; so, while any thing eases and contents the heart, there is no desire after Christ. Hos. iv. 11. 'Whoredom and wine have taken away the heart.' "[42] Shepard can also coin the memorable epigram, such as the following, which illustrates that humans prefer easy, handy remedies: "Kitchen physic is not far to seek";[43] or an apothegm that derides those with a merely formal faith: "And so their faith, like a bucket without a bottom, draws up nothing."[44] Encouraging patience in prayer, he remarks, "The Lord ever gives his importunate beggars their desires, either in pence by little and little, or by pounds; long he is many times before he gives, but payeth them well for their waiting."[45] And

[40] *The Parable of the Ten Virgins*, in *Works*, II, 31.
[41] *Op. cit.*, II, 73.
[42] *Op. cit.*, II, 29.
[43] *Op. cit.*, II, 37.
[44] *Op. cit.*, II, 281.
[45] *The Sincere Convert*, in *Works*, I, 12.

cheek by jowl with this image is another, indicating that God's providential rule will become clear at the Great Assize at the end of history, but not in the confused picture of the present: "God is now like a wise carpenter, but hewing out his work. There is a lumber and confusion seemingly among us; let us stay till the day of judgment, and then we shall see infinite wisdom in fitting all this for his own glory, and for the good of his people."[46]

Hooker, too, can use domestic images. Here is one from the kitchen, urging the maintenance of purity: "You may conceive it by a similitude, if a pot be boyling upon the fire, there will a scum rise, but yet they that are good housewives, and cleanly, and neat, they watch it, and the scum riseth up, they take it off and throw it away, happily more scum will arise, but still as it riseth they scum it off."[47] Cotton also recalls the domestic scene on washing day:

> And so an Houswife that takes her linning, she Sopes, and bedawbs it, and it may be defiles it with dung, so as it neither looks nor smels wel, and when she hath done, she rubs it, and buckes it, and wrings it, and in the end all this is but to make it cleane and white: and truly so it is here, when as Tyrants most of all insult over Gods people, and scourge them and lay them in hee, or dung, so as the very name of them stinks, yet what is this but to purge them, and to make them white, and it is a great

---

[46] *Ibid.*
[47] Hooker, *The Saints Dignitie*, 4–5. This reference, as also the next, I owe to Babette May Levy, *Preaching in the First Half Century of New England History* (Hartford, Conn.: The American Society of Church History, 1945), 114.

service they doe to the people of God in so doing.[48]

It takes real insight to find a simple similitude for the subtle issue of how much preparation can be made for the reception of grace by the elect, and this Hooker finds from watching a game: "The ball must fall to the ground, before it can rebound back againe; for the Lord Jesus must first dart in his love into the soule, before the soule can rebound in love and joy to him again, we must receive in grace before wee can rebound backe any love to God: as I Tim. 1:7."[49]

No one listening to the plain preachers could have missed their meaning, especially when abstract truths became concrete in such vivid illustrations drawn from day-to-day experiences.

The other striking characteristic of Puritan preaching was its psychological penetration in anticipating and answering the objections of the critical or half-hearted members of the congregations. It was exemplified in the sermons of every early major New England preacher, such as Hooker or Shepard. Shepard frequently offers us in his sermons a dialogue between the minister, as Christ's representative, and the wounded soul, with its objections to accepting the promises of Christ as applying to him or her. For example, in his sermon entitled *The Sincere Believer*, the weakened soul successively complains that sin prevails; that the devil will be busy with him and he cannot be cheerful; that there will be much opposition in the world; that he lacks outward comfort;

---

[48] John Cotton, *Christ the Fountaine*, 71–72; also cited by Levy, *op. cit.*, 115.
[49] "Spirituall Love and Joy" in *The Soules Implantation*, 182.

that he will be mocked and reproached; that his prayers are cold and comfortless; that he fears death; that he will not be able to endure suffering if it comes; and that he might fall away from God. Shepard has a ready answer to each of these objections, and his reply to the last is a ringing assurance: "None can pluck thee out of Christ's hands, neither sin nor devil."[50] But the poor soul is still unsatisfied, and the discussion continues for a few minutes more, when Shepard finds a final biblical promise if only the half-hearted soul can say that it would wish to feel a sense of compunction.

The struggle for the souls of the congregation, so characteristic of Shepard's preaching, had been anticipated by John Cotton, who, under the guidance of Sibbes, learned to substitute for intellectual conviction the psychological preparation of his hearers. As his contemporaries phrased it (and the same held true for most New England preachers), Cotton, in his preaching and writing, sought the substance of Paul rather than Plato, and the manner of Moses rather than the Muses.[51] According to John Norton, Cotton's Puritan style indicated that he "distinguished between the Word of wisdom and the wisdom of words"—and his preaching was "not with the enticing words of man's wisdom, but in the demonstration of the Spirit and of power."[52]

But, of course, unlike the opposing style of Lancelot Andrewes and the metaphysical preachers, Cotton re-

---

[50] "The Saint's Jewel," in *Works*, I, 290–92. The citation is from p. 291.

[51] *John Cotton on the Churches of New England*, ed. Larzer Ziff (Cambridge, Mass.: Harvard University Press, 1968), 10.

[52] *Abel Being Dead Yet Speaketh* (London, 1658), 14.

fused speculation such as Donne's wondering how a man swallowed by a fish or eaten by a cannibal or an animal would retrieve his own body at the General Resurrection.[53] Nor did he use fanciful illustrations drawn from "unnatural natural history," like Hacket, who believed that the crocodile "hath both eyes so befilmed that he perceives afar off and is not perceived." Neither did he crumble his text, like Andrewes, who rejoiced to preach on the syllables of one word as meaningful fractions. All Puritan preachers aimed to be psychologically persuasive.

Biblical Fidelity

Since the New England Puritans were determined to be servants of the Word of God, it is important to consider their mode of interpreting the Scripture in their sermons. While occasionally the first generation of preachers took topics from the Bible on which they expatiated at length (such as the hundreds of pages Shepard spent on the *Parable of the Ten Virgins*, extending it to the dimensions of a phenomenology of soteriology, and in the process illuminating a vast quantity of the Scripture), some preachers, like Cotton, in their lecture sermons managed to expound *seriatim* their study of entire books of the Old and New Testament. Regarding Cotton's nineteen years in Boston:

> Here, in an expository way, he went over the *Old Testament* once, and a second time as far as the thirtieth chapter of Isaiah; and the whole *New Testa-*

---

[53] *The Sermons of John Donne*, eds. G. R. Potter and E. M. Simpson, 10 vols. (Berkeley: University of California Press, 1953–1962), III, 96–97.

ment once, and a second time as far as the eleventh chapter to the *Hebrews*. Upon *Lord's-days* and *lecture-days*, he preached thorow the *Acts of the Apostles*, the prophecies of *Haggai* and *Zechariah*, the books of *Ezra*, the *Revelation*, *Ecclesiastes*, *Canticles*, second and third Epistles of *John*, the Epistle to *Titus*, both epistles to *Timothy*, the Epistle to the *Romans*, with innumerable other scriptures on incidental occasions.[54]

The weekday lectures often took the form of warnings against heresies. Shepard, for example, spent four years warning his congregations in Cambridge of the dangers of Arminianism and Antinomianism, while Cotton concentrated on the errors of Roman Catholicism.[55] By contrast, the Sabbath-day sermons were inclined to be less polemical and more inspirational, moral, and hortatory in character, contrasted with the catechetical and polemical[56] lecture sermons. Still, the contrast should not be drawn too boldly. In the earliest days in New England, there were two ministers (as at Boston and the larger towns) for a single congregation, one the pastor (John Wilson) and the other the teacher (John Cotton). The former would be chiefly concerned with the application of the gospel of redemption to the different states of progress of the soul, preaching "chiefly in *exhortations* and *admonitions* and good wholesome *councils*, tending to excite

---

[54] *Magnalia*, I, Bk. iii, 247.

[55] Shepard's lecture sermons were printed as *The Parable of the Ten Virgins*, and Cotton's were published as *The Powring Out of the Seven Vials*.

[56] Cotton Mather noted that although Thomas Hooker was of a choleric disposition, "he would hardly ever handle any *polemical divinity* in the pulpit" (*Magnalia*, I, Bk. iii, 314).

good motions in the minds of his hearers."[57] Cotton, the theologian, would be expert in warning against such heretical errors as Familism, Pelagianism, Arminianism, and Antinomianism. Yet, according to Cotton Mather, Wilson would preach "on the same texts that were doctrinally handled by his colleague instantly before."[58] In smaller communities, the single minister had to be both pastor and teacher, comforter and critic of developing souls, and expositor of doctrine.

One is astonished to read of the assiduity with which the ministers studied the Bible in both Testaments, and of their ability to find spiritual sustenance in apparently desiccated genealogies. The Reverend George Phillips was so learned in the Scriptures "that he was able on the sudden to turn unto any text without the help of Concordances."[59] Cotton Mather relates that when John Wilson called upon Nathanael Rogers just prior to family morning prayers, and the reading was the first chapter of the first book of Chronicles, on the spur of the moment Wilson "from a paragraph of mere *proper names*, that seemed altogether barren of any edifying matter, he raised so many fruitful and useful notes."[60] The New England preachers squeezed the last drop of juice from the fruit of their studies of the oracles of God. John Warham produced twenty-seven sermons on the single verse of Romans 5:1, whereas Thomas Hooker spent almost a year expounding Acts 25:1–13 (Paul's defense before Governor Festus), and Thomas Shepard was four

---

[57] *Op. cit.*, I, Bk. iii, 282.
[58] *Ibid.*
[59] *Op. cit.*, I, Bk. iii, 342.
[60] *Op. cit.*, I, Bk. iii, 282.

years explaining the meaning of a single parable of Jesus, that of the ten virgins (Matthew 25:1–13).[61]

But even when the text of the sermon was brief, it was not unusual to fortify it by citing numerous other texts, which constituted the "reasons" or supports of the doctrine. John Davenport, pastor of Roxbury, was admired for sermons fortified by many textual references, for he was "a notable *text-man* and one who had more than forty or fifty *scriptures* distinctly quoted in the one discourse."[62] Such attention to the letter of Scripture, even when the attempt was being made to find its spirit, combined with an insistence upon the literal and historical meaning (to the exclusion of allegorical meanings) and a demand for a plain pulpit style, cumulatively force the modern reader to wonder whether the interpretation of the Bible was not too flat and homogeneous, and whether the single meaning could be consistently maintained. It is appropriate, therefore, to consider the hermeneutics or principles of biblical interpretation of our preachers.

Principles of Interpretation[63]

The Puritans, like their Reformed predecessors, rejected the four-level medieval exegesis clarified by St. Thomas Aquinas as the literal or historical, the tropological, the allegorical, and the anagogical senses of Scripture.

---

61 Babette May Levy, *Preaching*, 89.

62 *Op. cit.*, II, Bk. iv, 49.

63 For much of the information on typological interpretation as employed by the ministers of New England, I am indebted to the fine monograph of Mason I. Lowance, Jr., a former student, author of *The Language of Canaan: Metaphor and Symbol in New England from the Puritans to the Transcendentalists* (Cambridge, Mass.: Harvard University Press, 1980), 1–177.

They retained the literal or historical sense, but rejected the tropological or moral sense, the allegorical sense which was widely interpreted as being concerned with the progress of the Church, and the anagogical sense concerned with eschatology. Thus, to use a convenient if commonplace illustration, Jerusalem in the Bible, for medieval interpreters, referred literally to the city located in Palestine, allegorically to the Church, tropologically to the seeker after divine peace, and anagogically to the heavenly resting place of the saints in glory. The rejection of the three senses was founded on the Puritan conviction that the extra senses weakened the primary sense, leading to uncontrolled subjectivity in interpretation.

Although the Puritans in America yielded to none in their conviction of the absolute primacy (in many cases, exclusively so) of the literal and historical sense of Scripture as used in their sermons, they emphasized that the Bible was also understood as having three tenses necessary for its exposition—past, present, and future. As Mason Lowance argues: "It is important to understand that history for the New England Puritans was believed to be a related series of divinely inspired events, so that the guiding hand of Providence might be perceived in human experience. The record of these historical events—the Bible— . . . became for the Puritans a rich source for describing their own contemporary history."[64]

Scripture's prophetic language became for the preachers a primary means through which later events could be understood. Clearly, first consideration had to be given

---

[64] Lowance, *The Language of Canaan*, vii.

to the mighty acts of God in past history, witnessed by prophets, judges, kings, and priests, culminating in the incarnation, crucifixion, and resurrection of Christ, and the founding of the Church as Christ's body in the Pentecostal descent of the Holy Spirit as the Illuminator, Strengthener, and Sanctifier of the Church. That always remained the primary sense of Scripture. But these providential actions of the same Triune God afforded a pattern and precedents for interpreting the divine will in the present, in which, to use their own terms, they discerned the "smiles" and "frowns" of God.

The profound Calvinist sense of particular Providence motivated the preachers both early and late. It inspired Captain Edward Johnson's *Wonder-Working Providence of Sions Saviour (1628-1651)*, which interpreted the Puritan errand into the wilderness as part of God's providential design to establish a pure Church, consisting of saints following Christ's own ordinances, unpolluted by human traditions or by too easy terms of admission to church membership and to the Lord's Supper. It was the same conviction that inspired Increase Mather to gather his collection of case histories of divine intervention in recent history, entitled *An Essay for the Recording of Illustrious Providences* (1684). As Robert Middlekauff reports, "In Increase Mather's hand, typology became more than a technique for penetrating the puzzle of Scripture: it became a method for understanding the history of his own time."[65]

It is significant that, as was described in the previous chapter, the American Puritans institutionalized the

---

[65] Robert Middlekauff, *The Mathers: Three Generations of Puritan Intellectuals* (New York: Oxford University Press, 1971), 107.

doctrine and experience of particular providence in their days of thanksgiving and days of humiliation; these were kept sometimes by the whole of New England, sometimes by several churches or a single church, sometimes by a family, and occasionally by a private individual. By preaching and by institution, the prophetic interpretation of Scripture spoke in contemporary terms.

In yet another sense, however, Scripture was interpreted in the future sense. The Puritans developed what Sacvan Bercovitch has termed a "developmental typology," "which enabled them to relate Old Testament figures and events not only to Christ's Incarnation, but also to the Second Coming."[66] This was eagerly and conveniently linked to chiliasm, or the belief that Christ would rule on the earth with His saints for a thousand years before the Great Assize and judgment seat of Christ at the end of history. The jeremiads,[67] or sermons reminding the second and third generations of New Englanders of how they were less pious than their ancestors who first reached New England's shores, weakened the conviction of many that this land would be the location of Christ's millennial reign on earth; but Increase Mather continued in this belief, even calculating by numerology that Christ's earthly reign would begin in 1716.[68] His son,

---

[66] *Typology and Early American Literature*, ed. Sacvan Bercovitch (Amherst: University of Massachusetts Press, 1971), 107.

[67] See Bercovitch, *The American Jeremiad* (Madison: University of Wisconsin Press, 1978). Two notable examples of such sermons were Samuel Danforth's election sermon of 1670, *A Briefe Recognition of New England's Errand into the Wilderness*, and Increase Mather's, preached and published thirty-two years later: *Ichabod; or, The Glory Departing*.

[68] Lowance, *The Language of Canaan*, 150.

Cotton Mather, also maintained millenarianism, as did the great Jonathan Edwards in the middle decades of the eighteenth century. This futuristic approach is part of the enthusiasm found in the sermons of Cotton, Shepard, and Hooker, as well as in those of the conservative Increase and Cotton Mather, and accounts for the frequency of typological interpretation in their sermons, and the exciting conviction that true religion had moved westward, leaving Europe for the "New Israel," New England.

The "type" in typological exegesis is an anticipatory shadow of the "antitype" or fulfillment of a person or event in the future, and is ultimately derived from the way the Fathers of the early church linked the Old and New Testaments. A type is distinguished from a trope, figure, allegory, or metaphor because of its anchorage in the authenticity of history, whereas the trope is a product of the imagination, such as the medieval Everyman, or Milton's *Comus*, or Christian, the hero of Bunyan's *Pilgrim's Progress*. The type exists in history and is factual, but the allegory, the simile, and the metaphor are products of human fancy and can mean whatever their inventors intend. Thus the historical Abraham is a type or adumbration of God the Father reluctantly willing to sacrifice His own Son, and the crossing of the Red Sea by the Hebrews is a foreshadowing of the *transitus* from death to life by the resurrection of Christ, as the receipt of the divine manna in the wilderness by the Israelites is the anticipation of the Eucharist founded by Christ. Oddly enough, although allegorical interpretation, because unhistorical, was rejected by the Puritans of New England at first, it was revived in the last two decades of the seventeenth century and became popular in the early eighteenth century.

There were three typological interpreters who chiefly influenced the American Puritans: Thomas Taylor, with his *Moses and Aaron, or the Types and Shadows . . . Opened and Explained* (1635); Samuel Mather, with his *Figures or Types of the Old Testament by which Christ and the Heavenly Things of the Gospel were Preached and Shadowed to the People of God of Old* (1683, with a second edition in 1705 that was the work of a son of the New England patriarch, Richard Mather); and Benjamin Keach, who wrote *Tropologia: A Key to Open Scripture Metaphors and Types* (1681).

Some New England preachers using typology are careful, as Shepard is, not to assume that all Old Testament persons or events are types with antitypical fulfillment in the New Testament. The New Testament also manifests the abrogation of the Old, as in the case of the covenant of works which God established with Adam, and the covenant of grace which was established in the sacrificial death of Christ, according to Romans 11:6. In his *Theses Sabbaticae*, Shepard argues that there were three types of laws "eminently appearing among the Jews: 1. Moral. 2. Ceremoniall. 3. Judiciall." It is the moral law, he insists, "contained in the decalogue," which "is nothing else but the law of nature revived, or a second edition and impression of that primitive and perfect law of nature, which in the state of innocency was engraven upon man's heart, but is now again written upon tables of stone, by the finger of God."[69] The moral obligations of the Decalogue are permanently valid, and the

[69] Theses 28 and 39 from Thomas Shepard's *Theses Sabbaticae* in *Works* (Boston: Doctrinal Book and Tract Society, 1843), I, 151.

Sabbath belongs to both moral and ceremonial systems, and so has continued efficacy. It is significant, however, that Samuel Mather disposes of all the Anglican ceremonial law that was claimed to be typologically adumbrated in the Old Testament by denying the claims of the ceremonial law, which he affirms is wholly abrogated in the New Testament.[70]

If we want examples of the excitement which typological exegesis at early and late dates was able to induce, we shall find them in sermons of both Shepard and Sewall. Shepard delights in reminding his congregation of the Second Coming of Christ:

> The church and people of God . . . now are no more of this world, but look out of it, and verily expect the second coming, and glorious appearing of Christ.
> REASON 1. Because they really foresee and see such a day. 2 Pet. iii. 3, 4. "In the last days shall come scoffers saying, 'Where is the promise of his coming? All things are as they were,' " and hence live in their lusts, die in their own dung, and never look for it. But these foresee it really, and hence look for it. . . .
> REASON 2. Because they see nothing else in this worth looking after; no, not for the present. For if a man sees the day of the Lord, yet has some prey in his eye, in this world, and his game before him, he will follow his hunting to catch his venison, though he comes too late for the blessing. But the Lord makes his people to see nothing in the world

---

[70] The views of Samuel Mather on the abrogation of the ceremonial law in the Old Testament are expressed in detail in his *Testimony of Scripture against Idolatry and Superstition*, and were briefly echoed in his *Figures or Types of the Old Testament*.

worth the hawking and catching.[71]

Samuel Sewall, the son of the judge, produced a most vivid account of his impression of the end of the world in *Phaenomena quadam Apocalyptica, or, Some Few Lines Towards a Description of the New Heaven as It Makes to Those Who Stand upon the New Earth* (1697). This is his prophecy of North America as a future paradise to replace that lost in Eden where God's elect shall be gathered:

> *The Land was as the Garden of Eden*, or *Paradise, Before Them; and Behind Them a Desolate Wilderness.* They have fulfilled, and surpassed the Mischievousness of *old Babylon, in Making the World as a Wilderness, and Destroying the Cities Thereof. Now the Good Lord by His Good Spirit Lift Up a Standard Against the Cruel Enemy of Christ and Mankind: That Such Enemies May be Scattered. And Let the Lord Lift* Up His Hand: Declare *His Power To the Gentiles, that They May Be Gathered To, and By the Standard of* the Gospel.[72]

The most striking *volte face* or turnaround in biblical interpretation was the enthusiastic acceptance of allegorical interpretation by the New England preachers. Carefully avoiding such interpretation as Romanist, contrived, fanciful, and idiosyncratic, they came to supplement the biblical source of revelation by the observation of the Creator's ways in nature and in human reason. Their exemplar in this respect was an English Presbyterian divine, John Flavel, in his *Husbandry Spiritualised*,

---

[71] Shepard, *The Parable of the Ten Virgins*, in *Works*, II, 143ff. The sermons can be no later than the early 1640's, since he died in 1645.
[72] p. 57.

published in London in 1669. Its subtitle, *Or, The Heavenly use of Earthly Things*, provides a clue to his method, which is the inverse of biblical exegesis, since it does not look to nature for verification of Scriptural truth, but as a separate source of divine revelation. Flavel can use a text as a pretext for his title in 1 Corinthians 3:9: "Ye are God's husbandry." Nature is his real text, and his genuine concern is for the similitude's and figures that teach the nature of God as effectively as Scripture, and much less mysteriously or darkly, but even so the lessons are not understood by the unregenerate. Flavel also asserts that poetry may reveal spiritual lessons for the laymen deaf to the preached Word: "That of *Herbert* is experimentally true: 'A Verse May Find Him That a Sermon Flies, and Turn Delight into a Sacrifice.' "[73] His "Propositions" derived from husbandry are—and this is the difference from typological exegesis—independent of historical verification, and extraordinarily vague. For example, the second proposition reads:

> *Husbandmen* divide and separate their lands from other mens, they have their Landmarks and their Boundaries by which property is preserved. So are the People of God wonderfully separated, and distinguished from the People of the Earth. It is a special act of Grace, to be inclosed by God out of the Waste Howling Wilderness of the World (Deut. 33:16).[74]

Even as conservative a divine as Cotton Mather copied this technique in his imitation of Flavel, termed

---

[73] Sig. A4.
[74] *Ibid.*, sig. A4 verso.

Agricola, or the Religious Husbandman (1727), not forgetting an earlier book of spiritualized instruction, *The Religious Mariner* (1700), in which maritime figures were introduced to teach spiritual lessons. Other ministers, however, such as John Davenport, in his *Knowledge of Christ* (1652), continued to maintain the truth of all the scriptural types of the Messiah as proving that the crucified Jesus was the only true Messiah—while other divines regarded reason surveying nature as an accessory source of divine truth, parallel to the progress of research in the natural sciences encouraged by the Royal Society of London, founded in 1660, and of which Cotton Mather was a proud member.

The topics of the sermons covered the whole range of Christian development from conviction of sin, to contrition, to vocation or calling, to justification by faith through grace, conversion, sanctification, finally looking to glorification. These stages were those that had been marked out in the Pauline epistles, and it is significant that these were more frequently cited than the four Gospels, with the exception of John's Gospel. In a letter to a brother minister, Charles Chauncey, Harvard's president for seventeen years, offered the following advice: "Preach much about the *misery* of the state of *nature*, the preparatives to *conversion* or *effectual calling*; the necessity of *union* and *communion* with Christ; the nature of saving and justifying *faith*, and the fruits thereof *love and good works*, and sanctification."[75] To this list may be added the practical gift that Shepard and Hooker had abundantly—to preach on "cases of conscience"—that is, the capacity to dress the wounds of the soul, making their

---

[75] Mather, *Magnalia*, I, Bk. iii, 399.

hearers ready for the transfusions and transformations of grace provided by the Great Physician Himself.[76]

Some series of sermons were extensive *seriatim* expositions of entire books of the Bible, such as Cotton and Chauncey delivered. Others were expositions of important parts of them, as Shepard's of a single parable. Yet others were topical, especially on artillery or election days, or at executions, dealing with the problem at hand. Yet others, like the jeremiads, were denunciatory or imprecatory in character. All attempted to be plain, persuasive, practical, and faithful proclamations of the living God, preached without fear or favor.

The sermons prepared for special occasions required a different rhetoric from the evangelical approach employed on Sundays. On such occasions, the ministers were less ambassadors of reconciliation than custodians of New England's social and cultural heritage. Hence, as Harry S. Stout observed, "their primary focus shifted from God's mercy to man's responsibility to honor the conditional terms of God's national covenant."[77] The ministers appealed to fear as they depicted the divine desertion of an impenitent people, and they acknowledged that personal salvation was divinely given (not humanly earned), while the national covenant demanded good works from the citizens of the Bible commonwealth.

The Length, Delivery, and Gestures of Sermons

The Puritans of New England relished sermons as the

---

[76] See the excellent study of theological preparationism by Norman Pettit: *The Heart Prepared: Grace and Conversion in Puritan Spiritual Life* (New Haven, Conn.: Yale University Press, 1966).

[77] *The New England Soul*, 24.

nourishment of the soul, and also as the iron rations of the serious pilgrim bound for eternity. They were prepared for, and very often received on many occasions, lengthy discourses so that their mental "stomachs" were "stuffed." It is well known that in Commonwealth days in England the length of the sermon, especially if it was genuinely extemporaneous, was the index of a powerful preacher. Cromwell, the Protector, was anxious to test the homiletical power of John Howe, a Presbyterian minister, with a view to appointing him one of his chaplains. So, after the conclusion of the prayer before the sermon, Cromwell changed the text he had given Howe to preach on. The worthy divine preached from the substituted text until the monitory sands of the first and second hours of the hourglass had run out, and was called upon to stop the spate of his oratory only when he was about to turn the glass again.[78]

Ordinary occasions did not require such marathon performances. On an extraordinary occasion—before the execution of a criminal and in front of a vast crowd—Cotton Mather preached a sermon lasting almost two hours. His own vivid, if smug, account reads: "The greatest Assembly, ever in this Countrey preach'd unto, was now come together; it may be four or five thousand Souls. I could not gett unto the *pulpitt*, but by climbing over *Pues* and *Heads:* and there the Spirit of my dearest Lord came upon mee. I preached with a more than ordinary Assistence, and enlarged, and uttered the most awakening Things, for near two hours together. My Strength and my Voice failed not; but when it was near

[78] Edmund Calamy, *The Continuation of the Ejected Ministers* (London, 1727), I, 250f.

failing, a silent Look to Heaven strangely renewed it."[79] Mather was given to prolixity. Even on the day of his ordination to the ministry on May 13, 1685, he offered a public prayer lasting ninety minutes and a sermon of an hour and three quarters in length, and this despite the fact that his ordination was delayed because he was a stutterer![80]

The earliest New England ministers were not as long-winded, although they were not short-winded either. Thomas Shepard preached a sermon on one occasion, according to Edward Johnson, who was fascinated by him, that must have been over two hours in duration, since "the glasse was turned up twice."[81] Charles Chauncy preached brief, concise, and pointed sermons on Sundays of forty-five minutes' length.[82] It seems that sermons lasting less than an hour were generally regarded as insufficient spiritual diet, even for those who listened to three sermons each week.[83]

It is clear that a gift for extemporaneous speech was admired by both ministers and congregations in a community that had rejected liturgical forms of prayer, since both read sermons and read prayers were considered a limitation on the inspiration of the Holy Spirit. Even so, the same ministers devoted long hours in their studies preparing their sermons, which must have demanded extremely retentive memories for their delivery from the

---

[79] *The Diary of Cotton Mather*, 2 vols. (Boston: Massachusetts Historical Society, 1911–1912), I, 279.

[80] *Op. cit.*, I, 80.

[81] *Op. cit.*, I, 98.

[82] Mather, *Magnalia*, I, Bk. iii, 423.

[83] Samuel Eliot Morison, *The Puritan Pronaos*, 162, citing Johnson's *Wonder-Working Providence*, 1910 edition, 135.

pulpit, or, as a remedy for poorer memories, the taking of notes into the pulpit. The latter practice was much frowned upon in the earliest years of settlement. As an aid to his memory, Samuel Danforth used to write his sermons out twice in full.[84] When Thomas Hooker, as a visitor from Hartford, tried to preach an extemporaneous sermon in Boston before a large gathering, the experience was humiliating:

> When he came to preach, he found himself so un-accountably at a loss that after some shattered and broken attempts to proceed, he made a full stop; saying to the assembly, *That everything which he would have spoken, was taken both out of his mouth and out of his mind also:* wherefore he desired them to sing a psalm, while he withdrew about half an hour from them; returning then to the congregation, he preached a most admirable sermon, wherein he held them for two hours together in an extraordinary strain both of pertinency and vivacity.[85]

The use of notes must have been rare in the early years, since Cotton Mather, echoing the oral tradition of his grandfathers passed on by his father, reported that the Reverend John Warham, pastor of Windsor, Connecticut, was the first to use pulpit notes in New England, and that this practice aroused controversy.[86] This information Mather prefaced by the reminder that the great English

---

[84] Morison, *ibid.*

[85] Mather, *Magnalia*, II, Bk. iv, 50: "But instead of venturing on any *extemporaneous performances*, it was his manner to write his sermons twice over; and it was in a fair long hand that he wrote them."

[86] *Op. cit.*, I, Bk. iii, 311.

Puritan, Richard Baxter, also used notes when preaching. Cotton Mather himself, when contemplating ordination in 1685, was advised by his Uncle Nathanael Mather not to use notes in a letter that provides important information from a Harvard graduate of 1647 on the pulpit practice of those days:

> I had forgot [he writes from England] to say to yourself, by any means get to preach without any use or help by your notes. When I was in N. E., no man that I remember used them except one, and hee because of a speciall infirmity. . . . Neither of your grandfathers [John Cotton and Richard Mather] used any, nor did your uncle [Samuel] here, nor do I tho wee both of us write generally the materialls of all our sermons.[87]

Solomon Stoddard, who on most issues disagreed with Increase and Cotton Mather, concurred with them in disapproving the taking of notes up into the pulpit. His view was:

> when Sermons are delivered without Notes, the looks and gestures of the Minister, is a great means to command Attention & stir up Affection. Men are apt to be Drowsy in hearing the Word, and the liveliness of the Preacher is a means to stir up the Attention of the Hearers, and beget suitable Affection in them: Sermons that are read are not delivered with Authority, they savour of the Sermons of the Scribes, *Mat. 7.29.* Experience shows that Sermons Read are not so profitable as others.[88]

---

[87] *The Diary of Cotton Mather*, I, 5, fn. 1.
[88] *The Defects of Preachers Reproved in a Sermon Preached at Northampton, May 19th, 1723* (New London, Conn., 1724), 24.

Stoddard allows a single exception: a concession to elderly pastors who "may lose the strength of their Memories."[89]

If sermons were memorized, then ministers could concentrate on the mode of their delivery and the character of their gestures to enforce the meaning. Perkins advised that the voice should be moderate when teaching doctrine, but "more fervent and vehement" when exhorting. As for gestures, he recommended gravity so that the body may grace the messenger of God: "It is fit therefore that the trunk or stalke of the bodie being erect and quiet, all the other parts, as the arme, the hand, the face and eyes, have such motions as may expresse and (as it were) utter the godly affections of the heart. The lifting up of the eye and the hand signifieth confidence. 2 Chron. 6. 13–14 . . . Acts 7. 55 the casting down of the eyes signifieth sorrow and heaviness. Luk. 18. 13."[90]

This advice seems to have been taken by many New England ministers, for Cotton Mather contrasts the pleading and accusatory voices of the apostle to the Indians, John Eliot: "His delivery was always very graceful and grateful; but when he was to use reproofs and warnings against any *sin*, his voice would rise into a warmth which had in it very much of energy as well as decency; he would sound the trumpets of God against all *vice*, with a most penetrating liveliness, and make his pulpit another Mount *Sinai*, for the flashes of lightning therein displayed against the breaches of the *law* given

---

[89] *Op. cit.*, 23.
[90] *The Art of Prophesying*, in *Works*, II, 672. (This title has been reprinted in a modern format by the Banner of Truth Trust.)

upon that burning mountain."[91] Probably in both delivery and gestures, there was more enthusiasm expressed in the Puritan than in the Anglican pulpit, and the Anglican don and parson Robert South must have been criticizing the more extreme radical Puritans of the Commonwealth in England, rather than the learned Puritans of New England, when he asked:

> Can any tolerable Reason be given for those strange new Postures used by some in the Delivery of the Word? Such as shutting the Eyes, distorting the Face, and speaking through the Nose, which I think cannot so properly be called Preaching, as Toning of a Sermon.[92]

He may have been nearer the mark in sarcasm about the "whimsical cant" of references to "Breathings, Indwellings, Rollings, Recumbencies," but he was right on target in claiming, "How mighty civil these persons are to their people, how careful to caress all their followers with the glorious names of God's Saints; the Lord's holy ones; the dear people of God, the little flock, the Lambs of Christ Jesus, the Redeemed ones of Sion, the true Remnant of Jacob, and the precious elect Seed."[93] The Puritans could have answered that they had the authority of Scripture for their use of these terms, and they preached faithfully, not flatteringly, to urge their congregations to live as became a community of men and women committed by covenant to Christ for time and eternity.

Inevitably there were times when the covenant was forgotten, worship became formal, and sermons seemed

---

[91] *Magnalia*, I, Bk. iii, 495.
[92] *Sermons* (Oxford, 1823), III, 34.
[93] *Ibid.*

dry, stale, and irrelevant. During a heavy summer Lord's Day in June of 1646, the Reverend Samuel Whiting was preaching when a certain man, Tomlins, fell too obviously asleep, and a witness reported that the mild minister "doth pleasantlie say yet from ye pulpitt hee doth seem to be preaching to stacks of straw with men sitting here and there among them."[94] On another occasion, he interrupted the service, reached for his hat, and went to feed his chickens, after observing that he would be back when his parishioners were awake again. And so desperate was he about this reprehensible behavior that he said he could wish for the Anglican service, for the frequent rising and responses would keep the congregation alert and awake. The general decline in reverence at worship is also prominently expressed in the Reforming Synod of 1679 and 1680 at its first session, meeting at Boston, which listed this as a major factor responsible for God's judgments on New England. This is the accusation:

> There is a great profaneness, in respect of irreverent behaviour in the solemn Worship of God. It is a frequent thing for men (though not necessitated thereto by any infirmity) to sit in prayer time, and some with their heads almost covered, and to give way to their own sloth and sleepiness, when they should be serving God with attention and intention, under the solemn dispensation of his Ordinances.

The minatory paragraph ends with a sting in the tail: "We read but of one man in the Scripture that slept at a Sermon, and that sin hath like to have cost him his life.

---

94 *The Journal of Obadiah Turner*, cited in William Whiting's *Memoir of Samuel Whiting*, 2nd ed. (Boston: 1873), 95, 170.

Acts 20.9."[95] Even the agapaic Thomas Shepard protest-
ed a generation earlier: "Oh how many men are there that
become quite sermon-proof nowadays! Are not men
blockish, dull, senseless, heavy under all means, they
taste not, they smell not whereas elsewhere, O how
lively and spirited are they!"[96] He is particularly disap-
pointed, too, that the fine old habit of taking notes of sermons is dying out. Hooker also complained that many
persons were reading, praying, or chattering during sermons, and that others resented the severity of the
preaching of the Word, which is "the sword of the
Spirit."[97] It was clear that the disaffected people had
never thought of the poet Herbert's temporary solution:

> The worst speaks something good; if all lack sense,
> God takes a text and preacheth Patience.[98]

---

[95] Willison Walker, *The Creeds and Platforms of Congregationalism*
(Boston: Pilgrim Press, 1960), 428–29.

[96] *The Parable of the Ten Virgins* (1660), Part II, 6, and *The Sincere
Convert* (1641), 69.

[97] *The Paterne of Perfection* (1639), 278, and *The Unbeleevers Preparing
for Christ* (1638), 111.

[98] *A Priest to the Temple, or The Country Parson* (1652), "The Church
Porch," lxxii.

5

Praises

If prejudice were to be given the last word on the contribution of the Puritans to praise, this chapter could be reduced to the following single sentence: The Puritans in England and New England rejected anthems, chants, chorales, hymns, choirs, and organs, as well as all musical instruments, in worship, in favor of unison singing of metrical psalmody.

It has been the important scholarly contribution of Percy A. Scholes, distinguished musicologist and editor of *The Oxford Companion to Music*, in his book *The Puritans and Music in England and New England* (1934), to rebut the charge that all Puritans were tone-deaf iconoclasts, fanatical Philistines, apostles of gloom and doom, and utterly antagonistic to music, dancing, and the visual arts.

The classic caricature is vividly portrayed in Lord Macaulay's *History of England* in the opening chapter:

> It was a sin to touch the virginals. . . . The solemn peal of the organ was superstitious. The light music of Ben Jonson's masques was dissolute. Half the paintings in England were idolatrous, the other half indecent. The extreme Puritan was at once known from other men by his gait, his garb, his lank hair, the sour solemnity of his face, the upturned white of his eyes, the nasal twang with which he spoke, and, above all by his peculiar dialect.

But the caricature of Puritanism is older than Macaulay; it goes back to Jacobean days. Shakespeare depicts the Puritan Malvolio in *Twelfth Night* as a killjoy when he is reproved thus by a hedonist: "Dost thou think because thou art virtuous, there shall be no more cakes and ale?"[1] In similar fashion, Ben Jonson, the Catholic playwright, has a Puritan character who is displayed as a boastful hypocrite and an interfering busybody in *Bartholomew Fair*. His name is Mr. Zeal-of-the-land Busy!

The charge against Puritanism of cultural philistinism is easily rebutted by pointing out that the Puritans included such poets as Edmund Spenser, Sir Philip Sidney, John Milton, and Andrew Marvell in England, together with Anne Bradstreet, Michael Wigglesworth, and Edward Taylor in New England. As far as the Puritan attitude toward music is concerned, it should be recalled that Cromwell loved it, entertained distinguished visitors with music at meals, and provided an orchestra of forty musicians to celebrate his daughter's wedding.[2] It was also at the height of his regime that Playford published his *English Dancing Master* (1651). Moreover, "opera, so far as Britain is concerned, was an importation of Puritan times."[3] Milton's *L'Allegro* delights in music, as might be expected from an amateur organist whose father was a musical composer, and his dramatic allegory *Comus* was set to the music of Henry Lawes, to whom he wrote a famous encomiastic sonnet.

---

[1] Act II, Scene iii, line 24.

[2] P. A. Scholes, *The Oxford Companion to Music*, 3rd rev. ed. (London: Oxford University Press, 1941), 766a.

[3] Scholes, *op. cit.*, 195.

And John Bunyan's religious allegories are replete with musical references, and he is said to have made a flute from a chair when in prison.

How, then, did this caricature of music-hating Puritans arise? It was partly due to a failure to recognize that the Puritans objected to *elaborate* church music because it distracted the attention of the worshippers and was a mere murmur to humbler believers. This strict view they inherited from Calvin's Geneva. It was also due to a failure to recognize that Puritans welcomed instrumental music in their homes while refusing its assistance in their meetinghouses. This restriction is based, in part, on the demand for simplicity and sincerity in worship, but also on their interpretation of Scripture and the finality of the authority of the New Testament for them.

The Restriction to Metrical Psalmody in Worship

It has been perhaps sufficiently stressed already that the Puritans insisted in their worship on the divine mandate, and that therefore every "ordinance" had to be plainly instituted or approved in the New Testament as the final Word of God. It was not enough that the Book of Psalms was ancient Israel's anthology of praise unless it was also used and approved by Christ or His apostles, and therefore ratified as the continuing will of God. If there was no evidence of the use of instrumental music in the gatherings of the early Christians, then it must be rejected by seventeenth-century Christians too.

One has only to look at the frontispieces of the two volumes of metrical psalmody used respectively by the Pilgrims and the New England Puritans to discover their New Testament authority and attestation for their practice. Henry Ainsworth's *The Booke of Psalmes, Englished both in Prose and Metre; with Annotations opening the words and sentences by conference with other Scriptures* (1612) was published in Amsterdam, where he was doctor or teacher of an English Separatist church in exile, and a distinguished Hebraist. His metrical psalmody in this volume was used by the 1620 Pilgrim Fathers until their Plymouth colony was merged in that of Massachusetts. Its frontispiece includes Ephesians 5:18–19 as its authority: "Be ye filled with the Spirit: speaking to your selves in Psalms, and Hymnes, and spiritual Songs, singing and making melodie in your hart to the Lord." This clearly combines the apostolic authority of St. Paul and sincerity of the heart as illuminated by the Holy Spirit.

The Bay Psalm Book was the first book to be printed in New England in 1640. Prepared by the Puritan ministers of the country, its full title was *The Whole Booke of Psalmes Translated into English Metre*, with the subtitles, *Wherein is prefixed a discourse declaring not only the lawfullness, but also the Necessity of the heavenly Ordinance of singing Scripture Psalmes in the Church of God.* Its frontispiece bore two authorizing texts. The first was Colossians 3:16, which reads, "Let the Word of God dwell plenteously in you, in all wisdome, teaching and exhorting one another in Psalmes, Himnes, and spirituall Songs, singing to the Lord with grace in your hearts." The second text was James 5:13: "If any be afflicted, let him pray, and if any be merry let him sing psalmes." Thus the first text emphasized sincerity, and the second joy.

It may be recalled from chapter 3 that the basic hermeneutical distinction of Calvinists (as contrasted with Lutherans and Anglicans) was that the former insisted that what God did not command in His Word was forbidden (*Quod non jubet, vetat*), whereas the latter took the more permissive attitude that what God did not forbid was allowable (*Quod non vetat, permittit*).[4]

The restriction of praise to metrical psalmody is defended through three generations of New England ministers at the very least. Its justification is found in the writings of John Cotton and of his grandson, Cotton Mather. Cotton's defense is seen in the influential book, *Singing of Psalmes a Gospel Ordinance*. Here he argues that instrumental music found in the ancient Jewish temple is merely a type or shadow of the edifying and untheatrical singing with the heart and voice approved and practiced in the New Testament. He explains:

> Singing with Instruments was typicall, and so a ceremoniall Worship, and therefore is ceased. But singing with heart and voyce is morall worship, such as is written in the heart of all men by nature; as to pray in distresse, so when we are merry and have cause of solemne thanksgiving unto God, then to sing Psalmes, which the Holy Ghost by the Apostle James approveth and sanctifieth. James 5:13.[5]

Cotton continues by arguing that even if it had no typical or foreshadowing significance in the Old Testament for the New, and it was "onely an externall solemnitie of worship, fitted to the solace of the outward sences of children under age (such as the *Israelites* were under the Old Testament, Galatians 4. 1, 2, 3), yet now in the grown age of the heires of the New Testament, such

---

[4] See my *Worship of the English Puritans* (Morgan, Pa.: Soli Deo Gloria, 1997), 13–24, for a consideration of the different attitudes toward tradition of the Lutherans (followed by the Anglicans) and the Calvinists.

[5] *Op. cit.*, 5–6.

externall pompous solemnities are ceased, and no externall worship reserved, but such as holdeth forth simplicitie and gravitie; nor is any voyce now to be heard in
the Church of Christ, but such as is significant and edifying by signification (1 Corinthians 14. 10, 11, 26) which
the voyce of instruments is not."[6] But Cotton also makes
it clear that if musical instruments are forbidden in
church, they may be used in the home. "Nor do we forbid," he writes, "the private use of any instrument
therewithal, so that attention to the instrument does not
divert the heart from attention to the soul."[7]

Cotton Mather says flatly: "Now there is not one
word of institution in the *New Testament,* for *instrumental
Musick* in the Worship of God. And because the holy God
rejects all he does not command in his worship, he now
therefore in effect says unto us, *I will not hear the melody of
thy organs.*"[8] Hence he argues that when the use of organs
is limited commonly to cathedrals, on the analogy of the
Temple of the Old Testament (as contrasted with syna-
gogues), where instrumental music was permitted, "it
seems too much to Judaize."[9] Then by a *reductio ad absur-
dum*, he declares that if instrumental music is admitted in
worship, then dancing will be allowed as well and "a
whole rabble of church-officers" (presumably organists
and choir directors) will be needed also.[10]

Even as late as the eighteenth century there were
some American Puritans with tender consciences who

---

[6] *Ibid.*
[7] *Ibid.*, 5–6.
[8] *Magnalia Christi Americana*, II, Bk. v, 228.
[9] *Ibid.*
[10] *Ibid.*

scrupled the use of metrical psalmody in worship. This is evident from a pamphlet, approved by a Church Council meeting on January 30, 1722. It is the work of three Independent New England ministers, Peter Thacher, and John and Samuel Danforth. It is entitled *An Essay Preached by Several Ministers of the Gospel for the Satisfaction of their Pious and Conscientious Brethren, as to SUNDRY QUESTIONS and Cases of Conscience Concerning the Singing of Psalms in the Publick Worship of God, under the Present Evangelical Constitution of the Church-State Offered to their Consideration in the Lord*.[11] This statement also dealt with controversial issues such as the cacophony caused in congregations where some sing a line of the psalmody ahead of the rest, whether Paul's prohibition of women speaking in church also applies to psalmody, whether the unconverted should join with the converted in psalm singing, and what is to be understood by the term "singing in the Spirit." The conclusion of the last issue is:

> Singing in the Spirit imports and implies the acting and exercise of Grace in Singing of Psalms, the fervency of it; the up-flowings of it towards Heaven in the Devotions of superlative Love to God and Delight in God, and Praises of God, and the Lord Jesus Christ; and Joy in the Holy Ghost.[12]

---

[11] This essay was printed at the request of a Council of Churches. It was reissued in full in Samuel Hopkins Emery's *The Ministry of Taunton with Incidental Notes of Other Professions*, 2 vols. (Boston, 1853), I, 269–287.

[12] *Ibid.*, 21.

The Ancestry and Character of *The Bay Psalm Book*

The Puritans of New England were not anxious to associate themselves with the Separatist production, Henry Ainsworth's metrical psalter of 1612, because it implied a more radical dissent from the Church of England than their own. Furthermore, Ainsworth's stanzas were not merely variations of four-line common meter (as were the majority of verses in *The Bay Psalm Book*), but some were five, six, seven, eight, nine, and twelve lines in length. Furthermore, the thirty-nine tunes Ainsworth supplied were "angular"[13] and difficult to sing, although Ainsworth declared he had taken for the longer stanzas the "gravest and easiest tunes of the French and Dutch Psalmes."[14] Despite this, his metrical psalmody went through six editions in the seventeenth century, and was used by the Puritans in England and even in New England until *The Bay Psalm Book* appeared in 1640.

The remoter ancestors of *The Bay Psalm Book* included the so-called "Old Version" of Sternhald and Hopkins to which William Whittingham, Knox's successor as minister of the English Church in Geneva and the Elizabethan Dean of Durham, had added a further seven metrical

---

[13] Longfellow referred to Ainsworth's psalter in "The Courtship of Miles Standish": "Open wide on her lap lay the well-known psalm-book of Ainsworth, / Printed in Amsterdam, the words and the music together, / Rough-hewn, angular notes, like stones in the wall of a churchyard / Darkened and overhung by the running vine of the verses." Cited by Waldo Selden Pratt, *The Music of the Pilgrims* (Boston: Oliver Ditson, 1921), 14.

[14] *Op. cit.*, 13. In Salem and Ipswich, however, the Ainsworth version remained in use as late as 1667. See P. Benes, *The Masks of Orthodoxy* (Amherst: University of Massachusetts Press, 1977), 31.

psalm, as well as polishing some of the psalms of his predecessors. This Anglo-Genevan Psalter of fifty-one
psalms was combined with the prayer book known as *The
Forme of Prayers and Ministration of the Sacraments, &c, used
in the Englishe Congregation at Geneva; and approved by the
famous and godly man, John Calvin* (Geneva, 1566).[15] This
psalter, because it emerged from the holy city of Geneva
and was partly the work of an English reformer of Puritan
stripe, was acceptable to the American Puritans until
they produced what they considered to be a better and
more accurate, if less mellifluous, version of their own.
The verses of the Old Version are in common meter, long
meter, and short meter, and common meter—the "dog-
trot" measure—dominates throughout so that it can be
easily remembered and sung. The completed Old
Version of all the Psalms became immensely popular. It
was bound up with the Book of Common Prayer and, by
1828, had been published in over six hundred editions.[16]

The first promoter of metrical psalmody was John
Calvin himself. In 1539, when minister of the French
Reformed Church in Strassburg, he published in the
same city his *Aulcuns Pseaumes et Cantiques mys en chant.*
This contains eighteen metrical psalms, together with the
Song of Simeon, the Creed, and the Decalogue, and is accompanied by melodies. It is conjectured by John Julian,
the hymnologist, that thirteen of the metrical psalms
were the work of Clement Marot, and that the other five

---

[15] For its history and remarkable influence, especially on the
Church of Scotland, see William D. Maxwell, *John Knox's Genevan
Service Book* (Edinburgh: Oliver and Boyd, 1931).
[16] Scholes, *The Puritans and Music in England and New England*,
256.

with the metrical version of The Song of Simeon's Song were the work of Calvin.[17] A complete psalter appeared in Geneva in 1562 in which revisions by Marot of his earlier versions and additional translations by Theodore Beza appeared. This psalmody was used on the battlefield in France in the Wars of Religion and also was sung by Huguenots burning at the stake after the revocation of the Edict of Nantes. Considerations such as these would endear metrical psalmody to the American fellow Calvinists, the Puritans.

Calvin also produced a remarkable *Commentary on the Psalms*. In his introduction to it, he indicated how they had strengthened and sustained him in his distressingly difficult days in Geneva with so much opposition to his reforms. Indeed, he affirmed:

> I have been accustomed to call this book, I think not inappropriately, "An Anatomy of all the Parts of the Soul"; for there is not an emotion of which any one can be conscious that is not represented here as in a mirror. Or rather, the Holy Spirit has here drawn to the life all the griefs, sorrows, fears, doubts, hopes, cares, perplexities, in short, all the distracting emotions with which the minds of men are wont to be agitated. It is by perusing these inspired compositions that men will be most effectually awakened to a sense of their maladies, and at the same time instructed in seeking remedies for their cure.[18]

---

[17] *A Dictionary of Hymnology setting forth the origin and history of Christian Hymns of all Ages and Nations*, ed. John Julian, revised edition (London: John Murray, 1907), 932b.

[18] John Calvin, *Commentary on the Psalms*, trans. James Anderson (Edinburgh: The Calvin Tract Society, 1845), Author's Introduc-

The first generation of New Englanders had been through similar bewilderment and the acute testing of their faith by enemies without and within. Like the Huguenots, they had endured persecution, and their feelings were mirrored in the Psalms. As Scholes expresses it, "they enrolled David as a Puritan."[19]

It may be worth comparing the opening of the Twenty-Third Psalm as Englished by Sternhald and Hopkins, Ainsworth, and the authors of the *Bay Psalm Book*. The Old Version goes:

> My Shepherd is the living Lord;
> Nothing therefore I need,
> In pasture fair near pleasant streams
> He setteth me to feed.

Ainsworth's quintet proceeds:

> Jehovah feedeth me, I shall not lack
> In grassy fields he down dooth make me lye:
> He gently leads me quiet waters by.
> He dooth return my soul for His name sake
> In paths of justice leads me quietly.

The *Bay Psalm Book* version begins:

> The Lord to mee a shepheard is,
> Want therefore shall not I.
> Hee in the folds of tender-grasse
> Doth cause mee down to lie:
> To waters calme mee gently leads,
> Restore my soul doth hee;

---

tion, xxxvi-xxxvii.
19 Scholes, *The Puritans and Music*, 254.

> He doth in paths of righteousness;
> For his names sake lead mee.

There are, of course, defects in all three versions considered from a literary standpoint, including awkward inversions and weak feminine rhymes, but each is a careful attempt to convey the sense of the Hebrew original. However, in *The Bay Psalm Book* there is also a fine implicit metaphor in the vivid phrase, "in folds of tender-grasse," which perfectly expresses the tenderness of God the Father helping His child to sleep.

The preface, previously considered to be the work of Richard Mather, is thought by Zoltan Haraszti, after considerable research, to be John Cotton's writing.[20] He deals with the contentions that have arisen in three issues. They are: (1) Are David's Psalms to be sung in church, or psalms invented by other holy persons? (2) If the scriptural Psalms are preferred, should they be translated into prose, or into the natural meter of English poetry with rhymes? and (3) Is a single person to sing the psalm, with the rest of the congregation remaining silent until the communal "Amen," or should it be sung by the entire congregation of spiritual and unspiritual persons? The first issue is resolved in favor of the Davidic Psalms (contrary to Smith, the English Se-Baptist who urged the alternative, though he is not mentioned by Cotton). The second issue is resolved by approving metrical psalmody, since much Hebrew praise is rhythmical, if unrhymed, while English poetry is both rhythmical and rhymed,

---

[20] See *The Enigma of the Bay Psalm Book*, 2 vols. (Chicago: Chicago University Press, 1950), II, v. ff. Haraszti's first volume is a facsimile of the 1640 edition of *The Bay Psalm Book*.

and such translations will be "familiar to an English ear."[21] As to who should sing, it is insisted that the spiritual and unspiritual members of the congregation should join together, since animals and humans are both commanded to sing to the Lord, yet animals have not the spiritual insight reserved for human beings. A resort to an argument from silence is made in defense of the tunes recommended, claiming that "the Lord hid from us Hebrew tunes lest we should think ourselves bound to use them," and, as a result, every nation has the right to follow the graver kinds of tunes in their country's songs and so also the graver sort of verses in their country's poetry. Moreover, the translators have avoided errors in Hebrew found in the commoner psalm books in English, and they have rejected detractions, contractions, and paraphrasing. The aim is "a plain and familiar Translation of the Psalms and Words of David into English Metre."[22]

It is acknowledged that the verse may not be as smooth and elegant as some may desire or even expect, but let such consider "that God's altar needs not our polishing (Exodus 20)." Plainness has been preferred to smooth paraphrase; conscience has precedence over elegance, and fidelity is more important than poetry. The final hope is "that we may sing in Sion the Lords songs of prayse according to his owne will; untill he take us from hence and wipe away all tears, & bid us enter into our Masters ioye to sing eternall Halleluiahs."[23]

Who were the composers of the metrical psalms included in *The Bay Psalm Book*? Cotton Mather indicates

---

[21] Introduction, 8–9.
[22] *Ibid.*, 12.
[23] *Ibid.*, 13.

that "the chief divines in the country took each of them a portion to be translated; among whom were Mr. Welds [Weld] and Mr. Eliot of Roxbury, and Mr. [Richard] Mather of Dorchester." He adds that these, like the rest, were of so different a genius for their poetry, that Mr. Shepard of Cambridge, on the occasion addressed them to this purpose:

> *You* Roxbury *poets keep clear of the crime*
> *Of missing to give us very good rhime.*
> *And you of Dorchester, your verses lengthen,*
> *But with the test's own words, you will them strengthen.*[24]

Shepard's reminder has, however, given the wrong impression that Weld, Eliot, and Mather were exclusively the composers of these metrical translations. The research of Zoltan Haraszti[25] concludes that in all probability, in addition to the trio mentioned, John Cotton, John Wilson, and Peter Bulkeley were also involved. He claims that Cotton probably translated the Twenty-Third Psalm; that Wilson, a facile versifier, produced Psalm 74 and may very well have translated Psalms 69, 72, 86, 89, 118, and 148; and that Bulkeley probably composed the version of Psalm 90 and possibly Psalm 29. This composite endeavor reflected very honorably on the Hebrew scholarship of the first generation of New England ministers, even if their verses were hardly of the standard of poets laureate. It was suggested that common meter tunes found in Ravenscroft or other English psalmodie compilations would prove satisfactory, and the pragmatic min-

---

[24] *Magnalia*, I, Bk. iii, 367.
[25] Haraszti, *The Enigma of the Bay Psalm Book.*

isters also provided common meter substitutes for six
psalms written in long meter, namely Psalms 51, 85, 100,
117, 133, and 138. The popularity of *The Bay Psalm Book*
can be divined from the fact that it appeared in some 57
editions: 26 or 27 at Boston or Cambridge, Massachusetts;
21 at London or Cambridge, England; 7 at Edinburgh and
2 at Glasgow.[26] It is significant that John Cotton advertised the psalmody with pride in his *Way of the Churches
of Christ in New England*, prepared while the Westminster Assembly was sitting and reforming the worship of
England and Scotland. Thus he showed the large number
of Presbyterians, and the small minority of English
Independents, what an established series of Independent
churches would look like. He stated:

> Before Sermon and many times after, we sing a
> Psalme, and because the former translation of the
> Psalmes, doth in many things vary from the
> Original . . . we have endeavored a new translation
> into English meetre, as neere the originall as wee
> could express it in our English tongue . . . and those
> Psalmes we sing both in our publike Churches and
> in private.[27]

If the impression has been given that it was only the
Puritans who took the Psalms seriously, it is a mistaken
one. Cavaliers and Roundheads, and Anglicans and
Calvinists (whether Presbyterian or Independent) found
them to be mirrors of their moods and circumstances, as a

---

[26] See Edward Gallagher and Thomas Werge, *Early Puritan Writers:
A Reference Guide* (Boston: G. K. Hall, 1976), 156, and Thomas J.
Holmes, "The Mather Collection of Cleveland," *The Colophon: A
Book Collector's Quarterly*, Part 14, No. 3, (1933).

[27] *The Way of the Churches of Christ in New England* (London, 1645).

single incident reported by R. E. Prothero (Lord Ernle) will make plain. It appears that King Charles I, when his power was broken at the Battle of Marston Moor, was a prisoner in the Scottish camp at Newark. The triumphant Presbyterian ministers of the Church of Scotland insulted him by ordering Psalm 52 to be sung, which included the taunt, "Why boastest thou thyself, thou tyrant, that thou canst do mischief, whereas the goodness of God endureth yet daily?" The King retaliated by asking for Psalm 56, which included the plea: "Be merciful unto me, O God, for man goeth about to devour me; he is daily fighting, and troubling me. Mine enemies are daily in hand to swallow me up; for they be many that fight against me, O Thou Most High."[28]

"Lining Out"

Between the theory and the practice of metrical psalmody, between the idea of an act of adoration of God and the cacophonous doggerel of reality, there was a great gulf fixed. This became a target of poetical abuse. Lord Rochester, the Restoration rake, poked fun at the Old Version:

> Sternhold and Hopkins had great qualms
> When they translated David's Psalms,
> To make the heart right glad:
> But had it been King David's fate
> To hear thee sing and them translate
> By ---, t'would set him mad.[29]

It was, however, "lining out" that produced the worst

---

[28] *The Psalms in Human Life* (New York: E. P. Dutton, 1903), 183.

[29] Cited in Julian, *A Dictionary of Hymnology*, 865a.

noises. Its purpose was that by a clerk or precentor reading out each line of a psalm before it was sung, the illiterate could then join in the praise. The Westminster Directory had enjoined

> that the whole congregation may join herein, every one that can read is to have a Psalm book; and all others not disabled by age or otherwise, are to be exhorted to learn to read. But for the present, it is convenient that the minister or some other fit person appointed by him and other ruling officers do read the psalm, line by line, before the singing thereof.[30]

The problem of "lining out" by the precentor in New England (as for the parish clerk in England) was that it dammed the flow of thought, especially when the sense ran over into a second line, and the interruptions dampened the spirits that might have been raised by continuous singing.

The other practical problem of congregational psalm singing in New England was the fact that the precentor occasionally mixed up his tunes, starting with one and ending with another, or that he pitched the notes too high. The result was a dreadful dissonance. Judge Sewall occasionally acted as precentor in the Old South Church in Boston, and with disastrous results, as his *Diary* confirms. On December 28, 1705, he wrote: "Mr. Willard [the minister] . . . spake to me to set the Tune; I intended Windsor and fell into High-Dutch, and then essaying to

---

[30] *Reliquiae Liturgicae*, ed. Peter Hall, vol. III: *The Parliamentary Directory* (Bath: Binns and Goodwin, 1847), 81. The Directory was first published in 1644.

set another Tune went into a key much too high. So I
pray'd Mr. White to set it; which he did well, Litch.
Tune." He was no more successful eight years later, for
on July 5, 1713, he wrote: "I try'd to set Low-Dutch
Tune and fail'd. Try'd again and fell into the Tune of
119th Psalm."

The hideous confusion into which choirless and or-
ganless and untrained psalm singing could fall is described in the Thacher and Danforths *Essay* of 1722, referred to earlier:

> And many Congregations have sung near one third
> too long, and some syllables have been quavering as
> in the singing of Mass; and in their singing have
> borrowed and taken, some, half a line, some a whole
> line out of time, and put it into another; and the
> singing of the same pretended Tunes in one
> Congregation hath not been alike to the singing of
> them in another Congregation, and several singers
> in the same Congregation have differed from one
> another in the turns and flourishes of the Tune
> which they have sung, and have been too discordant;
> and sometimes he that has set the Tune has been
> forced to sing two or three lines before the general-
> ity of the Congregation know what Tune was set, so
> as to fall in with it: Nor are the Musical
> Counterparts set to the Tunes, as we sing the said
> Tunes, in the late Customary Way, to make the
> Melody most Harmonious; . . .[31]

Little wonder that Isaac Watts was to complain in
1707 in England that singing about unintelligible practices in the Old Testament and the torpor induced by
"lining out" produced this result: "To see the dull indif-

---

[31] *An Essay . . . Concerning the Singing of Psalms* (Boston: 1723), 6–7.

ference, the negligent and thoughtless air, that sits upon the faces of a whole assembly, when a psalm is on their lips, might tempt even a charitable observer to suspect the fervency of inward religion."[32] Watts's own versions of the metrical psalms, in which he taught David to sing like a Christian, with the transition he made to biblical hymnody, were to bring an end to the dissatisfaction with metrical psalmody.

It is significant that the Brattle Square Church in Boston, the most liberal Independent church in New England, eliminated "lining out" in 1699.[33] In 1711 this church was left a pipe organ in the will of Thomas Brattle; it refused the organ, which then went to King's Chapel (an Anglican foundation), also in Boston, which could boast of having the first organ in any church in the British Colonies. The better tempi and control of tunes brought about by the use of organ and choir must have struck some dejected Puritans in Boston as improvements on the disorderly metrical psalmody sung in their own meetinghouses. Organs were stoutly resisted by the Puritans on the authority accepted by Samuel Mather: "But there is no word of Institution of them under the Gospel."[34] However, it is worth noting that "lining out" was not practiced by the earliest New England settlers. It only began in Plymouth in 1681, and did not become general until the middle of the eighteenth century.[35]

---

[32] Preface to *Hymns and Spiritual Songs in Three Books* (London, 1707); also in *Works*, IV, 253.

[33] Scholes, *The Puritans and Music*, 264.

[34] Samuel Mather, *A Testimony . . . against Idolatry* (Boston, 1725), 65.

[35] Scholes, *The Puritans and Music*, 265.

Music in the Home

As we have seen, John Cotton placed no ban on instrumental music in the home, and even so conservative a minister as Increase Mather could describe the marvelous calming power of music as "*of great efficacy* against melancholy discomposures," claiming that "the sweetness and delightfulness of musick hath a natural power to lenifie melancholy passions." This he proceeded to illustrate from both classical and biblical sources, in recalling the restoration of reason to a frantic man as the result of music played by Pythagoras, and from David's calming the troubled spirit of Saul by playing the harp.[36]

At least two ministers took Cotton's advice to heart, and there must have been several more, since it is in their wills that these two clerical musicians were made known. Edmund Brown of Sudbury left a "base vyol" in his will, as well as several music books, and Nathaniel Rogers of Ipswich left a "treble viall."[37] However, Babette May Levy suggests that the sparing references to music in the sermons of New England ministers imply that music played only a minor role in their lives and in those of their congregations.[38] Against this we must set the primary role of metrical psalmody in public worship on every Sabbath in New England, as seen in the proliferation of editions of psalmody, and the not-infrequent

---

[36] In Chapter VIII of his *Essay for the Recording of Illustrious Providences* (1684), reprinted in *Remarkable Providences Illustrative of the Earlier Days of American Colonization* (London: Reeves and Turner, 1890), 197.

[37] Samuel Eliot Morison, *Harvard College in the Seventeenth Century* (Cambridge, Mass.: Harvard University Press, 1936), 115.

[38] *Preaching in the First Half Century of New England History*, 125.

references to the joy of psalm singing at home. Judge Samuel Sewall must be our interpreter of the delight of the devout in singing at the Lord's Supper. He recorded on the Sabbath of February 26, 1688: "I sit down with the Church of Newbury at the Lord's Table. The Songs of the 5th of Revelation were sung. I was ready to burst into tears at that word, *bought with thy blood*."[39]

The ideal of singing the songs of Zion in preparation for the celestial Zion was maintained well into the eighteenth century. Benjamin Colman, one of Boston's most liberal ministers, renowned for the elegance of his preaching style, preached a sermon published as *A Discourse of the Pleasures of Religious Worship in our Publick Assemblies* (Boston, 1717). In referring to the singing of psalms, he said: "Gracious Souls taste much of Heaven in this part of Worship. It surely dilates & opens the Soul to God and he comes into it." His encomium of music at the Creation and at its ending is an exciting tribute to the elevated, if austere, joy of Puritan singing of the Psalms:

> Before this world was there was Joy and Singing, and the one expressed in the other. I mean when at the foundation of the Earth and *Morning Stars sang together, and all the Sons of God shouted for joy.* And when this World ends Singing will continue with Everlasting Joyes; *The Song of Moses and the Lamb.* We hold communion now with Heaven, we are preparing for Heaven, we already get some foretaste of Heaven in the holy Exercise of Singing.[40]

---

[39] Sewall's *Diary* (ed. M. Halsey Thomas), I, 161.
[40] This sermon is appended to *Sermons Preached at the Lecture in Boston . . . to which is added a Discourse from Psalm CXX. 1.* (Boston, 1717). It runs from pp. 133–163 and the citation is from pp. 150–51.

The relative iconoclasm in music of the New England Puritans is not to be attributed to any aesthetic deficiency. It was not that they disliked music, but that they loved the religion of Christ's ordinances more. The sublime intent (and the occasional achievement) of Puritan psalm singing was admirably expressed by John Cotton with deep conviction and from his own experience of its benefits:

> In Singing of Psalms we must endeavour to Sing to the Lord, looking up unto, and Trusting in God the Holy Ghost, for His Influences to Irradiate, Elevate, Invigorate, and Fix our Hearts, that so from our own Experience we may be able to say in Truth, as the Holy Psalmist, Our Hearts are Fixed, O God; We will Sing and Give Praise.[41]

---

[41] *Singing Psalms a Gospel Ordinance*, 286–87.

6
Prayers[1]

If sermons were the climax of Puritan worship, prayers, like praises, were an important response to the exposition of the oracles of God and the daily as well as Lord's Day preparation for the preaching. Prayer even made the preaching efficacious. Moreover, Puritanism had its own insight into the nature of prayer as sincere, serious, spontaneous, heart-deep conversation with God. One of the earliest New England definitions of prayer came from John Cotton: "Prayer (in generall, comprehending both lawfull and unlawfull) is the lifting up (or powring out) of the desires of the heart for Divine blessings . . . according to his will in the name of Jesus Christ, by the helpe of the Spirit of Grace."[2] In the basic demand for sincerity, his definition is echoed by that of Thomas Shepard, who wrote, "Holy prayers . . . are such desires of the soul left with God, with submission to his will, as may best please him."[3] In addition to sincerity, which might also characterize an egotistical petition, both

---

[1] I am happy to acknowledge the help of the Reverend Dr. Bryan Sellick in preparing this chapter.

[2] *A Modest and Cleare Answere to Mr. Balls Discourse of Set Formes of Prayer* (London: R. O. and A. D., Printers, 1642), 1.

[3] *The Works of Thomas Shepard*, "The Sound Believer" (Boston: Doctrinal Tract and Book Society, 1853), I, 265.

definitions stress the necessity of obedience to the divine will, and Cotton adds that this will be found in following the pattern of Christ, with the enabling assistance of the Holy Spirit.

The first New England form and order of public worship at the morning diet began with prayer which, according to Lechford,[4] lasted fifteen minutes, and concluded with a longer prayer and blessing. The same informant tells us that in the afternoon worship the minister prayed before and after the sermon. At the Lord's Supper both of the elements of bread and wine separately are consecrated by prayer, and there is a prayer after all have received Communion, and a final blessing.

There are three indicators of the importance of prayer in Puritanism. One is that ministers regarded the capacity to frame their own conceived or extemporary prayers as one of the gifts of the ascended Christ to His Church. Cotton Mather, for example, in his church history of New England, praises John Norton's exceptional ability in this regard: "It even transported the souls of his hearers to accompany him in his devotions, wherein his graces would make wonderful salleys into the vast field of entertainments and acknowledgements with which we are furnished in the new covenant, for our prayers." Mather reports that an Ipswich man would walk the thirty miles to Boston to attend the weekly lecture there, "and he would profess, that it was worth a great journey to be a partaker in one of Mr. Norton's prayers."[5]

A second factor marking prayer's importance was the great length at which some ministers prayed and the in-

---

[4] *Plaine Dealing: Or, Newes from New-England* (1642), 16.
[5] *Magnalia Christi Americana*, Bk. iii, 274.

tensity of their private piety. Some ministers prayed for as long as they preached. This is not only the report of a critic such as Jasper Danckaerts, the Dutch Labadist who visited Boston in 1680, who tells of one Puritan minister "who made a prayer an hour long, and preached the same length of time,"[6] but is admitted by the delighted ministers themselves. Thacher wrote once that he stood about three hours praying and preaching, and on a later occasion, "God was pleased graciously to assist mee much beyond my Expectation. Blessed be his holy name for it. I was near an hour and a halfe in my first prayer and my heart much drawne out in it, and an hour in the Sermon."[7] In Charles Hambrick-Stowe's opinion—and he is the authority on New England piety—"the norm on a common Sabbath seems to have been a major prayer for sixty to ninety minutes."[8]

The third sign of the significance of prayer was the recognition of the importance of importunity. Persistence in prayer was needed because "the work of Prayer is not to move or remove God . . . but to move or remove hearts near to the Lord; and then we have prayed to purpose, when by Prayer our hearts and spirits are in a more celestial frame."[9] Samuel Sewall was himself an admirable

---

[6] *The Journal of Jasper Danckaerts (1679–1680)*, eds. B. B. James and J. F. James (New York, 1913), 261–262.

[7] Thacher, *Diary*, MS, I, 121–22, as cited by C. E. Hambrick-Stowe, *The Practice of Piety* (Chapel Hill: University of North Carolina Press, 1982).

[8] *Op. cit.*, 104.

[9] Thomas Cobbett, *A Practical Discourse of Prayer* (London: printed by T. M. for Joseph Cranford, 1654), 6. This book was reprinted in 1993 by Soli Deo Gloria under the title *Gospel Incense: A Practice Treatise on Prayer*.

example of importunity in piety, as when worried about the mortal sickness of his son, Henry. Successive entries in his diary show how he called in ministers to pray for the boy, and finally and desperately, he prayed himself. The record is as follows:

> Satterday Dec. 19 [1685] Mr. Willard Prayes with my little Henry, being very ill.
> Sabbath-day Dec. 20. Send notes to Mr. Willard and Mr. Moodey to pray for my Child Henry.
> Monday, about four in the Morn the faint and moaning noise of my child forces me to pray for it.
> 21. Monday even Mr. Moodey calls. I get him to go up and Pray with my extream sick Son.
> Tuesday Morn. Dec. 22. Child makes no noise save by a kind of snoaring as it breathed, and as it were slept.

Later Sewall read the fourteenth chapter of John's Gospel on the theme of heaven and prayed with the family. The diary continues:

> By that time had done, could hear little breathing, and so about Sunrise, or little after, he fell asleep, I hope in Jesus, and that a Mansion was ready for him in the Father's House.[10]

It is a moving record of a man who, despite his doubts, continued to pray and handed his son over to God.

Ministers were seen as ambassadors to God who could prevail in prayer, as is evidenced by Sewall's frequent recourse to them, despite the fact that he had also been theologically trained. Cotton appeared to think that

---

[10] *Diary* (ed. M. Halsey Thomas), I, 89.

a minister's prayers were almost as important as his preaching: "The more that others hearken to us, the more need have we that Christ should hear of us."[11] The best of the ministers offered themselves as a sacrifice to God in their devotions. John Cotton understood that he had to be a witness to the threefold offices of Christ the Mediator, and that while preaching he was a prophet, while a king he ruled over his own temptations and over those in his family for whom he was responsible, and as a priest he offered up the "sacrifices of prayer and praise, and alms" as well as soul and body as "an acceptable sacrifice unto him."[12] Thomas Shepard's journal shows us in the entry for April 11, 1641, his total consecration and sacrifice in prayer:

> I gave myself up to the Lord, thus:
> 1. I acknowledged all I had or was was his own . . .
> 2. I resigned not only my goods and estate but child, wife, church, and self unto the Lord, out of love . . .
> 3. I prized it as the greatest mercy, if the Lord would take them. . .
> 4. I desired him to take all for a three-fold end:
> (1) To do with me as he would; (2) To love me; (3) To honour himself by me, and by all mine.[13]

Prayer for the Puritans had also a strongly corporate and communal aspect. God's elect souls are not solitary pearls side by side on a necklace; rather, they are an

---

[11] *A Brief Exposition with Practical Observations upon the Whole Book of Canticles* (New York: Arno Press, 1972), 235.

[12] *An Exposition of First John* (Evansville, Ind.: Sovereign Grace Publishers, 1962), 116.

[13] *Works*, "Meditations and Spiritual Experiences" (Boston: Doctrinal Tract and Book Society, 1853), 403.

army of the Lord, spiritual Ironsides, warmed by their proximity at worship. Benjamin Colman expressed this devotional cohesiveness and mutual inspiration perfectly: "At present we need more the assistance of one another in our Devotions. As Iron sharpens Iron, so do the devout Faces of Christian Brethren hearten & brighten one another in the publick Solemnities of God's House."[14] Cotton insisted that God is unwilling to receive the prayers of those who despise their brethren: "You can never look up to God and say, 'Our Father', if you despise and neglect your brethren."[15] Indeed, he insists that "the greatest love we can show to God is to love his image in his servant."[16]

The Critique of Set Forms of Prayer

Two theologians associated with New England expounded the necessity of free or extemporary prayers. One of them, Samuel Mather, attacked the imposition of the Book of Common Prayer, while the other, John Cotton, argued biblically for the superiority of extemporary prayers. Samuel Mather advances six considerations for the refusal by Puritans to employ the Book of Common Prayer. Firstly, "to introduce another Book beside the Book of God, into his church, is a dishonour, and an affront to the Scripture." Secondly, there is no precept in Scripture for the use of "stinted Liturgies," nor any promise that it will be accepted by God.[17] In the

---

[14] *A Discourse of the Pleasure of Religious Worship in our Publick Assemblies* (Boston: 1717), Preface, "To the Reader."

[15] *An Exposition of First John*, 500.

[16] *Ibid.*, 446.

[17] Samuel Mather, *A Testimony from the Scripture against Idolatry and*

third place, it derives from Rome's Breviary, Ritual, and Pontifical. Fourthly, "it undermines the great Ordinance of the Ministry, the principal duties of which office are Preaching and Prayer, Acts 6.4. in the one whereof they are the mouth of God to the people, in the other they are the mouth of the people unto God."[18] Further, even if it was lawful for those who cannot pray without it to use such a crutch, "yet it is unreasonable and absurd to force a man to go with crutches when he is not lame." Furthermore, the imposition of the Book of Common Prayer is "the arming of Persecutors with a bloody Weapon and Instrument of Violence, whereby to oppress the Consciences of Gods faithful Ministers and People."[19] Finally, it would fill a volume to enumerate all the "Corruptions of the Matter in it." Mather briefly lists some of the major blemishes in it: the assertion that baptized children according to God's Word are certainly saved; giving lessons from the Apocrypha a place with canonical Scriptures; superstitious observance of holy days; Churching of women; Signation of the Cross; and those "absurd broken responds, and shreds of Prayer, whereby they toss their Prayers, like Tennis balls between the Priest and People; Tautologies—*O Lord deliver us*, eight times;

Superstition in Two Sermons upon the Example of that Great Reformer Hezekiah, 2 Kings 18.4. The first, Witnessing in generall against all the idols and Inventions of men in the worship of God, The second more particularly against the Ceremonies, and some other Corruptions of the Church of England (originally published in Dublin, 1660; reissued in Boston, 1725), 68.

[18] *Ibid.*, 70.

[19] *Ibid.*, 70–71.

We beseech thee to hear us good Lord, twenty times; etc. etc."[20]

John Cotton attempts to refute arguments of the defenders of the Book of Common Prayer. He argues that if uniformity is desired above all, then why should there be any variation from one service to another? Nor is he willing to accept the argument that set forms of prayer are useful helps for poorly trained clergy:

> . . . if tying to set formes be requisite to supply the defects of the gifts of ignorant Ministers, then thereby a cloake is made for the covering and sheltering of ignorant Ministers; who had more need to be shouldered speedily out of the church. . . . And besides, if such set formes be prescribed for the succour of ignorant Ministers, then such Ministers as have received the gift of prayer, have no need at any time, nor use of prescribed and set formes of prayer at all.[21]

Cotton also objected to the imposition of a prayer book, as unwarranted by God's Word, which was the only necessary book in worship: ". . . and therefore [we] do see no more warrant to read out of a Prayer-Booke, the publique Prayers of a Church: then out of a book of *Homylies* to read the publique Sermons of the Ministers of the Church."[22] Positively, he insisted that God "*hath commanded us to pray in the Spirit,* Eph. 6.18, which implies not only with such affections as his Spirit kindleth and stirreth up, but also with such matter and words as

---

[20] *Ibid.,* 72.

[21] *A Modest and Cleare Answere to Mr. Balls Discourse of Set Formes of Prayer* (1642), 3.

[22] *Ibid.,* 5.

his Spirit helpeth us unto: For his Spirit is said to helpe us what to pray, which else we should not know, Rom. 8.26."[23] By contrast, a prescribed form of prayer assumes that we know how to pray without the Holy Spirit's aid, which is blasphemous arrogance. He adds that 1 Corinthians 14.16 assures us that the Spirit does provide assistance in prayer. He cannot, however, deny Ball's point that all the Reformed churches not only tolerate but approve a set form of liturgy. Rather lamely, he argues that no Reformed church imposes a liturgy on its ministers, forbidding them to pray their own prayers.[24]

Cotton's ultimate argument was that God had so ordered it that humans must worship Him as He had commanded them without addition or subtraction in worship. As far as set forms are concerned, he insisted:

> We finde no Commandement nor Patterne for them in the Word; nor any promise for their acceptance; They are injoyned for helpes, and means of Gods worship; which God hath not sanctified, and for forms of worship, which God hath not acknowledged, and therefore we know not how to excuse them from sinne, against the true meaning of the second *Commandement*.[25]

Now it is true that the Puritans were not the first to use extemporary prayers. From at least the times of Justin Martyr and Tertullian down to the Separatists[26] of the

---

[23] *Ibid.*, 14.

[24] *Ibid.*, 44 f.

[25] *Ibid.*, 19.

[26] See "The Worship of the Separatists," which is Chapter IX of my *Worship and Theology in England from Cranmer to Hooker, 1534–*

sixteenth century in England, prayers conceived by the leaders of worship independent of a fixed liturgy had been practiced. Even in Calvin's Geneva, although there was *La Forme et Maniere des Prieres selon la Coutume de l'Eglise Ancienne* used as a liturgy, with alternative prayers, the minister employed his own words in the prayer for illumination before the sermon. What was radical and revolutionary in New England was the provision of only extemporary prayers in divine worship *for an entire colony* before the Westminster Directory[27] appeared to plan the themes, but not the words of the prayers, and the structure of worship for England's Presbyterian and Independent Puritans. It was a bold and daring strategy in devotion and it was later followed by whole denominations of the Protestant stripe, and in our own day by charismatics wishing to supplement historic liturgies with free prayers. In this respect it was a historic and far-reaching contribution to worship, despite its potentials for misuse, including repetitiousness, prolixity, subjectivism, faddist topicality, occasional naiveté, and a rambling irrelevance. But the qualities outweighing its possible defects were simplicity, spontaneity, a moving directness and immediacy of approach, and the pastoral insights into the heartaches and temptations of the members of the congregation, expressed in warm particularities instead of in cold generalities. The innovative free prayer has become a vigorous tradition that is widely influential to this day, and even the strongly liturgical

---

27 For *The Parliamentary* or *Westminster Directory* (1644), see my *Worship and Theology in England from Andrewes to Baxter and Fox, 1603-1690* (Princeton, NJ.: Princeton University Press 1975), 406–426.

churches have since Vatican II dropped the invariable formula conception of prayer to provide even alternative prayers of consecration for the Eucharist. This itself may be a belated recognition of the Puritan plea for variety in the approach to God in prayer.

The Parts of Prayer

John Cotton began his description of worship in New England by referring in typical fashion to his New Testament authority for the types of prayer employed: "First then wee come together in the Church, according to the Apostles direction, 1 Tim. 2.1. Wee make prayers and intercessions and thanksgivings for ourselves and for all men." He continues, after a reference to the dependence upon the Holy Spirit that characterized their free prayers, by stating that "wee have respect therein to the necessities of the people, the estate of the times, and the worke of Christ in our hands."[28] Thus Cotton adumbrates two types of prayer, thanksgiving and intercession, and by implication, a third, petition. It is clear from the descriptions of the special days of fasting and humiliation that confession was also another part of prayer in common use, and dedication or consecration a fifth, since this was used in the "contribution" or collection in the regular service, and in the Lord's Supper the "blessing" or consecration of the elements of bread and wine. Thus there are five parts of prayer in all, which in logical and psychological order lead from thanksgiving and adoration to the contemplation of unworthiness which is expressed in

---

[28] *The Way of the Churches of Christ in New-England* (London, 1645), 66. The fivefold and standard analysis of the moods of prayer is not directly derived from Cotton.

confession; to a petition for forgiveness and the graces of the Christian life, with a concern for one's family also expressed in petitionary prayers; leading to a concern for the Church and kingdom of Christ and the wider world in prayers of intercession; ending with consecration or dedication of one's self and one's time, talent, and substance to the service of Christ. We shall next examine these five parts of prayer—thanksgiving, confession, petition, intercession, and consecration—in the public and private devotional life of the American Puritans.

For all these kinds of prayer the basic prerequisite was faith, which brought with it four needed graces. John Cotton listed them thus:

a) Faith producing reverence to God.

b) Faith breeds in us humility, by which we come before God with a sense of our unworthiness . . .

c) Faith works fervency and earnestness of spirit, that we will give God no rest . . .

d) Faith works in us a holy confidence that what we ask God will undoubtedly grant.[29]

Moreover, it is necessary to recall how the Puritan's life was filled throughout the week with individual and family prayers, quite apart from Sabbath worship, and special days of thanksgiving or humiliation, not forgetting the weekly lecture in a context of worship. What prayer could mean in the life of a patriarchal saint of New England, that of John Eliot, first Puritan missionary to the

---

[29] *An Exposition of First John*, 401–2.

Indians, is summed up by Cotton Mather in describing his spiritual regimen: and this is a model for other ministers in New England:

> . . . a good part of the week will be spent in sabbatising . . . we have our private meetings wherein we pray, and sing, and repeat sermons, and confer about the things of God . . . we perform *family-duties* every day; we have our morning and evening sacrifices, wherein having read the scriptures to our families, we call upon the name of God . . . we shall also have our daily devotions in our *closets*; wherein unto *supplication* before the Lord, we shall add some serious *meditation* upon his word; a *David* will be at this work no less than thrice a day. Seventhly, we have likewise many scores of *ejaculations* in a day; and these we have like *Nehemiah*, in whatever place we come into. Eighthly, we have our occasional *thoughts* and our occasional *talks*, upon spiritual matters . . . lest there should not be enough, lastly, we have our *spiritual warfare*. We are always encountring the enemies of our souls, which continually raises our hearts unto our *Helper* and *Leader* in the *Heavens*.[30]

This is an almost totally comprehensive account of the discipline of Puritan prayer, apart from the fact that it omits the necessary blessing over every meal. The frequency, seriousness, intensity, and persistence of Puritan prayers are impressive.

Except on days of thanksgiving, and in the table graces, one has little sense of gratitude in Puritan prayer, and almost none of the rapture of adoration. In this

---

[30] *Magnalia*, I, 484. See Cotton's similar practice in *The Diary of Cotton Mather* (New York: Frederick Ungar, 1911), I, 4.

respect its piety was less extrovertedly Lutheran than introvertedly Calvinistic.

Puritan diaries, reflecting their belief in original sin, abound in confessions. Sewall's diary, for example, shows an overwhelming sense of his inadequacy in considering accepting the covenant which would admit him to the Lord's Supper. "I have been a long time loth to enter into strict Bonds with God, the sinfullness and hypochrisy of which God hath showed me,"[31] he writes, and one is acutely aware of his scruplosity. The most famous act of confession he made was as a judge at the Salem witchcraft trials before the congregation at a fast day. The confession was in the form of a prayer bill which he handed to the Reverend Mr. Willard as he passed to his pew in the Old South Church, Boston. While it was being read, he stood up and bowed when it was ended:

> Samuel Sewall, sensible of the reiterated strokes of God upon himself and family; and being sensible, that as to the Guilt contracted upon the opening of the late Commission of Oyer and Terminer at Salem (to which the order for this Day relates) he is, upon many accounts, more concerned than any that he knows of, Desires to take the Blame and shame of it. Asking pardon of men, And especially desiring prayers that God, who has an Unlimited Authority, would pardon that sin and all other his sins; personal and Relative: And according to his infinite Benignity, and Sovereignty, Not Visit the sin of him, or of any other, upon himself or any of his, nor upon the Land: But that He would powerfully defend him against all Temptations to Sin, for the future; and vouchsafe him the efficacious, saving

---

[31] *Diary* (ed. M. Halsey Thomas), I, 39. See also 41, 42.

Conduct of his Word and Spirit.[32]

This is a manly confession for a public figure to make (without any attempt to excuse his conduct), compassionate in its concern for his family, others who have suffered through him, and for his own country. Its plea for forgiveness is rightly accompanied with a plea that his future conduct may be guided by Scripture and enabled by the Holy Spirit. It was, one may guess, typical except in its dramatic humility coming from the one who had presided over the Salem court in its panic and superstition. A devout man, Sewall occasionally set aside a whole day for prayer.[33]

Cotton Mather set aside a day in August of 1681 for devotional discipline. Typically it began by listing "Causes of Humiliation." He listed three:

> My *old Sins*, never to bee forgotten with my mourning Soul.
> My *late Falls* into old Sins, in regard whereof my *broken Vowes* give mee *broken Bonds*.
> My *great* Unsteadiness, in observing and performing, my *Resolutions*.[34]

This was not an unusual procedure for him, as again in January 11, 1698/9, when he recorded, "I sett apart this Day, for Prayer with Fasting in my Study. . . . I made a

---

[32] *Ibid.*, I, 366–67.

[33] *Diary*, I, 589. See the full account of his activity in prayer on February 10, 1707/8.

[34] *The Diary of Cotton Mather, 1681–1724*, ed. W. C. Ford, 2 vols. (Boston: 7th series, Vols. 7 and 8 of Collections of the Massachusetts Historical Society), I, 25.

Recapitulation of the humbling Things that had befallen me; and I confessed and bewayled the Special Miscarriages, by which I had rendered myself most worthy to be Humbled with such Dispensations of Heaven." This, as in the case of Sewall, was followed by firm resolutions, such as, "I implored the Favours of God, upon my Opportunities to glorify Him; and commended into His Hands, my particular Intentions to glorify Him."[35]

Earlier we saw how integral the conception of the covenant relationship between God and His elect people was to the formation and continuation of Puritan ecclesiology. It also clearly underlies the understanding of prayer. Cotton, for one, saw confession as the people's part in the covenant, in which they expressed their unworthiness of God's mercies, their inability to live without divine grace, and their need of forgiveness to restore the right covenantal relationship:

> Wee open the doore of our hearts, when wee goe to God and openly confesse . . . all the despight and contempt we have put Gods grace to, when wee in confession open the mouth and the heart together, and confess that all God hath spoken to us of our dangerous course, hath beene the Word of his truth and goodness, when wee confesse former and latter sins, and judge our selvs as unworthy of any mercy, he that thus confesseth and forsaketh his sins shall find mercy. Pro. 28.13.[36]

Petitions and intercessions also presupposed the

---

[35] *Ibid.*, 530.

[36] Cotton, *Gods Mercie Mixed with His Justice or His Peoples Deliverance in Times of Danger* (London, 1641; Gainesville, Fla.: Scholars' Facsimiles & Reprints, 1958), 21.

covenant relationship. The intercessions and petitions of the church reflect not only Christ's own intercessions as Mediator of the New Covenant, but also the bond uniting the covenanted community. Such prayers give life to our brethren (according to 1 John 5:16) because they channel our love, and because God knits together the members of the Body of Christ by making them serve each other.[37]

There is considerable evidence of the nature of the petitions of congregations from the prayer "bills" they placed in the hands of their ministers as they prepared to mount the pulpit, which they desired to be included in the long prayer of petition and intercession. Several examples can be cited. Sewall reports on April 18, 1686, that "Capt. Ephr. Savage puts up a bill to have God's hand sanctified in sending the Small Pocks into his family."[38] Then Samuel Sewall himself reports that at a gathering of the church at Sherburne "I put up a Note to pray for the Indians that Light might be communicated to them by the Candlestick, but my Note was with the latest, and so not professedly prayed for at all."[39]

Cotton Mather took these prayer bills or notes with the utmost seriousness and not only included them in his public pastoral prayer, but even resolved "to take the Bills, that are Putt for Prayer or Praise, in our Congregation, and afterwards present the particular Cases, there exhibited, before the Lord in my Study, where I may more particularly implore the Grace of God, for each of them, than I did in the public." Several of these very bills presented to Dr. Cotton Mather survive and are ap-

---

[37] Cotton, *First John*, 87, 571, 574.

[38] *Diary*, (ed. M. Halsy Thomas), I, 108.

[39] *Op. cit.*, I, 59. The entry is for March 26, 1685.

pealing in their simple expression of divine help. One reads thus: "Benjamin Elton Bound to Sea Desires prayers for him, that God would bless and prosper him and in Safety Return him." Another goes: "Anne Williams would Returne thanks to God for Hire safe deliverance in child bead, and desires your prayers for Hir Absent Husband Abroad at sea." Yet a third acknowledges: "Thomas Diamond Returned from see Desirs to Returne thanks to God for his mercies to him."[40]

This custom of handing prayer notes or bills to the minister had the advantages of including personal petitions in the parson's prayer and therefore of democratizing the worship. Anglicans had the advantage, otherwise denied to the Puritans, of being able to make responses to the prayers of the priest leading worship. Puritan congregations otherwise only participated in prayer by passive listening and adding their "Amen" at the end. John Cotton asserted, "The prayer of the Minister is the prayer of them; the matter of his prayer is the matter of all their prayers; the forme of his prayer (I speak of the externall forme, which is that wherein they can joyn) is the forme of them."[41] It is interesting that the new custom adopted by American Puritans was also used in Old England at the very same time. This is known from a report of the Reverend Robert Kirk, a Scottish Episcopal church priest who attended a Dissenting service in a hall near Charterhouse Hospital in London on November 10, 1689, with the hope of hearing Richard Baxter preach. Almost incidentally his account states, "Then the minister, reading the prayers of the troubled and sick in mind

---

[40] *Diary of Cotton Mather*, ed. W. C. Ford, I, 65-66, 1.

[41] *A Modest and Cleare Answere* (London, 1642), 47.

and intending a journey, he prayed and preached a sermon on popery." The members of the congregation sought the minister's petitions for themselves or intercessions for others by writing them down on a paper and by having them conveyed to him in a slotted stick.[42]

The Styles of Prayer

It is, of course, common knowledge that Puritans in old as well as New England liked their sermons plain. It might therefore be imagined that their public prayers would be the same, in line with their desire for sincerity and a total submission to the will of God. Moreover, since their extemporaneous prayers rarely found their way into print, how can we know how they prayed? Our information is derived from the reputations of the more distinctive, from those who liked to recall some of their better-framed prayers in their journals, such as Increase Mather, and the later, fuller printed accounts of important prayers made at the ordinations of ministers.

Of the earliest group of New England ministers, it is known that the Reverend Thomas Hooker's prayers were distinguished by their concision and the emotional climaxes and conclusions to which they rose.[43] The Reverend John Norton's outstanding gift for conceived prayer did not prevent him from relevance or orderliness, in both of which he was outstanding, and the men-

---

[42] The source of this information is Donald Maclean, *London at Worship* (Manchester: The Presbyterian Historical Society of England, 1928), 16. The editor has taken a catena of interesting citations from the manuscript of Robert Kirk's small commonplace book, now in the library of Edinburgh University.

[43] Hambrick-Stowe, *The Practice of Piety*, 106f.

tor of younger ministers. Cotton Mather boasted, "New England can show, even Young Ministers who never did in all Things Repeat One Prayer twice over in that part of their Ministry wherein we are First of All to make Supplications, Prayers, Intercessions, and Thanksgivings; and yet sometimes, for much more than an Hour together, they pour out their Soules unto the Almighty God in such Fervent, Copious, and yet Proper Manner, that their most Critical Auditors, can complain of Nothing Disagreeable, but profess themselves extreamly Edifyed."[44]

Other characteristics of the public prayers of New England ministers were their great length (which could be described as copious if imaginative and interesting, or simply prolix if wearisome and dull), and their strongly biblical diction and imagery. One must suppose that the George Herbert of New England, namely, the poetical parson, Edward Taylor, must have prayed with moving metaphoric vividness. In addition, it is evident that, with the advent of the eighteenth century and the recession of the wilderness in New England, a new elegance in spirit and diction found in the sermons also crept into the prayers. There is at this time a change from thinking of worship as a solemn duty to viewing it as a delight, and instead of the earlier disjunction between nature and grace, a profound sense of pleasure is derived from contemplation of the creatures as God's handiwork supplementing the Scriptures. The new attitude is best de-

---

[44] Cotton Mather (alias "Piscator Evangelicus"), *Johannes in Eremo. Memoirs relating to the Lives, of the Ever-Memorable Mr. John Cotton . . . Mr. John Wilson . . . Mr. John Davenport . . . and Mr. Thomas Hooker* (Boston, 1695), 38, cited in Hambrick-Stowe, op. cit., 106f.

scribed by the Reverend Benjamin Colman of Boston in
*A Discourse of the Pleasure of Religious Worship in our Publick
Assemblies* (Boston, 1717). The joy the preacher extols derives from his text, Psalm 122:1: "I was glad when they
said unto me, Let us go into the house of the LORD."
The sovereignty of God seems secondary to the glorification of the congregation, as when this encomium is offered:

> Here are the most Excellent Persons in their best
> Frames, Uniting in the most just & solemn Acts of
> their Lives, Confirming their Love to GOD and
> one another, Promoting each his own and every
> Man his Brother's Eternal Salvation. Here are the
> best Friends met together, the best, the greatest,
> and wisest of Men, in Whom is the Spirit of the
> Holy GOD: who are of Angelical Tempers, and in
> Heavenly Frames; the most nobly Imploy'd that
> Created Spirits, Humane or Celestial, in bodies or
> out of them, can possibly be—One in the Love,
> Admiration and Reverence of the High GOD, and
> breathing after the fullest Conformity to Him and
> Complacency to Him! Brethren—going hand in
> hand to Heaven![45]

What has happened to the overriding concern of Thomas
Shepard of the first generation to avoid hypocrisy in the
church? Has the doctrine of original sin entirely disappeared among the gentry of Boston? Has this elegant and
impeccable congregation already sprouted wings?

It is a relief to turn to the prayer of a second-generation leader, Increase Mather, offered at the Lord's
Supper, which addresses the hope of the covenant:

---

[45] *Op. cit.*, preface "To the Reader."

O Heavenly Father and our God in Jesus Christ,
  wee have avouched thee to be our God,
  and now we know that thou hast avouched us to
  be thi people,
  because thou hast given us thi son,
  and thou wilt with him give us all things.

Father, wee humbly expect from thee,
  that according to thi Covenant, even the new
  Covenant, thou wilt forgive us our iniquities.

Such is the grace of thi Covenant
  as that thou wilt not impute our infirmities to us,
  if they be our burden,
  and thou knowest that they are so.

Wee put the Answer of our prayers upon that,
  and are willing to be denied if it be not so.

But thou that searchest hearts,
  knowest that thou hast created such a spirit
  within us.

Wee are willing to be delivered from all sin,
  and we are willing to yeild Holy perfect obedience
  to all thi commands,
  tho' how to perform wee find not.
Father, Father, deal with us as with thi children.[46]

The simplicity and dependence upon the divine
promises sealed in Christ's sacrifice, and its echo of the
central image of the Lord's Prayer, make it most moving.

---

[46] Hambrick-Stowe, op. cit., 106f., has arranged the prayer in poetical form. His source is Ed. Hall, "The Autobiography of Increase
Mather," *Proceedings of the American Antiquarian Society, New Series,*
71 (1961), 316–317.

It was a distinguished third-generation minister, Cotton Mather, the son of Increase Mather, who was given in his daily devotions to spiritualizing the creatures and extracting lessons from casually observed objects, persons, or events. Often these prayers took the form of "ejaculations," in which he darted brief appeals to God for assistance. No fewer than four pages of his *Diary* list such events and the appropriate ejaculatory prayer. A few of them are listed in tabular form below:

Casting my Eye upon:	Ejaculations:
The Gentlewoman that *carved* for us.	*Lord, carve* of thy Graces and Comforts, a *rich portion*, unto that Person.
A Gentlewoman very *beautiful.*	Lord, *beautify* the Soul of that Person with *thy Comeliness.*
A Gentlewoman very *gay in her Apparel.*	Lord, give that Person an *humble Mind*, and lett her Mind bee most concern'd for the *Ornaments*, that are of *great Price in thy Sight.*
A *Physician.*	Lord, lett that Person be successful in his *Practice*; and let him carry all the Distemper of his own Soul unto thee, as the *Lord his Healer.*[47]

Cotton Mather adds that even when passing people on the street, "I have sett myself to *bless* thousands of per-

---

[47] *Op. cit.*, 81–82.

sons, who never knew that I did it; with *secret Wishes*, after this manner sent unto Heaven for them."[48] These ejaculations are also arranged in tabular form:

Upon the Sight of:	Ejaculations:
A *tall* Man.	*Lord*, give that Man, *High Attainments* in Christianity: lett him fear God, *above many*.
A *Negro*.	*Lord*, wash that poor Soul *white* in the *blood* of thy Son.
A Man on *Horseback*.	*Lord*, thy Creatures do *serve* that man; help him to serve his *Maker*.
A Man, who going by mee took no Notice of mee.	*Lord*, help that Man, to take a *due Notice* of the Lord Jesus Christ, I pray thee.
One who (as I had heard) had spoken very *reproachfully* and *injuriously* of mee.	Lord, bless and spare and save that Person, *even as my own Soul*. May *that* Person share with mee, in all the *Salvations* of the Lord.[49]

These ejaculations are simple, often simplistic, but some of them reveal that this potentially pompous parson and Fellow of the Royal Society knew how to turn the other cheek and forgive those who had maligned him. No one

---

48 *Ibid.*, 83.
49 *Ibid.*, 83–84.

was more indefatigable in his devotional discipline, which appears Herculean in its energetic vigor, variety, and frequency.

The earnestness, anxiety, and emotional intensity of Cotton Mather's spiritual life are matched by the variety of the techniques he employed to further it. These included sacramental meditations, fasting, secret prayers, vigils, pious ejaculations, daily spiritualizing of the creatures, and the singing of psalms. As Robert Middlekauff reports, "For most of his life he set aside six periods in his day in which to worship; four years before his death he increased this number to seven. . . . Sometimes he stretched himself prone on the floor of his study; and many times he went without food and sleep." Even this was not enough, and from his fortieth year he added "midnight vigils, all-night assaults on the Lord filled with prayer and hymns."[50]

The family training in spirituality in Puritanism is admirably illustrated by the devotions of Mariah Mather, wife of Increase and mother of Cotton. Increase Mather, in a letter addressed to his children, prefacing *A Sermon Concerning Obedience and Resignation to the Will of God in Every Thing* . . . (1714), commemorating his wife's death, wrote that he found in her private papers that she spent many whole days fasting and in prayer for her husband, family, and the country, during the four years he was in England engaged in the spiritual business of New England. From these papers he cites the summaries she left of her supplications and intercessions. She wrote on

---

[50] *The Mathers: Three Generations of Puritan Intellectuals* (New York: Oxford University Press, 1971), 205–6. For the vigils, see *Diary,* I, 421–422.

December 17, 1688:

> I kept a Fast alone in the Study, to request of God
> that he would afford Assistance to my Dearest now
> in England; that he may do Service for God, and for
> His New England Israel. And that he and Samuel,
> might be brought in Safety to us again: And for my
> dear son Cotton, that God would abundantly Bless
> him in the Work of the Lord; and Increase his
> Family. And for all my Children; and that all of us
> might be bro't nearer to God by the Death of dear
> Nathaniel; and that Sin may be pardoned, which has
> been the cause of his Death. And I do humbly give
> thanks to God this Day, for great Answers of Prayer
> since I kept a Fast in this Study last.[51]

On a later occasion, she recorded the following:

> It pleased the Lord to afflict my Son Nathaniel
> with long Weakness of Body: I often Prayed to God
> for his Recovery; and that the Lord would accept of
> Service from him: But the Holy God saw meet to
> Cut down this Young Tree before it had time to
> bear Much fruit to His Glory. But he has left great
> evidence of Grace; and was willing to Serve God to
> the uttermost of his Ability. I desire to rest satis-
> fied with the Holy Pleasure of God.[52]

In these citations we have a private glimpse not into
an extraordinary spirituality, but into the devotion of a
good, responsible Puritan woman, who loved her God,
her husband, and family and accepted the loss of a son
with resignation and hope. In days of frequent child

---

[51] *Op. cit.*, iii.
[52] *Ibid.*, iii–iv.

mortality, this must have been a typical loss and a typical fortitude, comforted by faith. What was atypical was her capacity to run a minister's home with a large family and to maintain its devotional life for four years in her husband's absence. Her faith also has a calm that contrasts with the febrile nature of her son's devotion.

Posture in Prayer

Much is known about the interior posture of prayer in Puritanism, with the emphasis on sincerity of heart, fervency, importunity, humility, repentance, absolute obedience to the divine ordinances, complete dependence upon the leading of the Holy Spirit, resignation in sickness and death, and the exercise of the three theological virtues of faith, hope, and love. In contrast, little is known about exterior posture in Puritan prayer. Roman Catholics and Anglicans knelt in prayer at worship, but kneeling was one of the "noxious ceremonies" rejected by Puritans ever since John Knox had insisted upon including the "black rubric" in the 1552 Book of Common Prayer, asserting that kneeling at Holy Communion did not imply a belief in the corporal presence of Christ. However, for private bedside prayer, kneeling was approved.

It appears that standing was the usual public posture in prayer, possibly with eyes uplifted to heaven in imitation of Jesus. John Cotton cites the two cases when Jesus is recorded to have lifted his eyes heavenward— John 11:41 and 17:1—as authority for recommending this posture.[53]

---

[53] *The True Constitution of a Particular Visible Church Proved by Scripture* (London, 1642), 6.

When the people confessed their sins, as on a day of humiliation, the posture might well have been bowing, as was clearly indicated when, as we saw, Judge Sewall confessed his vindictive role in the Salem witchcraft trials.

An Evaluation

Finally, one is deeply impressed by the determination of these Puritans to be visible saints, although uncloistered and intramundane. They really tried hard to live, as Cotton recommended, "in spiritual simplicity, without affectation of legal shadowes, of worldly pompe, of carnall excellence, decently, and in order, and to edification."[54] In truth, for all their backsliding, many maintained a serious dialogue with God, despite temptations, disappointments, and apparently unanswered prayers.[55] Shepard wisely recognized the importance of the priesthood of all believers because "sometimes a Christian can do others little good; yet he will wrestle for him in his prayers to God."[56]

Admirable as the personal, familial, and churchly devotions of the New England Puritans were, they were marred by three defects. Theoretically, as God's elect, they believed in the perseverance of the saints and, therefore, in the certainty of their salvation; yet their

---

[54] *Doctrine of the Church and its Government to Which is Committed the Keys of the Kingdom of Heaven*, 3rd ed. (London: B. Allen and S. Satterthwaite, 1644), 8.

[55] Thomas Hooker has a superb treatise on the reasons why God appears not to answer prayer. It is "The Soules Ingrafting into Christ" in *Redemption: Three Sermons*, 1637–1656 (Gainesville, Fla: Scholars' Facsimiles & Reprints, 1956).

[56] *Works*, III, 328.

empirical anxiety, as seen in persons as different as
Thomas Shepard, Samuel Sewall, and Cotton Mather,
weakened their hope of salvation, producing a feverish
and seemingly desperate devotion.[57]

Allied to this anxiety was the overpowering and
lugubrious sense of sin, original and actual, that over-
whelmed the adoration and thanksgiving which should
predominate in the Christian life and which are repristi-
nated by justification by faith, the assurance of divine
forgiveness, and the promise of everlasting life.

Furthermore, a dreary didacticism often characterized the exercise of ministerial prayer. This took place
when it became customary, when two ministers offici-
ated at worship, for the second one to pray over the
points made in the first one's sermon. Sewall proudly
records in his diary on August 20, 1710, that his son
Joseph preached, and adds, "In the afternoon Mr.
Pemberton traced much of his Discourse in his
Prayer."[58] Long prayers and long sermons must often
have produced the familiarity that breeds contempt. The
brief collects and responses of the Book of Common
Prayer the Puritans repudiated had at least the psychological advantage over their own form of piety.

Nonetheless, the Puritans in both England and New
England could take the justified pride that in their public
and private acts of piety they had fulfilled John Owen's
declaration of devotional aims:

> To sanctify the name of God; to own and avow our
> professed subjection to the Lord Jesus Christ; to

---

[57] Shepard even seriously contemplated suicide. See *Works*, I, 327.
[58] *Diary* (ed. M. Halsey Thomas), I, 643.

build up ourselves in our most holy faith; and, to testify and confirm our mutual love, as we are believers.[59]

Like Shepard, the Puritans could say, "I saw union with God to be the greatest good,"[60] and with Cotton, "A good prayer and a bad life can never meet."[61]

---

[59] *The Works of John Owen*, ed. W. H. Goold, "A Brief Instruction in the Worship of God" (London, 1851), IV, 455.

[60] *Works*, III, 407; entry for May 8, 1641.

[61] *First John*, 392.

7

The Sacraments

For the American Puritans, as for all Protestants, there were two sacraments of the Gospel, namely, baptism and the Lord's Supper, each of which proclaimed the death and resurrection of Christ and offered the gifts of forgiveness of sins and the promise of eternal life. The Puritan term for the sacraments was "the seals of the covenant." The term was popularized by the English Puritan theologian Richard Sibbes, and it was borrowed from him. Sibbes emphasized that baptism was a trustworthy seal of God's promises, and he analyzed the trope as having four significations. It was an impression, just as the image of a king is stamped on the wax of a seal, and in this manner the covenanted person was stamped as God's property. It was also a distinguishing mark, in the way a soldier bears the insignia of his company. It was further a mark of ownership or appropriation, as the branding of cattle.[1] In fact, Thomas Hooker describes the sacraments as "the *Brand* of Gods Sheep, the Livery of his household Servant: for amongst many other ends of the Sacraments, this is one, that its a brand-mark, and a separating note of the Sheep of Gods fold and such as are

---

[1] *The Complete Works of Richard Sibbes, D.D.*, ed. A. B. Grosart (Edinburgh, 1862) III, 458, from *Commentary on Second Corinthians.*

without."[2] The fourth and the final meaning of the seal, according to Sibbes, was ratification or certification, as found on documents authenticating genuineness. Admirable as this analogy was, it included one inherent defect.

Baptism

The analogy referred to above seemed to imply that those included in the covenant and sealed in baptism were God's forever, His elect who could not fall away from salvation. Though the New England Puritans believed in the doctrine of the perseverance of the elect, the diaries of their ministers and the narratives of individual conversions show there was a profound uncertainty in their hearts as to their status. Indeed, paradoxically, the anxiety about assurance was a required preparation for assurance.[3] And, ironically, the desire to save the churches and the sacraments from the pollutions of hypocrisy, and maintain the purity of Christ's ordinances, led in the end to the depreciation of the sacra-

---

[2] Thomas Hooker, *A Survey of the Summe of Church Discipline, Wherein, the Way of the Churches, of NEW-ENGLAND is warranted out of the Word, and all Exceptions of Weight which are made against it answered* (London, 1648), Part III, Chapter 2, p. 8.

[3] See Michael McGiffert, ed. *God's Plot: The Paradoxes of Puritan Piety, Being the Autobiography & Journal of Thomas Shepard* (Amherst: University of Massachusetts Press, 1972). The Puritan ethos, says McGiffert, was "one of anxiety and assurance" (Introduction, p. 10). No wonder, when Shepard himself believed that only one out of a thousand damned would be saved [*The Sincere Convert: Discovering The small number of true Beleevers, And the great difficulty of Saving Conversion*, 4th edition (London, 1646), 98]. Edmund Morgan, *Visible Saints*, 7c, summed up the paradox congently: "in order to be sure one must be unsure."

ments either by the small minority of each congregation
which fulfilled the requirement of a saving experience of
grace—which was, anyway, a gift and not to be earned—
or by, in Stoddardean fashion, admitting all comers in the
hope that they might be converted by the experience of
attending the Lord's Supper.

Neither alternative led to a larger attendance at the
Lord's Supper or to greater appreciation of it. The difficulty of the Puritan doctrine of the sacraments was admirably summarized by E. Brooks Holifield: "The
Puritans therefore considered baptism both a divine gift
and a problematic theological issue. They could not overcome the ambivalence inherent in the attempt to com-
bine sacramental benefits and inscrutable divine de-
crees."[4] The dichotomy of spirit and sense also caused a
depreciation of sacraments in the Puritan tradition which
was partly overcome only in the last decade of the seventeenth century in the appropriation of a more concrete
theology of the creatures which encouraged an appreciation of objects apprehended by the senses as reflections
of the Creator.

Few of the early accounts of the institution of the
sacraments in their simplicity and biblical fidelity gave
any indication of the future difficulties in store for those
who would safeguard these ordinances from pollution.
Thomas Lechford's *Plaine Dealing: Or, Newes from New-
England* (1642), is the exception to the rule. He reports
that baptisms were performed on the Sabbath afternoon
following the sermon:

---

[4] E. Brooks Holifield, *The Covenant Sealed: The Development of
Puritan Sacramental Theology in Old and New England, 1570–1720*
(New Haven, Conn.: Yale University Press, 1974), 48.

> After that [the sermon] ensues Baptisme, if there be any, which is done, by either Pastor or Teacher, in the Deacons seate, the most eminent place in the Church, next under the Elders seate. The Pastor most commonly makes a speech of exhortation to the Church, and parents concerning Baptisme, and then prayeth before and after. It is done by washing or sprinkling. One of the parents being of the Church, the childe may be baptized, and the Baptisme is into the name of the *Father*, and of the *Sonne*, and of the *holy Ghost*. No sureties are required.[5]

"Sureties" refers to sponsors, which were done away with in Puritan baptisms, since the covenant was to parents and their children, and the parents alone were responsible for the spiritual nurture and admonition of their children. In the same volume, with remarkable precision, Lechford predicted that demanding an experience of conversion as a prerequisite for owning the covenant (itself a prerequisite for the baptism of children) would result in the majority of New Englanders being unbaptized "in twenty years."[6]

Restricting the sacraments to a spiritual elite might be

---

[5] *Op. cit.*, 18. It should be noted that John Cotton's brief description in *The Way of the Churches of Christ in New England* (1645) specifically repudiates godparents: "The Father presenteth his owne child to *baptisme*, as being baptized by the right of his *Covenant*, and not of the Covenant unto God-fathers and god-mothers, (for there is no such covenant of God unto them and their god-sones) and therefore we have no use of them but omit them in Baptisme; as the Apostle cast out *love-feasts* from the Lords Supper, being both of them alike *superadditions to the Lords institutions.* I Cor. 11.23, 24." (p. 68).

[6] *Op. cit.*, 39.

intended as a proof of a pure Church, but it would only succeed in making the sacraments seem irrelevant to the majority of the population and the greater part of the congregations who listened to the preaching and joined in the prayers and praises, but forfeited the sacraments for themselves and their children. It was the smallness of the various elites that led to the "Half-Way Covenant" by which the unregenerate members in each church were enabled to transmit their church membership and right to baptism to their children, but being unregenerate rendered them incapable of attending the Lord's Supper. This compromise was the result of the Ministerial Convention of 1657 and the Synod of 1662.[7] Two other possibilities were open, both even more objectionable to the majority. One was to deny to the unregenerate the right to church privileges, but this would leave a tiny minority of full members in each church, for which English Puritans were already criticizing their American cousins. The other alternative would have been to admit to the full privileges of membership all instructed in Christian doctrine who were leading decent lives although unregenerate, which was virtually what Presbyterians and Anglicans did, and what Stoddard would later urge. This was rejected because it meant a total abandonment of the Puritan principle of visible saints in a pure Church.[8]

---

[7] See Robert G. Pope, *The Half-Way Covenant: Church Membership in Puritan New England* (Princeton, N. J.: Princeton University Press, 1964).

[8] For a discussion of the three possible strategies, see Williston Walker, *The Creeds and Platforms of Congregationalism* (Boston: Pilgrim Press, 1960), 245–50.

The important middle-way decision was affirmed in the following terms:

> Church-members who were admitted in minority, understanding the Doctrine of Faith, and publickly professing their assent thereto; not scandalous in life, and solemnly owning the Covenant before the Church, wherein they give up themselves and their children to the Lord, and subject themselves to the Government of Christ in the Church, their children are to be Baptised.[9]

The covenantal ecclesiology led to the depreciation of baptism, since membership in the church was dependent upon the parental acceptance of the covenant which included their seed and was prior to baptism. Baptism could not therefore be regarded as entering into membership in the church, and as the sacrament of initiation. While he was aboard the *Griffin*, Cotton refused to baptize his own newborn son because he was convinced that the appropriate context for the ceremony was a "settled congregation." Later he criticized English critics for assuming that baptized persons were church members by the instrumentality of baptism.[10] The theory that baptism was subordinate to the church covenant created severe practical problems as well. Was a child in the covenant only if its parents were members of covenanted churches? (As we have seen, the demand for regeneration on the part of the parents was dropped in the Half-Way Covenant.) Suppose a regenerated grandparent wished a grandchild to be baptized whose parents were not mem-

---

[9] Walker, *op. cit.*, Article 5, p. 314.
[10] Holifield, *op. cit.*, 145.

bers of a church, was this permissible? Were servants and adopted children to be regarded as in the church covenant?

Clearly, there was a continuing struggle between debate and devotion, between a discussion of the effects and value of the sacraments (instruments of grace or only pedagogical memorials) and the solemnity with which they were celebrated by ministers alone. As to the value of baptism, the most the New England ministers could agree upon in 1648 was that covenanted baptized children were "in a more hopefull way of attayning regenerating grace."[11]

Difficulties about admission to baptism did not go away. Increase Mather produced a treatise as late as 1680 entitled *The Divine Right of Infant Baptisme Asserted and Proved from Scripture and Antiquity*. Citing Calvin, Bullinger, and Beza as authorities for paedobaptism, he advances five main arguments. The first is that the covenant and the seal of the covenant should go together, and 1 Corinthians 7:14 asserts the federal holiness of children of believing parents. Secondly, he argues that all who are by divine institution members of the visible Church have a right to baptism. Next he insists that disciples have the right to baptism and some children are disciples. Further, he claims that those who have the inward grace signified by baptism have the right to the outward sign. Finally, he alleges that believers have a right to baptism and that some infants are believers. This he claims is proven by the fact that John the Baptist was filled with the Holy Ghost from his mother's womb, and Christ's invitation of the little children to come to Him.

---

[11] Walker, *Creeds and Platforms*, 224.

He also advances the view that if children of believers in the Old Testament had the right to circumcision, so should the children of believers in the New Covenant have the right to baptism. The arguments are not new, but they are presented with vigor and clarity.

Twelve years later, Increase Mather's son, Cotton, found it necessary to write a lengthy letter[12] to John Richards, an important merchant and elder of the First Church in Boston, in justification of "my purpose to administer the baptism of our Lord unto such as were instructed and orthodox in the Christian religion, and should bring testimony . . . that they are of a virtuous conversation . . . with a declaration of their study to prepare themselves further for the table of the Lord." He is clearly not willing to regard such persons as unregenerate, and is fearful that when so many persons have been baptized by the Devil into witchcraft, he has been remiss in not offering them Christian baptism as a way to the Lord's Supper, the church member's supreme privilege.

We shall leave the subject of baptism with two brief records of its celebration from the diary of Judge Samuel Sewall, the first the baptism of his own son John, and the second of his grandson baptized by his ministerial son, Joseph. The entry in the diary for April 8, 1677, reads:

> Sabbath day, rainy and stormy, in the morning but in the afternoon fair and sunshine, though a blustering Wind. So Eliz. Weeden, the Midwife, brought the Infant in the third Church when Sermon was about half done in the afternoon. Mr. Thacher

---

[12] *Selected Letters of Cotton Mather*, ed. Kenneth Silverman (Baton Rouge: University of Louisiana Press, 1971), 46–50. The letter is dated 14 December, 1692. The citation is from pp. 46–47.

> preaching. After Sermon and Prayer, Mr. Thacher
> prayed for Capt. Scottow's Cousin and it. Then I
> named him John, and Mr. Thacher baptized him
> into the name of the Father, Son, and H. Ghost.
> The Lord give the Father and Son may be con-
> vinced of and washed from Sin in the blood of
> Christ.[13]

The second entry in the diary is forty-two years later,
when his six-day-old grandson is baptized:

> Mr. Prince preaches in the Forenoon, Mr. Sewall
> in the Afternoon, from Act. 2.38. Baptised his Son
> Joseph, holding him in his Arms; baptised also
> Thomas Fayerweather, John [blank] and Grace, the
> daughter of Toby, the Ethiopian, who cuts his wood
> for him: so all are One in Christ.[14]

Despite all the arguments about baptism, the level of
piety is high, and the Reverend Samuel Sewall baptizes
his Caucasian son at the same time as Grace, the black
girl, to his father's obvious approval. It should also be
noted that, unlike an Anglican christening, there were no
godparents present or even designated, for the right of
baptism was solely through the regenerate parents. In
addition, one has reason to doubt whether there had been
any really significant change in the rite from the days of
John Cotton to Cotton Mather and Samuel Sewall. The

---

[13] *Diary* (ed. M. Halsey Thomas, 1973), I, 41–42.

[14] *Ibid.*, 925. Entry for July 19, 1719. When the judge's daughter
Judith was baptized on August 24, 1690, the diary supplies the following details: "I publish my little daughter's name to be Judith,
held her up for Mr. Willard to baptize her. She cried not at all,
though a pretty deal of water was poured on her by Mr. Willard
when He baptized her" (*Op. cit.*, I, 264).

child was sprinkled with water on its face in the name of the three persons of the Trinity, with a prayer that it might grow up in the nurture and fear of the Lord and with repentance and faith become a full member of the Church.

The theology underlying the rite of baptism has changed very little from the time of Thomas Hooker to the days of Samuel Willard. Hooker argues that both sacraments are alike in that "they must be dispensed publikely" and "they should have the preaching of the Word accompanying their solemn administration."[15] Baptism is defined by him as *"the Sacrament of our Initiation and ingrafting to Christ* . . . hence Baptisme is *once administered*, and never again to be repeated, because of the stability of the Covenant of Grace: It is an everlasting Covenant."[16]

For Samuel Willard, teacher at the Third or South Church of Boston, and a systematic theologian, whose *A Compleat Body of Divinity* was posthumously published in 1726, the sacraments are still seals of the covenant of grace. Baptism is an external sign with a spiritual meaning. Washing with water represents for him the initiation into the community of the covenant of grace and is a direct substitute for the Jewish rite of circumcision, and therefore the ground for infant baptism.[17] Acknowledging

---

[15] *A Survey of the Summe of Church Discipline* (1648), 28–29.

[16] *Op. cit.*, 30.

[17] *A Compleat Body of Divinity* (Boston, 1726), 848. According to E. B. Lowrie in *The Shape of the Puritan Mind: The Thought of Samuel Willard* (New Haven, Conn.: Yale University Press, 1974), 3, 18, it was a marathon lecture series, thirteen times as long as Calvin's *Institutes of the Christian Religion*, begun in 1688 and continued until Willard's death in 1710. This giant volume comprised two hundred

that the primitive Church immersed rather than sprinkled the candidates for baptism, he argues that as
Christianity spread to the colder regions, sprinkling became the commoner method of administration. The only
difference in his treatment of the sacraments is his stress
on the visibility or sensory character of them by which
they are distinguished from other ordinances of Christ.
Also, he maintains the Augustinian view that the sacraments were instituted or approved by Christ and empowered by the Holy Spirit, and the grace they convey is
not limited by the state of the person administering them.
Evidently for Willard, they are more than merely pedagogical in value, for they communicate as well as commemorate grace.[18]

Accounts of the Lord's Supper

If baptism was regarded as the sacrament of initiation,
the Lord's Supper was the continuing sacrament of
nourishment. The earliest New England accounts of a
Puritan celebration of the Lord's Supper are those of the
critical Anglican, Thomas Lechford, and of the patriarch
of the Puritans, John Cotton. Lechford's account follows:

> Once a moneth is a Sacrament of the Lords Supper
> whereof notice is given, usually a fortnight before,
> and then all others departing save the Church,
> which is a great deal lesse in number then those
> that goe away, they receive the Sacrament, the
> Ministers and ruling Elders sitting at the Table, the
> rest in their seats or upon forms; All cannot see the
> Minister consecrating, unlesse they stand up, and

---

and fifty expository lectures on the Westminster *shorter* catechism!
[18] *Op. cit.*, 837–842.

> make a narrow shift. Then one of the teaching
> Elders prayes before, and blesseth, and consecrates
> the Bread and Wine, according to the words of
> Institution; the other prays after the receiving of all
> the members: and next Communion they change
> turnes; . . . and the Ministers deliver the Bread in a
> Charger to some of the chiefe, and peradventure
> gives to a few the Bread in their hands, and they
> deliver the Charger from one to another, till all
> have eaten; in like manner the Cup, till all have
> dranke, goes from one to another. Then a Psalme is
> sung, and with a short blessing the congregation is
> dismissed.[19]

Lechford, explaining how as a non-Puritan he knows
about this service so carefully guarded, adds, "Any one
though not of the Church, may, in Boston, come in, and
see the Sacrament administered, if he will: But none of
any Church in the Country may receive the Sacrament
there, without leave of the congregation, for which purpose he comes to one of the ruling Elders, who pro-
pounds his name to the congregation, before they goe to
the Sacrament."[20]

   Lechford is struck by the simplicity of the Puritan
celebration of Communion, by its barring from the Lord's
Supper all who in the Puritan vernacular are not "visible
saints," and the fact that lay officers pass the bread and
wine to other lay members. He mentions the sitting
posture for reception, though he does not elaborate upon

---

[19] *Plaine-Dealing: Or, Newes from New-England* (1642), 16–17.
[20] *Ibid.*, 17. Lechford adds a marginal note on the same page to
prove his *bona fides:* "Once I stood without one of the doores; and
looked in, and saw the administration; Besides I have had credible
relation of all the particulars from some of the members."

it, but as an Anglican used to receiving the consecrated elements kneeling, this must have surprised him.

John Cotton's account, written three years later in *The Way of the Churches of Christ in New England* (1645), stresses five characteristics of the rite: the sitting posture for reception, the separate blessing of the bread and the wine in accordance with Christ's example as reported in the synoptic Gospels, the restriction of the administration to ministers, the conditions of admission being repentance and faith or by letters from other churches giving similar assurances, and the prayers, which are all extemporaneous. The sitting posture is explained as the privilege of Church members "as co-sessors with him [Christ] at the last Judgment (Luke 22.27 to 30) which maketh us looke at kneeling at the Lords Supper not only as an adoration devised by man, but also as a violation by man of the institution of Christ, diminishing part of the Counsell of God, and of the honour and comfort of the Church held forth in it."[21] In commenting on this passage, Stephen Mayor observes that it is no longer a question of avoiding idolatry by refusing to kneel, but that the sitting posture has its own symbolic meaning: "Whereas earlier Puritans sat or stood to show that the posture was not important, for Cotton it *is* important."[22] Significantly, an old rejected symbol is replaced by a different innovative symbol. The careful guarding of the Lord's Table from unworthy persons has been explained earlier in the

---

[21] *The Way of the Churches of Christ in New England* (1645).

[22] *The Lord's Supper in Early English Dissent* (London: Epworth Press, 1972), 89–90. For the origin of the new symbolism in John Archer, a fifth monarchist, see my *Worship and Theology in England*, II, 208*f*.

same book of Cotton's.[23]

Here is Cotton's fullest account of the Puritan celebration of the Lord's Supper:

> In time of solemnization of the Supper, the
> Minister having taken, broken, and blessed the
> bread, and commanded all the people to take and
> eate it, as the body of Christ broken for them, he
> taketh it himselfe, and giveth it to all that sit at
> Table with him, and from the Table it is reached
> by the Deacons to the people sitting in the next
> seates about them, the Minister sitting in his place
> at the Table.
>
> After they have all partaked in the bread, hee
> taketh the cup in like manner, and *giveth thankes a
> new*, (blesseth it) according to the example of
> Christ in the Evangelist, who describes the institu-
> tion Mat. 26.27 Mark 14.23 Luk. 22.17 All of them
> in such a way as setteth forth the Elements, not
> blessed *together*, but either of them *apart*; the bread
> first by it selfe, and afterwards the wine by it selfe;
> for what reason the Lord himselfe knoweth, and

---

[23] *Op. cit.*, 5: "But now for as much as wee all who are borne in
Christian Churches are baptized in our infancy, and such as are
baptized infants, are not admitted to the Lords Table in well ordered Churches, till they have approved, and in their own persons
publickly confirmed their profession of repentance and faith, which
their parents, or others in their stead professed and promised for
them at their Baptisme; it cannot be thought unreasonable, that
such a company of godly Christians, having been baptized infants,
should not make the like profession of their repentance, before
they are admitted into Church estate, which others made in the
Primitive times before Baptisme, and all growne up to ripe yeares
are wont publickly to make (or at least ought to make) before their
admittance to the Lords Supper." For the careful conditions upon
which members of other churches were admitted to Communion,
see Cotton's *The Keyes of the Kingdome of Heaven* (1644), 17.

> wee cannot be ignorant, that a received solemne
> blessing expresly performed by himselfe, doth ap-
> parently call upon the whole assembly to look againe
> for a supernatural and speciall blessing in the same
> Eliment also as well as in the former; for which the
> Lord will be againe sought to doe it for us.
>   After the celebration of the Supper, a Psalme of
> thanksgiving is sung, (according to Mat. 26:30.) and
> the Church dismissed with a blessing.[24]

It should be observed that the deacons distribute the
bread and the wine, which they receive from the minister, who first receives himself. This was unclear in the
Lechford account. Also, the Lord's Supper was celebrated monthly as a rule, a fact that Weld confirms.[25]

The rite for Communion has not changed significantly
by 1726, when it is described in great detail in Cotton
Mather's *Ratio disciplinae fratrum Nov.-anglorum.* He
gives extended consideration to the preparation for Communion and the conditions of admission requiring proof
of vital piety. Our own summary will emphasize the
rubrics of the rite as often as possible on Cotton Mather's
own words.

When the regular session of worship is concluded and
the people dismissed, "except for any devout persons
who stay scattered here and there at some distance from
the Communicants, to be the Spectators of the *Mysteries,*"
we learn that there are first-class and second-class

---

[24] *The Way of the Churches*, 68.

[25] In *A Brief Narration of the Practices of the Churches in New England*
(1651), 8, Weld writes, "We commonly have it monthely, though
we tye not ourselves to any set time, but alter it as often as good
reason appeares."

Christians present.[26]

The rite[27] begins when the minister descends from the pulpit to the Communion table, "which now stands furnished with the *Sacramental Elements* before the *Seat*, usually designed for the *Deacons*, in the sight of all the *Communicants*, and the *Deacons* do stand waiting before it." When the names of members from other churches desiring Communion have been read, some ministers in some churches exhort the communicants as a preparation for the solemnity. After a short passage, "equivalent to the *Sursum Corda* of the *Ancients*," the minister either reads as warrant for the sacrament the institution of the Lord's Supper from the Lukan or Pauline accounts, "or else, makes the Recitation by Parcels."

When he reaches Christ's reference to the bread, "he touches with his *Hand* the *Loaves* of *Bread* in the *Dishes* (or takes the *Dishes* towards him) now before him uncovered, where they were aforehand fitted easily to be *broken* in pieces." Meanwhile the communicants are standing and when he has said, "And HE BLESSED it," the minister prays in gratitude for the truths of the Gospel which the Lord's Supper recalls and asks for a blessing on the bread and the communicants. The fraction follows, either in silence or with the minister adding appropriate sentences of Scripture or "their own Pathetic Thoughts."[28] Then

---

[26] *Ratio disciplinae fratrum Nov.-anglorum*, 97.

[27] *Op. cit.*, 97–101, in which the rite of the Lord's Supper is described in detail.

[28] A rough guess at what brief monitions or encouragements were like may be obtained from Judge Sewall's report of his experience attending a Communion celebrated by Dr. Samuel Annesley in London, a Nonconformist minister: "In our Pue said—Now our Spikenard should give its smell; and said to me, Remember the

he receives the consecrated bread himself and eats it, and in turn hands the dishes containing the bread to the deacons, who transmit it to the communicants. After the deacons return to the Communion table, the minister asks if any have been omitted in the distribution, and if any such raise their hands, they also receive, and finally the deacons also receive the bread.

Then the pastor "takes a Cup of the Wine that is now in the *Flagons* and the *Tankards* on the Holy Table; and says, *Our Lord JESUS CHRIST after the same Manner TOOK THE CUP*; adding—*And, He GAVE THANKS*." The communicants now stand for a second prayer. Then the minister, "filling out the *Wine* from the *Flagons* into the *Cups*," recites the Dominical words: "*This Cup is the New Testament in my Blood, which is shed for you and for many for the Remission of Sins; TAKE it, and all you DRINK of it, and do it in Remembrance of me*." To this the minister adds: "*Wherefore in the Name of that most Gracious Lord, I invite you to TAKE and DRINK hereof, and to do it in remembrance of Him*." The minister receives first, and the deacons dispense the wine to the communicants, and, when it is ascertained that all have received the wine, partake of it themselves.

A psalm chosen (and in some churches read) by the minister is sung by the communicants, and the pastor then offers the third prayer, "consisting of the most Raised *Thanksgiving* to GOD, and *Assurance* of the Blessings in the *New Covenant* sealed by this Ordinance." Cotton Mather comments, "It may now be said, That some of the *Pastors* often pray with very much of the

---

death of Christ." *Massachusetts Historical Society Collections*, 5 (Boston: published by the Society, 1879), 253–254.

Spirit of a *Moses*, or an *Elias* on these *Eucharistical* Occasions." Then the "Contribution" or collection follows, which the deacons gather and eventually distribute to the poor, retaining some for the expenses of the Communion. Finally, the pastor pronounces a blessing to dismiss the assembly.

The reading of the institution narrative, the double consecration, and simplicity of the earliest celebrations are still retained, but the numbers celebrating have increased considerably or it would not be necessary to ask if all have received the consecrated elements. The atmosphere, however, is different. The language in which the rite is described is marked with a greater formality (for example, "eucharistical," "the mysteries," "holy table," and "consecration"), which may owe something to Cotton Mather's pedantry but also owes something to a desire to be as sacerdotal in manner as the priests of the Anglican church, and the triple prayers probably preach more than is desirable in the approach to God. But the structure remains intact and the prayers are still extemporaneous. The essential moments of dramatic ceremonial (otherwise so rare in Puritan worship)—the fraction and libation—may even stand out more prominently because of their rarity, and thus express the extreme costliness of redemption.

The Theology of the Lord's Supper

Sometimes the theology of the Communion accepted by the New England Puritans appears Zwinglian, at other times more richly Calvinian. Its emphasis on remembrance is strong, but it is never the remembrance of an absent Lord. Also it is strongly notional, and Zwingli associates mental eating with faith. In contrast, Calvin's

theology of the Eucharist emphasized both the presence
of Christ in the Lord's Supper, and the mystical, as well
as mysterious spiritual, noncorporeal union of the members of the Body of Christ with their Lord. It is an accommodation, according to Calvin, of the ascended Lord,
who, through the power of the Holy Spirit, unites faithful believers with Christ, and it is beyond human understanding. The Puritans considered the sacrament a
seal of the covenant of grace; for Calvin, however, it was
a seal of the promised presence of Christ Himself.[29]
Puritan sacramental theology, if weak, runs to early
Zwinglianism, and, if strong, to the Calvinian approach.

Weaknesses in Puritan sacramental theology were due
to several factors. One was the rigid dichotomy insisted
upon between the spiritual and the material, which made
it difficult to accept the possibility of a material sacrament conveying grace, and resulted in it only being regarded as a pedagogical sign. This was overcome in part
by the recognition, for example by Willard, that the seals
of the covenant actually exhibited and therefore conveyed grace. The second factor leading to weakness was a
concentration less on the presence of Christ in the

---

[29] For Zwingli's teaching on the Lord's Supper, see Walther
Koehler, *Zwingli und Luther: Ihr Streit uber das Abendmahl nach seinen
politischen und religiosen Beziehungen*, 2 vols. (Gutersloh, 1924–1954),
and Ernst Bizer, *Studien zur Geschichte des Abendmahlsstreits im 16.
Jahrhundert* (Gutersloh, 1940). For Calvin's teaching on the Lord's
Supper, see Wilhelm Niesel, *Calvins Lehre von Abendmahl* (Munich:
Chr. Kaiser Verlag, 1935) and Ronald S. Wallace, *Calvin's Doctrine
of the Word and Sacrament* (Edinburgh: Oliver and Boyd, 1953),
chapters XII-XVI. For English translations and introductions to the
Communion liturgies of Luther, Zwingli, and Calvin, see Bard
Thompson, *The Liturgies of the Western Church*, 9th printing
(Philadelphia: Fortress Press, 1980), 95–126, 185–210.

Communion, and more on the psychological benefits or effects of the rite, which led to excessive subjectivity, as is often demonstrated in the interpretations of Cotton Mather. A third factor was that by 1635 the demand for a saving experience of grace as a condition for admission to Communion meant that the dramatic inner conversion overshadowed the objective reality of the Lord's Supper. No longer was the Church defined, as by Calvin, as having three marks: where the Gospel was preached, the Gospel sacraments of baptism and the Lord's Supper were celebrated, and discipline was exercised. This reinforced the factors stressing subjectivity and the retrospective glance, and minimized objectivity and the contemporaneous and efficacious presence of Christ in the sacrament. The fourth factor weakening the appreciation of the Lord's Supper was the high wall with which it was surrounded; this produced the very gravest anxiety among many potential communicants, since their knowledge of Christian doctrine, the reality of their faith and repentance, and their experience of converting grace were all challenged, privately if they were women, and publicly if they were men. These were formidable obstacles to overcome before they could recite the church covenant, become full members, and receive Communion. Curiously, it was the continuing discussion and even dissension among proponents of differing views of the Lord's Supper in the later seventeenth century that ultimately helped give the sacrament greater importance.

Three main views appear to have been held. One was that the inner attitude of the recipient of the Lord's Supper was all-important, which inevitably took the focus away from the objectivity of the rite and the presence of Christ in the Communion. A second view, held by those who were distressed by the small minority of the congregation that was admitted to the Supper, reacted by claiming that the Communion itself was a converting ordinance, a view strongly propounded by Solomon Stoddard in western Massachusetts, and which was contested with equal vigor by Increase and Cotton Mather and the poet-parson, Edward Taylor. The third view was reaffirmed in the sacramental manuals of the period that it was the mystical presence of Christ in the Communion that was the basis of the efficacy of the sacrament. None of the parties, it hardly needs stating, affirmed the corporeal presence of Christ as in the transubstantiatory view of the Roman Catholic Church. The second and third groups affirmed the spiritual presence of Christ with power, and this is technically known as virtualism. The first group veered toward memorialism, but in fact believed in the spiritual presence of Christ communicated to the hearts of believers, and stressed the inwardness so much as to cast doubt on the objectivity of the presence. It was not always possible to distinguish members of the first and third groups, but both were opposed to the second group.

The anxiety in approaching or preparing for the Lord's Supper is apparent in both minister and laity. Shepard's journal shows that on January 23, 1642/3, he "had much trouble in spirit whether I did believe, for I saw Christ in the sacrament but it was for them that did believe."[30] On April 10, 1643, he has a long argument with himself as to whether sin predominates in him over love for Christ, and a rational worry troubles him: "Also I did then make a question how Christ could be in the

---

[30] *God's Plot*, 154.

sacrament and yet remain in heaven." This was resolved by understanding that "Christ in heaven might and did unite himself by his spirit as that thereby he did come to the sacrament and so come into the soul and so convey himself crucified spiritually yet really to the soul and spirit."[31] At Hartford on July 10th in the same year, he reports, "When the sacrament came, my heart not feeling the presence of the Lord, I began to mourn inwardly for my sins as standing between God and my soul."[32]

Fear was also created by wondering whether one was a hypocrite or not in claiming to be a visible saint, and whether, if one was, God might not take His revenge. The rigor with which discipline was practiced by the earliest pastors in "fencing" the Communion table, and its consequences, must have deterred many from seeking admission to the Lord's Supper. The Reverend Francis Higginson preached a sermon on Christ's words, "Give not that which is holy to the dogs," and was about to administer the sacrament to the waiting communicants when he observed a man known to all to live scandalously and dishonorably, and told him that he would only admit him to Communion when he professed his repentance to the satisfaction of the entire congregation. Higginson then asked the man to withdraw, which he did, "but he went out full of passion and poison against Mr. Higginson, and horror in his own conscience, that he fell sick upon it; and while he lay sick he was visited, as well by good people that endeavoured his conversion, as by bad people that had been his old companions, and now threatened what they would do against Mr. Higginson.

---

[31] *Op. cit.*, 172.
[32] *Op. cit.*, 181.

The wretch continued in an exorbitant frame of mind for a few days, and at last roared out, 'That he was damned, and that he was a dog, and that he was going to the dogs for ever.' So he cried, and so he died: and this was known to all people."[33]

As a notable case, like Shepard's, of introspection transformed into anguish, we must consider young Samuel Sewall's worries as he approached the Lord's Supper:

> And I could hardly sit down to the Lord's Table. But I feared that if I went away I might be less fit next time, and thought that it would be well to withdraw, wherefore I stayed. But I never experienced more unbelief. I feared at least that I did not believe that there was such an one as Jesus Xt., and yet was afraid that because I came to the ordinance without belief, that for the abuse of Xt. I should be stricken dead; yet I had some earnest desires that Xt. would, before the ordinance were done, though it were when he was just going away, give me some glimpse of himself; but I perceived none. Yet I seemed then to desire the coming of the next Sacrament day, that I might do better, and was stirred up hereby dreadfully to seek God who many times before had touched my heart by Mr. Thacher's praying and preaching more than now. The Lord pardon my former grieving of his Spirit, and circumcise my heart to love him with all my heart and soul.[34]

Preparation for the Lord's Supper

We have earlier referred to the grueling questioning about the faith, the morals, and the experience of conver-

---

[33] Cotton Mather, *Magnalia Christi Americana*, I, Bk. iii, 324–325.
[34] *Diary* (ed. M. Halsey Thomas), I, 40.

sion of intending communicants before their admission to the sacrament. This abstraction also needs to be illustrated. It now seems to be agreed that the English Puritans, while requiring evidence of faith and repentance, very rarely demanded an experience of conversion. What is intriguing, however, is the claim of Edmund Morgan[35] that this additional requirement came from the non-Separating Puritans of Massachusetts and returned to England via Plymouth, Connecticut, and New Haven. In this we have a clear case not only of the independence of New England Puritanism, but of its innovative power.

The Reverend Jonathan Mitchel, who died in 1668, and was president of Harvard College, was particularly careful about stressing the importance of a test of conversion as a necessity for admission to Communion. According to Cotton Mather, he wrote a series of "Propositions" of which the sixth is crucial to what was necessary in giving a relation of conversion or its equivalent. He prefaces this by stating that, apart from a doctrinal knowledge of the principles of religion, there is also required a way of life "wherein some positive fruits of piety do appear" and for a person to be able to speak "of the essentials of effectual calling, as doth signifie, not only a doctrinal, but a practical or spiritual acquaintance therewithal." The sixth proposition then reads:

> Hence, either a relation of the work of conversion, such as hath been ordinarily used in most of our churches, or somewhat equivalent thereto, is neces-

---

[35] *Visible Saints: The History of a Puritan Idea* (New York: New York University Press, 1963; repub. Ithaca, N.Y.: Cornell University Press, 1965), 33, 63–66.

sary in order to full communion, or to admission to the Lord's Table. There is an equivalent thereunto. 1. When an account of the essentials of conversion is given in way of answers, unto questions thereabout. 2. In a serious, solemn and savoury profession or confession, *de praesenti,* i.e. when a person doth with understanding and affection, express and declare himself sensible of his sin and misery, and absolute need of Christ, his believing or casting himself on Christ in the promise, for righteousness and life, and his unfeigned purpose and desire through the grace and strength of Christ, to renounce every evil way, and walk with God in the ways of new obedience; pointing also to some special truths, considerations or scriptures, that have or do affect his soul with reference to those things, though he do not relate the series of former passages and experiences. 3. When a person is eminently known to excel in gifts and grace, (as a long approved minister of the gospel, or other eminently holy christian;) this is more than equivalent to such a relation.[36]

The ministers expected the communicants to prepare themselves conscientiously for the reception of Communion by a thorough self-analysis and the offering of views that, aided by Divine grace, would lead to amendment of life. The ministers themselves prepared with assiduity, both in extensive and unsparing self-analysis as may be seen in the diaries of Shepard and Wigglesworth as well as in the case of Jonathan Mitchel, who spent a whole preparatory day every two months before each Lord's Supper and began it with fasting, as affirmed by Cotton

---

[36] *Magnalia,* II, Bk. iv, 83.

Mather.[37] It is interesting to note that the same Cotton Mather who, with his father Increase, was so insistent upon the relation of a saving experience felt by 1697 that an oral declaration of this experience before the entire congregation was in many cases an inordinately severe demand upon quiet and sensitive persons. The result was that "some truly gracious Souls have been discouraged from Offering themselves to join in Fellowship."[38] In the same passage he recounts Richard Baxter's report of a meeting of many ministers, only one of whom could answer the time and manner of his conversion, and himself saying, "I Answer from my Heart, that I neither know the Day nor the Year, when I began to be sincere." Mather's final judicious comment is: "For Churches then to expect an Account of *that* from all, that they *Receive* into their Fellowship, is *Unscriptural* and *Unreasonable*. Never-the-less it concerns them to Beware of the other *Extream* of *Laxness* in Admission to the Lord's *Holy Table*."[39]

Cotton Mather, and others who thought like him who were in the majority of the ministers, probably became over-rigorous in the demands for reception to the Lord's Table in reaction to the Reverend Solomon Stoddard: the latter was all for relaxing them, and based his case factually on the very small minority qualified under the existing rules to become communicants, and on two theological foundations. These foundations were the impossibil-

---

[37] *Op. cit.*, II, Bk. iv, 74–75. See also *The Diary of Michael Wigglesworth*, ed. Edmund S. Morgan (New York: Harper & Row, 1946), 76.

[38] *Ecclesiastes: The Life of the Reverend & Excellent Jonathan Mitchel* (Boston, 1697), 6, Epistle Dedicatory.

[39] *Ibid.*

ity for human beings to know the difference between a
true and a hypocritical communicant, and the conviction
that the Lord's Supper was itself a converting ordinance,
a belief originally propounded by the famous Puritan
lawyer William Prynne.

The Mathers and their followers wished to prevent
the unregenerate from attending the Lord's Table for a
variety of reasons. They wished to preserve it unpolluted, to maintain the traditions of their distinguished ancestors, and to make the half-way members embarrassed
enough by their exclusion from the sacrament to long for
communion and ultimately to receive it as a consequence
of God awakening their souls through their preaching.

Stoddard rejected this strategy, believing it to be arro-
gant to identify the regenerate, and unwise to encourage
the hopeful to consider themselves converted. As Brooks
Holifield remarks, "Though he did not share his oppo-
nents' exalted view of the sacrament, Stoddard, too,
helped to ensure that New England's concern for sacramental matters would be widespread and intense as the
eighteenth century began."[40]

A Sacramental Renaissance?

Brooks Holifield has argued that the striking proliferation of the printing of Communion manuals, and the
contentions between the disciples of the Mathers and of
the counterparts of Stoddard—together with a sensory
spiritualizing of creatures—cumulatively produced a
"sacramental renaissance."[41] One might even add that

---

[40] *The Covenant Sealed*, 224.

[41] *Op. cit.*, Chapter 7, which bears the title "The Sacramental
Renaissance."

the fourth factor corroborating this claim would be the demand for more frequent celebrations of the Lord's Supper. As against this there is a significant negative argument that, as will be seen, indicates a growing indifference toward the Lord's Supper that took place at the very same time. These various factors, both positive and negative, now fall to be considered in turn.

Certainly, one consequence of the lengthy and heated contention over whether the Lord's Supper was or was not a converting ordinance was that Communion manuals were published in astonishing numbers and frequency. Holifield points out that in the first fifty-one years of printing on the New England presses, not one set of sacramental meditations appeared, but in the following thirty-eight, New England printers produced twenty-one separate editions of manuals.[42] Two of the many manuals from English Nonconformist sources that were republished in New England deserve passing consideration. One is Thomas Doolittle's *Treatise Concerning the Lord's Supper*, which ran into twenty-six editions between 1665 and 1727, and which has been reprinted by Soli Deo Gloria; the other, Matthew Henry's *Communicant's Companion*, appeared in eight printings in its first twenty years.

Doolittle maintains that

> sacraments are glasses for our understanding, and monuments for our memories, that by mean and visible signs, we might perceive and call to mind sublime and invisible things. Here is bread, even bread of life to fill the hungry soul, and wine to sat-

---

[42] *Op. cit.*, 198.

isfy the thirsty, and to cheer the drooping soul.[43]

The strength of this exposition is that it emphasizes the three tenses that the sacrament affirms:

> This sacrament is a *signum rememorativum*, to bring to your remembrance the passion of our Lord, where he would testify to your conscience, and assure you that he died for you. It is *signum demonstrativum*, a demonstration of his love, where he would assure you that he loves you. It is *signum prognosticum*, or *proenuntiativum*, a prognostic of your future and eternal happiness, where he would assure you, that you shall undoubtedly be partakers of it, and will you yet neglect it?[44]

Henry's *Communicant's Companion* does not descend to the minute analysis of motivations characteristic of so many Puritan disquisitions, but it is clearly Calvinistic in its recognition that the sacrament "was appointed to be a *commemorating* Ordinance, and a *confessing* Ordinance; a *communicating* Ordinance, and a *covenanting* Ordinance."[45] He rejects memorialism outright by the statement that

> God in this Ordinance not only assures us of the Truth of the Promise, but, according to our present Case and Capacity, *conveys* to us, by his Spirit, the good Things promis'd; *Receive Christ Jesus the Lord*, Christ and a Pardon, Christ and Peace, Christ and Grace, Christ and Heaven; 'tis all your own, if you

---

[43] *Treatise concerning the Lord's Supper*, 9. The edition used is that published in Edinburgh in 1817.

[44] *Op. cit.*, 27.

[45] *The Communicant's Companion*, (London, 1704), 16.

> come to the Terms on which it is offer'd in the
> Gospel.[46]

This was an exhilarating and demanding proclamation of
the meaning of the Holy Supper.

By comparison, Cotton Mather's eucharistic treatises
are periphrastic, but Willard's *Sacramental Meditations*
(Boston, 1711) is as lively as Henry's work and exhibits
the new perspective which shows the dramatic and sensory approach to the sacraments. For Willard, the Lord's
Supper is a sacramental sign of the sustenance and nourishment of the Christian community, which supremely
exhibits the "mutual conjugal love between Christ and
His Spouse," the Church.[47] God's grace is conveyed
through the sacraments not from any inherent quality, but
solely through the work of the Holy Spirit in them. But
what is distinctive about Willard's teaching is its illustrative quality.

Bread is aptly suited to signify the Body of Christ, for
as bread is the basic food of man's physical life, so is
Christ the basic food of man's spiritual life. Wine naturally symbolizes "the refreshing and cheering of life,"
and as wine makes the body happy, so Christ cheers the
heart and soul of His people. Exact citations, rather than
summaries, will make the point more vividly: "Wine is
used in some countries for their drink; and it was more
especially liberally made use of at their feasts, weddings,
and more free entertainments, being accounted the more
noble sort of drink. . . . Wine is good to drive away sorrow, and make the man cheerful. . . . Wine is a cordial, it

---

[46] *Op. cit.*, 27.
[47] *Op. cit.*, 167.

comforts the heart, recruits the fainting spirits, and greatly refresheth them that drink it, when laboring of infirmities. . . . Wine puts boldness and courage into persons, and drives away fear, and this it doth by exciting the spirits of activity. . . . Wine will open the lips and make them that were silent to talk. . . . Wine is used in surgery, to cleanse and purge the wounds men have gotten."[48] His teaching is effective precisely because he sees a series of natural parallels between the elements and the work of Christ, though he insists that the efficacy of the Lord's Supper rests not in them, but in the divine appointment of them to convey grace. He further claimed that this sacrament "is a great mystery, and none can have a clear apprehension of it, but those who have the experimental tastes of the reality of it in their participation."[49] In all this theological use of natural earthly symbols to convey the benefits of Christ's crucifixion and resurrection, Willard sees Christ's humble accommodation to human capacities—which is a real *kenosis*, a humble self-emptying, like His incarnation. One example of this type of thinking only need be given: "Bread is not made without *Grinding* of the Grain to Dust and being prepared with *Water* and Fire; and Christ became Food for our Souls to live on, by being bruised for our Sins, and scorched in the Fire of God's Wrath, and so he is made fit for us to feed on."[50]

His prose is almost poetical, and it suggests how the orthodox Calvinist interpretation of the Lord's Supper finds a laureate in Edward Taylor, New England's muse

---

[48] *Op. cit.*, 13–16.
[49] *Op. cit.*, 21.
[50] *Op. cit.*, 11.

and minister. One poem is enough to give us a sense of how important the supreme sacrament became in New England during the last decade of the seventeenth and the first of the eighteenth century. His two series of *Preparatory Meditations* for the Lord's Supper were written between 1685 and 1725 when he was minister of the frontier settlement of Westfield, Massachusetts. The following stanzas come from the second series of meditations, No. 111, a meditation on 1 Corinthians 10:16, "The Cup of blessing which wee bless, is it not the Communion of the body of Christ?"

> Theandrick Blood, and Body with Compleate
>> Full Satisfaction and rich Purchase made
> Disht on this golden Table, spirituall meate
>> Stands. And Gods Saints are Welcom'd with this trade
> The Satisfaction, and the Purchase which
> Thy Blood and Body made, how Good? how rich?
>
> Oh! blesst effects flow from this table then.
>> The feeding on this fare and Spiritually
> Must needs produce a Spirituall Crop for them
>> That rightly do this table fare enjoy
>> Whatever other Ordinances doe!
>> This addeth Seale, and Sealing wax thereto.

The meditation ends thus:

> Lord, on thy Commons let my Spirits feed
>> So nourish thou thy new Born babe in mee.
> At thy Communion Table up mee breed
>> Communicate thy Blood and Body free.
>> Thy Table yielding Spirituall Bread, and Wine
>> Will make my Soul grow brisk, thy praise to Chime.[51]

---

[51] *The Poems of Edward Taylor*, ed. Donald E. Stanford (New

The spiritual rather than corporeal feeding is emphasized, as well as the "brisk" invigorating effects of the nourishment, which is also a seal of the covenant of grace.

The solemnity of this rite led to both sadness at its cost to Christ and joy for its recipients, who now have pardon and the promise of eternal life, as some of them still explain.

The normally solemn and controlled Increase Mather, on whose long face a smile would seem as unintended as a rictus, lost his sternness at the Lord's Supper, for, according to Robert Middlekauff, "only in his church, and especially at the Lord's Table did he unbend." Yet he often wept at the Supper, and these were tears not of terror but of happiness, as he recalled the sublime condescension of the most perfect act in all history.[52]

Samuel Sewall, too, was moved to tears at the Lord's Supper. His diary entry for Sunday, February 26, 1688, reads: "I sat down with the Church of Newbury at the Lord's Table. The Songs of the 5th of Revelation were sung. I was ready to burst into tears at that word, *bought with thy blood*. Me thought 'twas strange that Christ should *cheapen* us; but that when the bargain came to be driven, he should consent rather to part with his blood, then goe without us; 'twas amazing."[53]

The joyfulness of the Communion is stressed by

Haven, Conn.: Yale University Press, 1960), 287–288.

[52] *The Mathers: Three Generations of Puritan Intellectuals* (New York: Oxford University Press, 1971), 95. See also Michael G. Hall, ed. "The Autobiography of Increase Mather," *Proceedings of the American Antiquarian Society*, New Series, 71 (1961), 318.

[53] *Diary* (ed. M. Halsey Thomas), I, 161.

Benjamin Colman in *A Discourse of the Pleasure of Religious Worship in our Publick Assemblies* (Boston, 1717). He elaborates on the aspect of Christ's "conjugal love," as did Willard, for His Church:

> Here is the Banquet of Wine and the Sceptre of Grace held forth. . . . As some happy People keep with Joy the day of their Espousals, so is or should be the frequent Communion of Saints to them at the Table of Christ. . . . Let this be thy Wedding Garment, the Joy of thy Soul in Christ, and in Remembrance of his love.[54]

Colman even includes echoes of the Song of Songs in his jubilant and encouraging invitation as he continues:

> The Banner of Christ's love is over you at his Table, and holy Souls should be there solacing themselves in his love. It is a Love-feast, and a frame of love to God is the most joyful one that can be.[55]

It is surely significant that it is the religious leaders of New England who for the first time are cultivating a clearly sacramental piety. Earlier leaders among the clergy did not urge more frequent attendance at the Lord's Table. For example, when Richard Mather was requested by the governor of Massachusetts to advise him whether the Lord's Supper should be celebrated every Lord's Day, as in the New Testament Church (Acts

---

[54] This sermon is appended to *Sermons Preached at the Lecture in Boston . . . to which is added A Discourse from Psalm CXX*. 1. It runs from pp. 133 to 163. The reference is to p. 157.
[55] *Op. cit.*, 158.

20:7), the minister thought it commendable, but not a necessity.[56] With this should be contrasted Judge Sewall's desire to make it possible for Bostonians to be present, if they so desired, each Sunday at Communion at one of the four churches in the town. This plan is recorded on September 10, 1705, in his diary:

> In the Afternoon I went to speak to Mr. Allen that the Lord's Supper might be celebrated once in four weeks, as it was in Mr. Cotton's Time and Mr. Wilson's: He was just come out of his house with Elder Brigham, Elder Copp, Deacon Marion and Deacon Hubbard: I pray'd them to go back again, and open'd my mind to them. All save Mr. Hubbard plainly remember'd how it was in Mr. Wilson's days; and the Alteration upon the coming in of Mr. Davenport, upon his desire because he had it so at Newhaven: and seem'd inclinable enough to alter it. Then I went to Mr. Cooke, both he and Madam Cooke remember'd the change, and seem'd not displeas'd with my proposal. I discours'd with Mr. Pemberton, and told him it would be a Honor to Christ, and a great Privilege and Honor to Boston, to have the Lords Supper administered in it very Lords Day: we having nothing to do with moneths now; Their Respect now ceases with the Mosaical Pedagogy. [Gal. iii.24] It seems odd, not to have this Sacrament administered but upon the first day of each Moneth: and the rest of the Sabbaths always stand by.[57]

The change would involve a celebration of Communion in his own church once each month, instead of once ev-

---

[56] John Winthrop, *The History of New England from 1630 to 1649,* ed. James Savage (Boston, 1853), i:399.
[57] *Diary* (ed. M. Halsey Thomas), I, 528.

ery two months, and return New England to the usual monthly Communion reported by John Cotton and Thomas Lechford at the beginning. It was still a long way off from Calvin's wish for a weekly celebration of the Lord's Supper which the Church of Geneva would not consent to institute, despite his wish.[58]

In the absence of statistics it would seem impossible to tell how widespread or persistent this desire for more frequent Communion was, or whether Sewall's wish and that of his supporters were merely exceptions.

There appear to be two factors that make one cautious in readily accepting the view that there was a widespread and profound "sacramental renaissance" between roughly 1680 and 1720. The first and less important consideration is the adequacy of the view that the contention between the Mathers and Stoddard and their supporters about the terms of admission to the Lord's Supper would make interest in the sacrament all the greater. It could be argued that this very contention would make the sensitive and thoughtful persons minimize the sacrament and pronounce "a plague o' both your houses," as a disillusioned man said of the warring Montagues and Capulets. Also, it could well be argued that to regard the Lord's Supper, with Stoddard, as a converting ordinance was to reduce it to the level of preaching at which the unregenerate could be present, and thus lowering the barriers likewise lowered the value of Communion, so that the

---

[58] See *The Institutes*, Bk. IV, Section 43, paragraph 3 at the beginning: "Now to get rid of the great pile of ceremonies, the Supper could have been administered most becomingly if it were set before the church very often and at least once a week." (*The Library of Christian Classics*, Vol. XXXI 1961), trans. Ford Battles, 1421.

Communion was no longer a celebration for the spiritual aristocrats but only a Table for the masses.

A more serious doubt about the validity of the supposed renaissance is raised by the evidence during the same period of serious neglect of the Lord's Supper and even indifference toward it, as expressed by the leading ministers of New England of both contentious camps. In 1690 Cotton Mather complains in his *A Companion for Communicants* that "it is a Lamentable Thing to see what Multitudes and Quantites [sic] among us do dayly turn their Backs upon the Table of the Lord Jesus."[59] In 1707 Samuel Stoddard wrote *The Inexcusableness of Neglecting the Worship of God.* This, according to his biographer, Ralph J. Coffman, was a public confession of the inadequacy of the supposed converting power of the Lord's Supper. For after removing the restrictions to attending Communion, three-quarters of his own congregation were disinclined to celebrate the Supper.[60]

Nor were the more liberal members of the Brattle Street, Boston, congregation keener to attend the sacrament. Their minister, Benjamin Colman, preached a sermon before the sacrament which was entitled *Parents and Grown Children Should Be Together at the Lord's Table.* Having insisted that as the Jews were ordained by God to celebrate Passover, so Christians are obligated by Christ to celebrate the Lord's Supper by the positive command, "Do this in remembrance of Me," he proceeds to castigate the congregation: "What can we think or say in

---

[59] *Op. cit.*, 62.

[60] Coffman, *Solomon Stoddard* (Boston: Twayne Publishers, 1978), 134f. This interpretation of the purpose of Stoddard's book has, however, been greatly criticized by reviewers.

excuse of the easie *neglect* and careless observation of this Ordinance among *Christians*?"[61]

What is undeniable, however, is that the new sensory approach in explaining the meaning and relevance of the sacraments did help to overcome the dualism and dichotomy of spirit and flesh that had made it previously almost impossible for ministers in New England to take signs and symbols with the seriousness that is imperative for appreciating the sacraments.

Jonathan Edwards, in the later eighteenth century, would part company with his grandfather, Solomon Stoddard, in re-emphasizing the need for regeneration before admission to the Lord's Table, and in his conviction of the reality of the mystical union of Christ with His own at the same Table.

Throughout our period of study, however, there are constants in the celebration and the understanding of the meaning of the Lord's Supper. There is always the strong conviction that the New Testament warrants in the service proclaim that this is obeying the Lord's own mandate on the eve of *His* Passion, and in the simplicity and purity of His ordinance. Equally, this loyalty is evinced in the double consecration, as at the Last Supper. There is no diminution of the dramatic and prophetic symbolism in both sacraments, in the symbolical sprinkling of cleansing by water in baptism, and by the fraction of the bread and libation of the wine in the Lord's Supper, proclaiming both the destructive costliness of redemption and the banquet of the redeemed. Admission to both sacraments was generally carefully restricted, indicating their importance and the preparation necessary for atten-

---

[61] *Op. cit.*, 8.

dance at them. In the case of the Lord's Supper, the memorial aspect is never forgotten, nor that of deep thanksgiving, which is true eucharist. The aspect of mystery is often overshadowed by excessive pedagogical explanations that succeed in explaining away, but it is never wholly lost. Increasingly, as the seventeenth century ends, the sense of the banquet shared with Christ is dominant, though rarely is there any adumbration of the eschatological banquet in eternity.[62] The sense of the communion of saints is weak, although that of the union of the "visible saints" as God's elect in the churches is strong. The renewal of Christian hope in life after death is not strongly stressed in the rite (the Crucifixion overshadows the Resurrection, though both Resurrection and Ascension are presupposed by the presence of Christ in the Holy Supper), nor is there any sense of the sacrifice of the Church as linked with the sacrifice of Christ. There is, however, full agreement with Edward Taylor that "Thy Table, yielding Spirituall Bread and Wine will make my Soul grow brisk." The Communion never ceased to be a spur to Christian ethics and a stimulus to sanctification.

---

[62] One significant exception is Increase Mather's *A Discourse Concerning the Danger of Apostasy*, 56, where he perceives the earthly Lord's Supper as a foreshadowing of the visible saints sitting beside Christ and judging at the end of history. The important phrase, referring to the sacrament, is "type and emblem of the New Jerusalem."

8

Marriages and Funerals

At first glance, the Puritans made little of the rites of passage, although soon after birth the child of faithful parents was baptized in the sacrament of initiation. Even here, however, the Puritans reduced the ceremonial, omitting oil, candles, the crossing, and godparents, and eliminated the Anglican postbaptismal service, "The Churching of Women," since there was no biblical authority for it. In the case of both marriages and funerals, the superficial impression is that neither was of any ecclesiastical or possibly even religious importance, since at the outset marriage was not celebrated in the meeting-house, nor by the minister, but in the home by the magistrate. In addition, so empty of any trace of pomp was the funeral in the earliest days in New England that it is best described as a "burial," since there was neither service in the home nor at the graveside. Such austerity, or even vacuity, whether real or only apparent, demands explanation.

Marriages
It might be thought that the Puritans insisted upon marriage by the magistrate and in the home rather than in church because they were squeamish about sex, but Edmund S. Morgan has demolished this misunderstand-

ing[1] declaring: "In short, the Puritans were neither prudes nor ascetics. They knew how to laugh and they knew how to love."[2] Leading divines such as John Cotton in the middle decades of the seventeenth century and Samuel Willard in the first quarter of the eighteenth century ridiculed the notion of Platonic love and the higher evaluation in the Roman Catholic Church of virginity over married love. John Cotton the younger esteemed marriages that refused the dues of the flesh as efforts of "blind zeal, for they are the dictates of a blind mind that follow therein, and not of the Holy Spirit, which saith *It is not good that man should be alone.*"[3] Willard twice expresses his detestation "at the Popish Conceit of the Excellence of Virginity."[4] The Reverend Edward Taylor, the nearest American analogue to the English poet George Herbert, wrote in his commonplace book that the refusal of sexual intercourse by either partner of a marriage "Denies all reliefe in Wedlock unto Human necessity, and sends it for supply unto Bestiality when God gives not the gift of Continency."[5] The only

---

[1] See his article "The Puritans and Sex" in *The New England Quarterly*, XV (1942), 591–607, and *The Puritan Family: Religion and Domestic Relations in Seventeenth-Century New England*, rev. ed. (New York: Harper & Row, 1966).

[2] *The Puritan Family*, 64. Robert Middlekauff would modify Morgan's view as follows: "They [the Puritans] acknowledged the necessity of the physical side of life and its legality but they did not extol the joys of the flesh even when legality was not an issue." *The Mathers: Three Generations of Puritan Intellectuals* (New York: Oxford University Press, 1971), 202.

[3] *A Meet Help: Or, a Wedding Sermon Preached at New-Castle in New England*, June 19, 1694 (Boston, 1699), 15.

[4] *A Compleat Body of Divinity* (Boston, 1726), 125 and 608f.

[5] The manuscript is in the library of the Massachusetts Historical

Puritan restraint on sexual pleasure in marriage was if it became "inordinate" (John Cotton the patriarch's word) and interfered with religious duty.[6] It was to be refused on a stated religious day of fasting, for example, or if it led either husband or wife to fulfill the obligations of religion with less affection to God.[7]

Puritan New England in the seventeenth century was in fact a much married society, in which everyone on reaching an early maturity was expected to be married. So much was this the case that the widow or widower usually remarried shortly after the loss of their first partner. Henry W. Lawrence, in a well-researched but iconoclastic volume, maintains that the Puritans of New England practiced "serial monogamy."[8] Richard Mather was a widower for only eighteen months before his remarriage, and his son Increase Mather reveals how supportive both his wives were to his father and how deeply he loved them:

> That which of outward Afflictions did most aggrieve him, was the death of his dear wife, who had been for so many years the greatest outward comfort and Blessing which he did enjoy. . . . After he had continued in the state of widowhood a year and a half, he again changed his Condition, and was Married to

---

Society.

[6] The adjective "inordinate" is applied to married love that takes precedence over the love owed to God by John Cotton in *A Practical Commentary upon the First General Epistle of John* (London, 1656), 126.

[7] Citations 3 through 6 in this paragraph are taken from Morgan's article, "The Puritans and Sex."

[8] Henry W. Lawrence, *The Not-Quite Puritans* (Boston: Little, Brown, 1928), 84–85.

> the pious widow of that deservedly Famous Man of
> God Mr. *John Cotton;* and her did God make a
> Blessing and a Comfort to him during the remain-
> der of her days.[9]

It was unusual for remarriages to take place after a briefer
interval. For example, the first marriage in New England
took place in 1621 between Edward Winslow, whose
first wife died in the great sickness, and Susannah,
widow of William White, the latter also a victim of the
first winter's ills for the Pilgrims of Plymouth Colony.[10]
The new wife had only been a widow for three months,
and the new husband a widower of less than two
months.[11] Marriage and procreation were clearly a necessity in a new colony to provide the hands necessary
for taming the wilderness. In fact, for a few generations
bachelorhood and (to a lesser degree) spinsterhood were
strongly discouraged. In 1637, the Connecticut Colony
passed a law defining the penalties bachelorhood would
incur:

> It is ordered that no young man that is neither
> married nor hath any servant and be no public offi-
> cer shall keep house by himself, without consent of
> the town where he lives first had, under pain of 20s.
> per week.
> It is ordered that no master of a family shall give
> habitation or entertainment to any young man to

[9] *The Life and Death of the Reverend Man of God, Mr. Richard
Mather, Teacher of the Church in Dorchester* (New England, 1670; reissued in 1974 with introduction and notes by William J. Scherck).
[10] William Bradford, *Of Plymouth Plantation, 1620–1647*, new edition
of Samuel Eliot Morison (New York: Knopf, 1952), 86.
[11] Lawrence, *op. cit.*, 62–63.

> sojourn in his family but by the allowance of the
> inhabitants of the said town where he dwells, under
> the penalty of 20s. per week.[12]

This legislation was directed against the social dangers posed by the presence of single males of social standing.

Since neither squeamishness about sexuality nor a failure to appreciate the importance of marriage was responsible for the simplicity of the ritual and ceremonial for the Puritans, how is it to be accounted for? Four factors call for consideration. The first is biblical and of primary importance. The second is the traditions of the Separatists (who were the embarrassing ancestors of the Independents), the Pilgrims (their more reputable successors), first in Holland and later in Plymouth Colony, and the confirmation of these traditions in English and New England Puritanism. The third factor is Ramism. The fourth factor is a strong, if guarded, element of anti-Anglicanism in which the Puritan sons accused their mother church of compromising with Rome in both ritual and ceremonial.

We have already seen in reference to the biblical factor that John Cotton quotes Genesis 2:18, "Then the Lord God said, 'It is not good that the man should be alone; I will make him a helper fit for him,' " as a sufficient refutation for Puritans of the Roman Catholic assertion of the superiority of virginity to the married state. For the Puritans no authority could be higher than the command of the Creator recorded in God's own Word. And the very same basic text is their justification for regarding companionship rather than procreation or the

---

[12] *Ibid.*, 65.

avoidance of fornication as the primary aim and end of marriage.[13] The two other ends of marriage also have biblical justification,[14] but whereas the procreative end of marriage was primary for Anglicans, as the First and Second Prayer Books of Edward VI make plain,[15] for Puritans companionship had the priority, though they did recognize the subordinate validity of the other two ends of marriage.

The Puritans followed the English Separatists Greenwood and Barrow in believing that marriage was a civil, not a religious or ecclesiastical ceremony, and in

---

[13] See James T. Johnson, "English Puritan Thought on the Ends of Marriage," *Church History*, 38 (December 1969), 429.

[14] The other texts are: for procreation, Genesis 1:27–28: "So God created man in His own image . . . male and female created He them. And God blessed them and said to them, 'Be fruitful and multiply, and fill the earth and subdue it' "; for avoiding fornication the text is 1 Corinthians 7:9: "But if they cannot contain let them marry, for it is better to marry than to burn [with passion]." Johnson, however, credits the English Puritans with excessive originality in asserting the priority of companionship as the chief end of marriage in the relief of loneliness, since this was anticipated by the Renaissance humanists, such as Erasmus, as Margaret Todd affirms in "Humanists, Puritans, and the Spiritualized Household," *Church History*, 49 (1980), 18–34. I owe this reference to a former student, the Reverend Mary Doyle Morgan.

[15] The relevant part of the marriage service proceeds thus: "One cause [of matrimony] was the procreation of children, to be brought up in the fear and nurture of the Lord, and praise of God. Secondly it was ordained as a remedy against sin, and to avoid fornication, that such persons as be married might live chastely in matrimony, to keep themselves undefiled members of Christ's body. Thirdly, for the mutual society, help, and comfort that the one ought to have of the other, both in prosperity and in adversity." (The First Prayer Book of Edward VI, 1549).

the conviction that there was no biblical warrant for a church ceremony. Greenwood was the first Englishman to insist that marriage was no part of a minister's duty when he appeared before the Court of High Commission in 1587.[16] Barrow demanded, "I would fain know of the most Learned of them all, either Foreigners or Natives, whether they find in the Old or New Testament, That Marriage is an Ecclesiastical Action. . . ."[17]

It is also worth noting that John Robinson, pastor in Holland of the future Plymouth Pilgrims, referred in his *Justification of Separation* to "almost twenty severall scriptures and nine distinct reasons grounded upon them, to prove that the celebration of marriage, the bury all of the dead, are not ecclesiasticall actions, apperteyning to the ministry, but civill and so to be performed."[18] Chilton L. Powell observes that when a favorite Puritan pastor was invited to take a larger role, such as preaching a sermon, in an important social marriage, this was frowned upon and actually forbidden by the magistrates, in the case of the Reverend Peter Hobart in 1647 in Boston, and the reason given was that "they were not willing to bring in the English custom of ministers per-

---

[16] Benjamin Brook, *The Lives of the Puritans* (London, 1813),II:35. This scarce set was reprinted in 1994 by Soli Deo Gloria.

[17] Robert Barrow, *A Brief Discoverie of the False Church* (Dordrecht, 1591), 160. Leland H. Carlson has produced admirable modern critical editions of such Elizabethan Separatists as Penry, Barrow, and Greenwood, and Barrington Raymond White provides an excellent account of Separatists in *The English Separatist Tradition: from the Marian Martyrs to the Pilgrim Fathers* (London: Oxford University Press, 1971).

[18] Cited in the Chilton L. Powell article, "Marriage in Early New England," *The New England Quarterly*, 1 (1928), 325.

forming the solemnization of marriage which sermons at
such times might induce."[19]

The origin of the magistrate performing marriage derives from the practice of the Separatists in Holland and
Plymouth, New England. This William Bradford makes
clear in describing the first marriage in Plymouth:

> according to the laudable custome of the Low-cun-
> tries, in which they had lived, was thought to be
> most requisite to be performed by the magistrate,
> as being a civill thing . . . and most consonate to the
> scriptures, Ruth. 4, and no wher found in the
> gospell to be layd on the ministers as part of their
> office. . . . And this practise hath continued
> amongst, not only them, but hath been followed by
> all the famous churches of Christ in these parts to
> this time, Anno: 1646.[20]

As Perry Miller has pointed out, the Puritans shaped
many of their ideas under the influential logic of Ramus,
as they read it in his *Dialecticae Libri Duo* (London, 1669)
or in his commentators, Alexander Richardson or George
Downame.[21, 22] Applying his logic to human relation-

---

[19] *Ibid.*, 326. Powell's source is John Winthrop's *History of New England* (1853 edition), II:182.

[20] *History of Plymouth Plantation, 1620–47*, ed. Worthington C. Ford, 2 vols. (Boston, 1912), I:218–9.

[21] See Perry Miller's *The New England Mind: The Seventeenth Century* (Cambridge, Mass.: Harvard University Press, 1937), *passim* and especially 111–239. For a briefer introduction to relational thinking, see Edmund S. Morgan, *The Puritan Family*, rev. ed. (1966), 21–24.

[22] Alexander Richardson wrote *The Logician Schoolmaster, or a comment upon Ramus Logick* (London, 1657), and George Downame *Commentarii in P. Ramis Dialecticam* (London, 1669).

ships enabled the Puritans to insist that the God of order had so arranged human society in a web of relationships that one party was usually subordinate to the other, such as ruler and subject, husband and wife, parent and child, master and servant. The one natural relationship was involuntary, that of parents and children; the other relationships were dependent on the voluntary action of individuals, and these were based upon a contract, or "covenant"—the latter a profoundly significant theological term. Marriage was recognized as a free covenant between husband and wife in the sight of God, as the relationship of church members and their seed was also a covenant relationship with Christ ratified by the individual by reciting it or singing it in church meeting. Hence, however simple, austere, and even bare the ritual and ceremonial of Puritan marriage was, it was a profoundly religious act, the solemn taking of a covenant in the sight of God, Creator, Redeemer, and Sanctifier. Thus behind the simple marriage ceremony there lies the whole Puritan covenant theology which would be familiar to most of those who married in the Puritan theocracy in New England.

The Puritan-Anglican controversy dated from Elizabethan days and included an objection to the use of the marriage ring (along with kneeling at Holy Communion and making the sign of the Cross over the child at baptism) as one of the three "noxious ceremonies."[23] In the service of Holy Matrimony, the

---

[23] See my *The Worship of the English Puritans* (Morgan, PA.: Soli Deo Gloria, 1998), 61–67, and *Worship and Theology in England from Cranmer to Hooker, 1534–1603* (Princeton, N.J.: Princeton University Press, 1970), 70, 267.

Anglicans had also used the objectionable phrase, "With my body I thee worship," when worship was alone due to God. In addition, by permitting Holy Communion to be celebrated at a wedding, the Puritans felt that Anglicans were almost, as in Roman Catholic fashion, elevating an essentially civil ceremony into an ecclesiastical sacrament. It is also possible, if unlikely, that the Puritans objected to the marriage ring not only as an unbiblical requirement, but also, in James T. Johnson's view, as symbolizing a chattel.[24]

It is high time to ask and answer the question, What were these simple Puritan ceremonies like? First, it was necessary for the couple intending marriage to publish their intentions "in some public place and at some public meeting in the several towns where such persons dwell, at the least eight days before they enter into such contract."[25] The proof that the "banns" had been published was required before the magistrate would consent to marry them, in order to prevent clandestine, bigamous, or coerced marriages. According to Edmund S. Morgan,[26] no marriage covenant has survived in the records of New England, and therefore educated guesses are all that can be given as to its nature. Morgan adds, "The promises

---

[24] See Johnson, "English Puritan Thought on the Ends of Marriage," 435. His point of the priority of companionship among the ends of Puritan marriage is well taken, but he ignores the subordination of women to men in the social hierarchy and does not cite any Puritan text where the ring symbolizes or is equated with the status of a chattel.

[25] The citation is from a law passed in Connecticut Colony on 10 April, 1640, and given in Alden T. Vaughan, *The Puritan Tradition in America, 1620–1730* (New York: Harper & Row, 1972), 181.

[26] *The Puritan Family*, 30.

were made orally then as they are now, and although the
Puritans insisted upon a public record of every marriage,
they never recorded the covenant itself but simply the
fact of its having been made." If we are to guess at the
nature of that covenant, we have two choices, either to
take the Parliamentary Directory of the Westminster
Assembly of 1644, allowing for Independent divergence
from Presbyterian order, or the memory of what a third-
generation historian such as Cotton Mather had heard
from his second-generation father, Increase Mather, who
in turn had heard about first-generation marriages as reported by his father, Richard Mather, or his father-in-
law, the first John Cotton.

The former guess would lead us to eliminate from the
vow the words "before this congregation," since the ceremony in New England was not in the church or meetinghouse. In that case the covenant would read: "I N. do
take thee N. to be my married wife, and do, in the presence of God . . . promise and covenant to be a loving and
faithful husband unto thee, until God shall separate us by
death." The wife promised before God to be "a loving,
faithful, and obedient wife unto thee, until God shall
separate us by death."[27]

Cotton Mather indicates that prior to 1686 there were
public "espousals" corresponding to a modern engagement, at which a pastor "was usually employed and a
Sermon preached on this Occasion."[28] He adds that these
are entirely done away with in his own time. At the
marriage itself the magistrate presided in the home, and,

---

[27] *Reliquiae Liturgicae*, ed. Peter Hall, Vol. III: *The Parliamentary
Directory* (Bath: Binns and Goodwin, 1847), 64.
[28] *Ratio Disciplinae Fratrum Nov-Anglorum* (Boston: 1726), 112.

according to Cotton Mather, gave the covenant to the couple and even prayed over them, and he then suggests, counter to the Peter Hobart case referred to earlier, "However, if a *Minister* were present, he was desired usually, to make at least one of the Prayers."[29] But whether the ceremony approximated the order of the Westminster Directory, or Cotton Mather, it was streamlined, stripped down, and austerely simple.

The marriage ceremony gradually developed in complexity and social sophistication only after 1686, when the original charters were revoked and royal government was firmly established, and ministers were given the right to perform marriages, but only in the towns where they were pastors.

It was probably the existence of espousals that made the transition from magistral to ministerial performance of weddings an easy one after 1686.[30] Neither magistrates nor ministers appear to have objected strongly to the change. Judge Samuel Sewall's second marriage was conducted by his own son, the Reverend Joseph Sewall.

A full account of a church service for the solemnization of a marriage, as it had developed in a century, is provided in Cotton Mather's *Ratio Disciplinae Fratrum Nov-Anglorum: A Faithful Account of the Discipline professed and practised in the Churches of New England with Interspersed and Instructive Reflections on the Discipline of the Primitive Churches* (Boston, 1726).[31] It includes the fol-

---

[29] *Ibid.*

[30] E. S. Morgan, *The Puritan Family*, 32, makes this suggestion and describes an espousal sermon preached by Peter Thacher in his article, "Light on the Puritans from John Hull's Notebooks," *The New England Quarterly*, XV (1942), 95–101.

[31] *Op. cit.*, 113–117.

lowing elements:

- Pastoral Prayer, acknowledging marriage as God's ordinance.
- A brief charge to the couple concerning the covenant they make in the presence of God, followed by a request that the pair "Give therefore your Hands, with your Hearts, unto one another."
- The covenant taking the form as phrased below, formulated by the pastor to the groom, similarly to the bride, except for the additional requirement of obedience, as well as loving and honoring.
- The consent to the covenant is signified, and then the pastor makes the formal declaration: "I then declare you to be Married, according to the laws of GOD and of this Province. And what GOD has joined, Man may not separate."
- A final prayer of blessing on the couple.

The prefatory rubric states: "When the Wedding arrives, the Bridegroom with the Bride, having some Attendants, present themselves before the Pastor, and give him a Certificate of their Lawfull Publication, with which the Town-Clerk must furnish them." The pastor's charge and declaration to the man, as to the woman, takes a form partly reminiscent of the Anglican Order for Holy Matrimony. His words to the husband are as follows:

> The person whom you now take by the Hand, you take to be your wedded Wife; Depending on the Grace of Heaven, you promise to Love her, to Honour her, to Support her; and to treat her in that Relation, as it becomes a Professor of the Glorious Gospel of our Lord JESUS CHRIST, so long as you live both together in this World. This Promise you

make as in the Presence of the Great GOD, and before these Witnesses.

Finally, the minister is instructed to return to the Town Clerk a record of the Marriage. The parallel with the earlier form of the marriage service is still clear, despite the additions of piety, not least in the prohibition of the use of a wedding ring.[32]

An entry from Judge Samuel Sewall's diary provides a vivid light on the celebration of the later New England marriages, showing that they were joyful occasions, but also it provides a transition from weddings to burials. The events took place on Thursday, November 9, 1682.

> Cous. Danl Quinsey Marries Mrs. Anne Shepard Before John Hull, esq. Saml Howell, esq. and Many Persons present, almost Capt. [Thomas] Brattle's great Hall full; Capt. B and Mrs. Brattle there for two. Mr. Willard begun with Prayer. Mr. Tho. Shepard concluded; as he was Praying, Cous. Savage, Mother Hull, wife and self came in. A good space after, when we had eaten Cake and drunk Wine and Beer plentifully, we were called into the Hall again to Sing. In Singing Time Mrs. Brattle goes out being ill... At length out of the Kitching we carry the chair and Her in it, into the Wedding Hall; and after a while lay the Corps of the dead Aunt in the Bride-Bed.[33]

---

[32] Cotton Mather writes (*ibid.*, 115–16): "In former Ages there was, and still in other Places, there is much stress laid upon the Wedding Ring. In other Roman Rituals, there is a Form of Benediction used by the Priest upon it. . . . We shall only say, that in the Weddings of New England, the Ring makes none of the Ceremonies."

[33] *Diary*, ed. M. Halsey Thomas (New York: Farrar, Straus &

Funerals

The development in the ceremonial for the dead greatly resembled that of weddings; in brief, it might be described as a gradual shift from a burial to a funeral. Moreover, the influence of the example of the Separatists, as of the English Puritans, was initially as powerful in both occasional ordinances, and in each case stressed the biblical authority for its austerity, as in its deliberate departure from the Anglican tradition.

As in the case of weddings, the Separatists regarded burials as civil rather than religious in character. Barrow gave the matter sustained treatment in *A Briefe Discoverie of the False Church*. He could find no authority "in the booke of God, that it belonged to the ministers office to burie the dead. It was a pollution to the Leviticall priesthood to touch a carcase or anything about it." Barrow also took exception to the costly trappings of funerals for poor men, with the demand for mourning gowns and other paraphernalia, and he particularly excoriated the insincerity that characterized many laudatory encomia for the dead: "To conclude, after al their praiers, preachment, where (I trow) the priest bestoweth some figures in his commendations (though he be with the glutton in the gulfe of hell) to make him by his rhetorick a better Christian in his grave than he was ever in his life, or else he yerneth his money ill." In addition, Barrow complained that "after al is done in church, then are they all gathered together to a costly and sumptuous banquet. Is this not jolly Christian mourning?"[34]

Giroux, 1973), I, 53.
[34] Cited in the L. H. Carlson edition of *The Writings of Henry Barrow, 1587–1590* (London, 1962), 459f.

These objections were also reasserted by the Puritans of the first generation in New England. Their gravest objection, however, was to the Book of Common Prayer's unbiblical assurance that every corpse was buried "in sure and certain hope of resurrection to eternal life." This was only a charter for rogues.

A description of a famous Separatist, Samuel Eaton, records that many of his adherents followed his body to the graveside, thrust his corpse into the grave, and stamped earth upon it without prayers, commendations, or exhortations.[35] Any Anglican bystanders must have thought it a good riddance rather than a good burial.

The earliest account of a New England burial is from Thomas Lechford, an Anglican critic, writing in 1642; his description would hardly seem to differentiate a Puritan from a Separatist burial, so iconoclastic is the absence of both ritual and ceremonial in those earliest days. Lechford writes:

> At Burials nothing is read, nor any Funeral Sermon made, but all of the neighbourhood, or a good company of them come together by tolling of the bell, and carry the dead solemnly to his grave, and there stand by him while he is buried. The ministers are most commonly present.[36]

Human nature abhors a vacuum, and it will be seen that the ceremonial of funerals in New England, both in the preparation and the accoutrements, developed in ways

---

[35] Champlin Burrage, *The Early English Dissenters in the Light of Recent Research* (Cambridge, Mass.: Cambridge University Press, 1912), II, 326f.
[36] *Plaine Dealing: Or, Newes from New-England* (London, 1642), 94.

that would have surprised and probably shocked the earliest generation of settlers.

The Westminster Directory also insisted on austere burials, in order to avoid superstitious or unedifying abuses, but permitted ministers, if present, to put mourners "in remembrance of their duty." The general rubric for burials was "When any person departeth this life, let the dead body, upon the day of burial, be decently attended from the house to the place appointed for public burial, and there immediately interred, without any ceremony." This simplicity is justified as a remedy for abuses, in cases where there was "praying by or toward the dead corpse . . . in the place where it lies" and also because "the praying, reading, and singing, both in going to and at the grave have been grossly abused, are in no way beneficial to the dead, and have proved many ways hurtful to the living; therefore, let all such things be laid aside."[37]

The New England Puritan burials were not, however, as bleak as those of the Separatists, even in desperately sad circumstances. The Reverend Samuel Danforth of Roxbury made an exhortation in his home just prior to the removal of the bodies of three of his children who were victims of an epidemic in 1659. The first known prayer made at a funeral, was also offered in the home prior to interment, when the Reverend Mr. Wilson prayed at the funeral of the Reverend William Adams of Dedham in

---

[37] *Reliquiae Liturgicae*, Vol. III: *The Parliamentary Directory*, 72-73. The Directory was first published in 1644. See also my *Worship of the English Puritans* for the service books of the English Puritans at Middleburgh and the burial directions.

1685, as recorded by Samuel Sewall.[38] While funeral sermons were not allowed to be preached on the day of the burial, it soon became customary for them to be given on the Sunday after the funeral, or on the following lecture day or a weekday, and eventually (later in the century) on the evening of the funeral. The custom was also for sermons commemorating notable persons to be printed. The first known sermon to be preached on the Sunday after a burial was John Cotton's, delivered on the death of John Oliver in 1646.[39] The first recorded graveside eulogy, an impromptu and most moving tribute to his mother by Judge Sewall on January 15, 1701, deserves citation for its poignant literary expression. As one Bricket was preparing to fill up the grave, the judge said:

> Forbear a little and suffer me to say amidst our bereaving sorrows We have the comfort of beholding this Saint put into the rightfull possession of that Happiness of Living desir'd and dying Lamented. She liv'd commendably Four and Fifty years with her dear Husband, and my dear Father: And she could not well brook the being divided from him at her death; which is the cause of our taking leave of her in this place. She was a true and constant Lover of Gods Word, Worship, and Saints: And she always, with a patient cheerfullness, submitted to the divine Decree of providing Bread for her self and others in the sweat of her Brows. And now her infinitely Gracious and Bountiful Master has promoted her to the Honor of higher Employments, fully and absolutely discharged from all manner of

---

[38] *Diary* (ed. M. Halsey Thomas), I, 74.
[39] See Gordon E. Geddes, *Welcome Joy: Death in Puritan New England* (Ann Arbor: University of Michigan Research Press, 1981), 113.

> Toil, and Sweat. My honoured and beloved Friends
> and neighbours! My dear Mother never thought
> much of doing the most frequent and homely of-
> fices of Love for me; and lavish'd away many
> Thousands of Words upon me, before I could return
> one word in Answer: And therefore I ask and hope
> that none will be offended that I have now ventured
> to speak one word in her behalf; when shee her self
> is become speechless![40]

Small wonder that after reporting the eulogy in his diary,
he added: "Note, I could hardly speak for passion and
tears."

If biblical authority was sought for funeral sermons,
which became more frequent and more elaborate in the
eighteenth century, or for the plethora of elegies which
were read in the house of mourning and often affixed to
the coffin, it was found in David's elegy over Jonathan.
Funeral sermons were delivered and printed at the request and expense of the family. They included such
themes as mourning, preparation for death, the joys of
heaven as the rewards of holy living, and advice to imitate the virtues of the deceased with divine assistance.
The extraordinary efflorescence and popularity of elegies
(at first they were handwritten; much later, elegies were
printed and circulated) clearly indicate that the bareness
of New England funerals gave insufficient opportunities
for the expression and control of grief. In addition, the
restrained and credible eulogies were the start of Puritan
hagiography. It was James Fitch at the funeral of Anne
Mason in 1672 who preached the first funeral sermon in

---

[40] *Diary* (ed. M. Halsey Thomas), I, 444.

New England.[41] The old guard were reluctant to recommend any eulogies, so that when Increase Mather records his father Richard as preaching in England at funerals, he adds, "but only with Instructing the Living concerning Death, the Resurrection, the Judgement to come, and the like seasonable truths."[42] There was an exponential increase in the publication of funeral sermons in the first three decades of the eighteenth century, with 15 in the first, 60 in the second, and 76 in the third decade.[43]

The sources of the grief felt in New England's mourning were threefold. There was inevitably the terrible sense of loss—the longing for "a touch of a vanished hand and the sound of a voice that is still"—but added to that was a sense of guilt in the divine judgment recognized in the death of sons and daughters. On the death of his son Henry, after nights when the child moaned in his agony, Sewall wrote immediately after the funeral, "The Lord humble me kindly in respect of all my Enmity against Him, and let His breaking my Image in my Son be a means of it."[44]

The third source of sadness was due to Puritan theology itself, which emphasized human depravity, the inability to assist one's own salvation or that of others, which depended upon the election of few or rejection of a multitude by an inscrutable God, and demanded doubt

---

[41] *Peace the End of the Perfect and Upright* (Boston, 1673).

[42] Increase Mather, *The Life and Death of That Reverend Man of God, Mr. Mather* (Cambridge, Mass., 1670), 50–51.

[43] Geddes, *op. cit*, 173. The danger of flattering the dead was stressed by Joshua Scottow in the preface to James Fitch's funeral sermon on Anne Mason, published as *Peace the End of the Perfect and Upright*, 1.

[44] *Diary* (ed. M. Halsey Thomas), I, 93.

of salvation as an essential preparation for salvation.[45] Moreover, the issue would remain in doubt until the general resurrection. The fears were admirably summed up in Leonard Hoar's sermon, *The Sting of Death* (Boston, 1680):

> So it may be said of every inhabitant of this earth when he comes to dye; the weight of sin, the insupportableness of Gods anger, the terrors of hell, the nearness of the danger, the difficulty of salvation will all appear nakedly to the naked soul.[46]

Perhaps the greatest frustration the mourners had in Puritan customs was their utter inability to do anything for the souls of the dead, the privilege open to those who believe that masses and prayers for the dead can reduce the time to be spent in the intermediate state of purgatory and speed the way to heaven. That Roman Catholic consolation was not open to Puritans. In addition, it threw a heavy responsibility on the individual believer's shoulders, for as Keith Thomas observed, "Every individual was now to keep his own balance-sheet, and a man could no longer atone for his sins by the prayers of his descendants."[47] If they were predestinarians, as most Puritans were—before the inroads of Arminianism (and possibly of preparationism)[48]—they believed that the ultimate

---

[45] See David E. Stannard, *The Puritan Way of Death: A Study in Religion, Culture, and Social Change* (New York: Oxford University Press, 1977), 83*f*.

[46] Stannard, *ibid.*, cites this reference.

[47] *Religion and the Decline of Magic* (London: Weidenfeld and Nicolson, 1971), 603.

[48] For preparationism, the practices that were encouraged to ready the believer for the gift of converting grace, see Norman Pettit's

destination of the soul was predetermined, and they could do absolutely nothing to change it. It is little wonder in these circumstances that burials were austere or that they later became much more elaborate, both to commemorate the deceased worthily and comfort family and friends.

As the seventeenth century advanced and the eighteenth arrived, there was a striking development in the impressiveness and the costliness of funerals, which occasionally reached sheer extravagance. As to expense, one has only to compare the cost of a funeral in Salem, where early charges (to include a shroud, a coffin, and the digging of a grave, as well as liquor for the mourners) cost between twelve shillings and two pounds sterling, with the funeral of Waitstill Winthrop in 1717 at a cost of over six hundred pounds sterling (incidentally consuming 20 percent of his estate) to mark the growth of extravagance.[49] So contradictory was this to the expected Puritan virtues of simplicity and thriftiness that a law was passed by the General Court of Massachusetts in 1721, the preamble of which read: "The charge or expense of funerals of later years (when the circumstances of the province so loudly call for all sorts of frugality) is becoming very extravagant, especially in the giving of scarves, to the great detriment of the province and the impoverishment of many families."[50] Extravagance, especially in scarves, was outlawed with a penalty of twenty pounds

---

excellent study, *The Heart Prepared: Grace and Conversion in Puritan Spiritual Life* (New Haven, Conn.: Yale University Press, 1966).

[49] Geddes, *op. cit.*, 142, and Alice M. Earle, *Customs and Fashions in New England* (New York: Scribner's Sons, 1893), 376.

[50] Lawrence, *The Not-Quite Puritans*, 178.

for infringement.

Extravagance marked not only the funerals of governors and judges, but, ironically, of famous ministers who had criticized such unnecessary costliness. One such case was Cotton Mather, who had condemned the increasing costliness of New England funerals in *A Christian Burial* (Boston, 1713), but whose own funeral was carried out with pomp and circumstance in 1728. The Reverend Mr. Gee, Mather's colleague, led the procession in deep mourning, followed by the deacons of the church and congregation, arranged according to their social ranking. The pall was carried by the first six ministers of the Boston Lecture, Benjamin Colman, Peter Thacher, Joseph Sewall, Thomas Prince, John Webb, and Thomas Cooper, while "several Gentlemen of the bereaved Flock took their turns to bear the Coffin." The relatives of the deceased followed in mourning, then came Lieutenant Governor William Dummer, the Council, the House of Representatives, and after them, "a large Train of Ministers, Justices, Merchants, Scholars, and other Principal Inhabitants, both of Men and Women." As the procession moved toward the grave, "the Streets were crowded with People and the Windows fill'd with Sorrowful Spectators all the way to the Burying Place."[51] The number and dignity of the mourners all reflected the respect in which Cotton Mather was held.

The costliness came from the necessary garb of

---

[51] This reconstruction of the scene on the way to Cotton Mather's burial is the work of Gordon E. Geddes in his *Welcome Joy*, 136–137, and is based upon *The New England Weekly Journal*, February 16, 1728, and Sewall's *Diary* entry for the previous day.

mourning,[52] requiring black suits and costumes, hats and
stockings; the scarves (white or black), gloves, rings it
was customary to send to those invited to funerals, and
the charges for the food, wine, and beer consumed by the
mourners at the home afterwards. The coffin also was
often made of excellent wood, lined with cloth, and had
the year of death hammered in small nails on its surface,
and it was occasionally covered with a mort-cloth, to
which the elegies of mourners were affixed.[53] An additional cost was for embalming, which was not necessary
in the early days in New England because bodies were
usually buried within two to four days after death, but
became commonplace in the last decades of the century
and in the first three of the eighteenth.[54] For most of our
period the procession to the grave was made by foot, but
by the 1730s in Boston it was possible to hire black
horses and coaches for the gentry.[55] When coaches were
used they took up the rear of the procession.

The gloves and scarves were usually made of linen,
but the more expensive were of corded silk. Sewall reported that for being present at 29 funerals, he had re-

---

[52] When the Reverend John Bailey's wife died in 1691, he bought a
mourning coat, mourning breeches, mourning stockings, a mourning
hat, and black crepe, some of which he used for the hat. These cost
more than eight pounds. See Geddes, *op. cit.*, 120, whose authority is
*Watertown Records, Comprising East Congregational and Precinct
Affairs 1697 to 1737*; also *Record Book of the Pastors 1686 to 1819*
(Boston: David Clapp & Son, 1906), IV, 177.

[53] Stannard, *The Puritan Way of Death*, 113.

[54] Stannard, *op. cit.*, 116, points out that Sewall mentions the matter
so casually in his *Diary* (II, 1020–21), as if it were not unusual to
embalm bodies, indicating that his daughter had expressed the wish
"not to be disembowelled."

[55] Geddes, *op. cit.*, 135.

ceived 26 scarves, 13 rings, and 5 pairs of gloves between March 29, 1697, and July 2, 1704.[56] Andrew Eliot, minister of the North Church in Boston, is reputed to have recorded the number of gloves he received for attending funerals, and it is said that in 32 years he had amassed 3,000 pairs, which he ultimately sold to Boston milliners for the equivalent of between 600 and 700 pounds sterling.[57] For the death of a notable person the family might be required to send out a hundred pairs of gloves and several rings to the intimates of the deceased. These mortuary gifts were both mementos of the occasion, and tokens to encourage attendance at the funerals.

Cotton Mather typically tried to make pious use of these "civilities":

> I would never putt on the Civilities (of a Glove, or a Ring, or a Scarf) given me at a Funeral, but endeavour to do it, with a Supplication, *Lord, prepare me for my own Mortality.* And, *Lord, lett me at my Death be found worthy of a Remembrance among the Living!* And inasmuch as I have a distinguishing Share above the most of them who ordinarily attend a Funeral, I would look at it, as an Obligation on me to press after the instance of Godliness and Usefulness, that may render me more excellent than my Neighbour; and particularly, in an holy Behaviour at a Funeral, exemplary in the Religion of the Funeral.[58]

It seems as if the ritual of the funeral had changed

---

[56] *Diary* (ed. M. Halsey Thomas), I, 469–470.

[57] Earle, *Customs and Fashions in New England*, 374–375.

[58] *Diary*, 8:96, cited by Kidran and Ann Tasjian, *Memorials for Children of Change: The Art of Early New England Stonecarving* (Middletown, Conn.: Wesleyan University press, 1974), 28.

only slightly during a century, while the ceremonial had become immensely elaborate, with processions in deep mourning, and the mourners following the hearse, the pallbearers, and the under-bearers in strict order. The closest relatives were at the head of the procession, with the husband leading singly at the funeral of his wife, and the wife, at her husband's funeral, leading but on the arm of a close male relative. After the relatives in pairs, as was seen in the Cotton Mather funeral, the other mourners marched in the strict order of social rank. For civic and military leaders, the corpse was accompanied to the graveside by troops in arms, and volleys were fired in honor of the deceased, as when William Adams in 1671 attended the funeral of Deputy Governor Willoughby, accompanied by eleven companies of foot soldiers, sounding trumpets and drums, as well as volleys.[59]

With all this developing impressiveness, elaboration, and costliness of funerals in New England, one is forced to ask: why does this differ so strikingly from the earlier austere funerals in New England and from the relatively restrained and modest funerals of the heirs of the Puritans, the Nonconformists of Old England? David Stannard may have the brief but comprehensive answer in the suggestion that "in meeting death, it seems clear, they [the Puritans] encountered something their English ancestors never had. What they encountered was themselves and their profound sense of tribal vulnerability."[60]

---

[59] The "Diary" of William Adams (Massachusetts Historical Society Collections, 4th series, 1 [1852]), 8–22, cited by Geddes, *op. cit.*, 12.

[60] Stannard, *op. cit.*, 117–18.

Many factors help to account for that vulnerability, including the diminishing number of conversions and therefore of covenanted church members, which no amount of preaching jeremiads could change; the increasing rationalism which fought against the old orthodox pietism; the growing materialism and secularism of life in the expanding cities and towns; the decrease of Calvinists and the increase of Arminians; the diversity of denominational allegiances permitted or rather demanded by the new royal charters; and the attractiveness the Church of England had in both ritual and ceremonial for some who felt that Puritanism had been too spare and too iconoclastic. These are all factors that hacked at the granitic exclusiveness of the old Calvinistic and Independent orthodoxy of the founders of the Puritan theocracy.

In the matter of funerals, it is seen most vividly in a new iconography which represented a new sensitivity, which Larzer Ziff has called in relation to death a change from the monitory outlook to the sentimental.[61] By the term "sentimental," Ziff means the "validation of divine truths by the pleasurable effect they had on the feelings." This John Flavel had encouraged in his books that found lessons in created things more easily assimilable than the transformations required by divine revelation and soteriological demands. "New England religion," writes Brooks Holifield about the early eighteenth century, "was infused with a new symbolic consciousness . . . and the spiritualizing of the creatures transformed all

---

[61] *Puritanism in America: New Culture in a New World* (New York: Viking Press, 1973), 253.

of nature into an instrument of the meditative life."[62]
Another explanation for the changed attitude to death is
offered by Gordon E. Geddes, namely, that the seventeenth-century Puritans identified death with the disso-
lution of the body—as seen in the death's heads on their
tombs—whereas their eighteenth-century successors
thought of death as the release of the soul—as seen by the
soul effigy replacing the death's head on tombstones.[63]
The latter suggestion may have merit, but Allan I.
Ludwig's fine study of New England tombstones, *Graven
Images*, provides illustrations of early soul effigies.[64]
   Geddes further avers that with the growing emphasis
on conversion, sermons became more a preparation for
death and heaven, and less a dangling of victims over the
flaming pit of Hell, and consequently both a rationalist
(like Benjamin Colman) and pietist (like Cotton Mather)
minimized death's terrors, turning it into an adventure
for the saints.[65] One incident exhibiting the views of a
major figure of the second generation would seem to support this view. According to Williston Walker, when
Increase Mather, the report of whose death (like Mark
Twain's) had been greatly exaggerated, was confined to
his house because of his weakening condition after
September 1719: "The thought of his approaching rest in

---

[62] *The Covenant Sealed: The Development of Puritan Sacramental
Theology*, 1570–1720 (New Haven, Conn.: Yale University Press,
1966), 196.
[63] *Welcome Joy*, 191–192.
[64] *Graven Images: New England Stonecarving and Its Symbols*
(Middletown, Conn.: Wesleyan University Press, 1966), 18–52 and
176–424. These pages provide a thorough analysis of mortuary symbols.
[65] Geddes, *op. cit.*, 191.

the presence of his Lord seemed increasingly attractive
to him. To his London friend, Thomas Hollis, who had
inquired if he were still in the 'land of the living', he sent
the message: 'No. Tell him I am going to it; This Poor
World is the land of the Dying. 'Tis Heaven that is the
true Land of the Living.' "[66]

The evidence of the iconography of tombstones is
particularly significant in mirroring changes of sensibility and the necessity for visual symbols when the ritual
and ceremonial of burial were so naked to begin with. So
iconophobic was the burial service, so depressing was
the finality of the disappearance of the dead into the
earth, that iconography was bound to fill the vacuum. It
is not surprising either that there were feasts to follow
the burial: the rum and wine and cakes were needed to
provide good cheer in a lugubrious situation, even if
Cotton Mather had to satirize the indulgence by remark-
ing rhetorically, "In the very Room where the Dead is
before our Eyes, how Frothy often are we?"[67]

This stonecarvers' art was a popular, if often uncon-
scious, protest against the bleakness of funerals, substitut-
ing vivid eschatological symbols which were abstract in
sermons but lively on stone and reflected on the retina of
the eye. The imagery was limited, but the emblems
ranged from death to resurrection. Death symbols were
early linked to time symbols, such as hourglasses,
scythes, and skeletons extinguishing candles, all of which
signified the king of terrors, and the earliest of all images
is a winged effigy that may be a soul effigy found on a

---

[66] *Ten New England Leaders* (New York: Silver Burdett, 1910), 212.
[67] *The Christian Funeral* (Boston, 1713), 20.

stone of 1668 in Haverhill, Massachusetts.[68] Later,
starting about 1690 and 1691, stones reproduce imps carrying hourglasses and deadly arrows, but do not reappear
after 1710.

Death symbols are followed on the tombstones by
resurrection symbols. Garlands of victory—flowers
sprouting from an urn—occur in 1697–1698 in Boston.
Trees of life in which doves nestle appear in 1725 and
1729, and between 1718 and 1725 crosses are carved (the
first of which has a blossom). A very ancient symbol of
resurrection, the peacock, appears in 1703 in Quincy,
Massachusetts, where two peacocks flank an hourglass.
Images of the soul's flight to heaven are seen on a
Providence, Rhode Island, stone in 1732; a host of angels
escorts the soul to the bosom of Abraham. In Charlestown, Massachusetts, a 1710 stone depicts a soul "sucking
on a stem at the top of a foliated border made up of gourd-
like shapes—imbibing, presumably, wine."[69] Such an
image is common, and it links the Lord's Supper with the
Celestial Banquet.

What may be the least expected is the discovery that
the Puritan imagination in New England designed new
emblems on its gravestones. Peter Benes argues convincingly that the frequently depicted winged skulls are not
symbols of death, as they seem to have been in England,
but rather symbols of the emancipated spirits released
from their bodies at death. This would explain the great
variety in their representation and the fact that their
faces often bear smiles, are occasionally caricatures, and,
in some cases, are portraits of the deceased. "By custom,"

---

[68] Allan I. Ludwig, *Graven Images*, Plate 209.
[69] *Ibid.*, 165.

writes Benes, "a spirit ideogram consisted of a core symbol (a skull, a geometric face, or an explicitly human face), to which was attached one or a pair of secondary symbols that suggested flight (birds' wings, bats' wings, feathers); eternal life (diamonds, hearts, books, and trees); radiance (suns, halos, or brightness markings); or heaven (suns, stars, and planets)."[70] Thus there was an increasing cheerfulness about the destination of human spirits after death, and this was the creation of the American Puritan imagination, characterized by originality, variety, and vividness.

It is fitting to close with the observation of Allan Ludwig: "Puritan funerary art shows a deep strain of passion and a naive delight in mystical symbolism" as well as "the vision of a life to come which was frozen for posterity."[71] It is good to know that where the institutional provision for ceremonial and ritual was inadequate, the people compensated for it by the supplementation of iconography.

---

[70] *Masks of Orthodoxy: Folk Gravestone Carving in Plymouth County, Massachusetts, 1689–1805* (Amherst: University of Massachusetts Press, 1977), 45.
[71] *Graven Images*, 5.

9
Ordinations

Independent or Congregational churches have rightly been proud of their democratic constitutions, and nowhere is this more clearly demonstrated than in their New England foundation. Strictly speaking, each Independent church is a combination of monarchical, aristocratic, and democratic powers. The relationship to Christ, as prophet, priest, and King, the founder and continuing enabler of the Church as His Body, is evidently monarchical, with the members as His majesty's humble subjects. The power of the ministry as leaders in the church is aristocratic, with the exception of the fact that the foundation of a new church, the invitation to a person to become a minister, and the admission and dismissal of members of a church require the concurrence of the majority of the members of the church, and in this sense it is a democracy. However, in the earliest New England churches it was the local church members who actually ordained their ministers, and it was only at the end of the second generation in New England that, as will be seen, a greater clericalization of the churches took place.

The Foundation of Churches
The democracy of churches is evident most clearly in the foundation of churches, as can be seen if we examine the procedure for the founding of Dedham Church in

1636 and Woburn Church in 1642, for both of which we have detailed information.

The gathering of a church was undertaken by a small number of charter members, ten in the case of Dedham, "whome we had best hope for soundnes of grace and meete guifts for such a work."[1] According to the Reverend Richard Mather, the number needed to found a church was typically "about eight or nine."[2] The usual custom was for this keen nucleus of a future church to meet regularly and, after fasting and prayers, to reveal to each other their experience of grace, and, finally, to agree on a devout person known to them to call as their minister. They would also decide on a day when, again after fasting and prayer, they would solemnly accept a covenant which they had previously drawn up as the expression of their engagement to Christ and each other. Then, after questioning by ministers of neighboring churches, and in the presence of a magistrate, they received the right hand of fellowship and the acknowledgment that their church was rightly and truly gathered.

It is clear from the Dedham church founding that it was no light matter. The future minister and church members prepared over a period of several months "lovingly to discourse and consult together," during which time each individual spent an entire day "to open each one his spiritual condicion to the rest, relating the man-

---

[1] For information about the origin and history of Dedham Church, see Kenneth A. Lockridge, *A New England Town, The First Hundred Years: Dedham, Massachusetts, 1636–1736* (New York, 1970), Chap. 2.

[2] Richard Mather's letter to William Rathband and Mr. T., June 25, 1636, in E. Emerson, *Letters from New England: The Massachusetts Bay Colony, 1629–1638* (Amherst: University of Massachusetts Press, 1976), 202.

ner of our conversion to God and the Lords following proceedings in our soules with present apprehensions of Gods love or want thereof."[3]

Edward Johnson, describing the gathering of Woburn Church, says that it is "as unnatural for a right N.[ew] E.[ngland] man to live without an able Ministry, as for a Smith to work his iron without a fire," and that the founders, "after some search meet with a young man, named Mr. *Thomas Carter*, then belonging to the Church of Christ at *Water-Town*, a reverend godly man, apt to teach the sound and wholsome truths of Christ," who exercised his gifts among them, especially on a day of fasting and prayer.[4] The day of the gathering arrived on the 24th day of the 6th month of 1642, when they met at 8 a.m. in the company of eight Massachusetts ministers, and the proceedings were directed by the Reverend Mr. Syms, who "continued in preaching and prayer about the space of four or five houres." Then, in the presence of the magistrate, Increase Nowell, "the persons stood forth and first confessed what the Lord had done for their poor souls, by the work of his Spirit in the preaching of his Word, and Providences, one by one." The "messengers" from the other churches questioned them, and, on being satisfied, held out "the right hand of fellowship unto them, they declaring Covenant, in words expressed in

---

[3] *Dedham Church Records*, 5, 10, cited by C. Hambrick-Stowe, *The Practice of Piety* (Chapel Hill: University of North Carolina Press, 1982), 127.

[4] *The Wonder-Working Providence of Sion's Saviour in New-England* (London, 1654), ed. with historical introduction by William Frederick Poole (Andover, Mass., 1867), 177.

writing to this purpose."[5] Three months later Thomas
Carter was ordained as their minister—be it noted—by
two of the lay members of the church by the imposition
of their hands on his head, saying, "We ordain thee
Thomas Carter to be Pastor unto this Church of Christ."[6]

To complete the picture of the foundation of Woburn
Church, the covenant will be cited, for this was the ligature of the polity and discipline of the new church. It
reads as follows:

> We that do assemble our selves this day before God
> and his people, in an unfeigned desire, to be ac-
> cepted of him as a Church of the Lord Jesus Christ,
> according to the rule of the New-Testament, do ac-
> knowledge our selves to be the most unworthy of all
> others, that we should attain such a high grace, and
> the most unable of our selves to the performance of
> any thing that is good, abhorring our selves for all
> our former defilements in the worship of God, and
> other wayes, and resting only upon the Lord Jesus
> Christ for attonement, and upon the power of his
> grace for the guidance of our whole after course, do
> here in the name of Christ Jesus, as in the presence
> of the Lord, from the bottom of our hearts agree
> together through his grace to give up our selves,
> first unto the Lord Jesus as our only King, Priest
> and Prophet, wholly to be subject unto him in all
> things, and therewith one unto another, as in a
> Church-Body to walk together in all the Ordinances
> of the Gospel, and in all such mutual love and of-
> fices thereof, as toward one another in the Lord;
> and all this, both according to the present light that
> the Lord hath given us, as also according to all fur-
> ther light, which he shall be pleased at any time to

---

[5] *Ibid.*, 178.
[6] *Ibid.*

reach out unto us out of the Word by the goodness of his grace, renouncing also in the same Covenant all errors and Schismes, and whatsoever by-wayes that are contrary to the blessed rules revealed in the Gospel, and in particular the inordinate love and seeking after the things of the world; every Church hath not the same for words, for they are not for a form of words.[7]

It is worth observing the salient features of this church covenant, which, although framed for the occasion, is typical of the genre of this period. It begins with repentance and faith—the preconditions of regeneration—as it affirms a total dependence upon Christ for salvation. It continues by asserting its sincerity ("from the bottom of our hearts"), and promises to observe all the ordinances of Christ together. Finally, it agrees to abide by the light of the Word of God as presently revealed and to be revealed. The simplicity, sincerity, and solemnity of this undertaking are cumulatively impressive, especially as this is wholly the work of laymen, not theologians.

By 1651, when Thomas Weld had published *A Brief Narration of the Practices of the Churches in New-England,*

---

[7] *Ibid.,* *179.* The final words may be part of the covenant or an editorial addition by Captain Edward Johnson, the author of the history. The early Salem Covenant of 1629 simply sums up the essence of all church covenants in the first years of settlement: "We Covenant with the Lord and one with an other; and do bynd our selves in the presence of God, to walke together in all his waies, according as he is pleased to reveale himself unto us in his Blessed word of truth." Williston Walker, *The Creeds and Platforms of Congregationalism* (Boston: Pilgrim Press, 1960), 116. It was considerably expanded in 1636.

the system of church gathering was fully regulated. The steps, as he lists them, are as follows. Firstly, those intending to start a church meet privately to examine each other's spiritual condition and are satisfied "in the judgment of charity of the truth of grace, of each other."[8] Next, they certify to the magistrate and to the adjoining churches their intention to found a church, and the day on which they intend to meet publicly. In this they have a triple aim: to show they are not ashamed of the Gospel; to beg the advice and prayers of their brethren in Christ; and to allow their brethren to see them and accept them more comfortably into communion.

Then on the day of gathering, the time is chiefly spent in fasting and praying. After this a deputed charter member requires the others to follow him in describing publicly the work of grace in their hearts: "Then he himself begins and makes confession of his faith in all the principles of Religion, and a declaration of his effectual calling to Christ, and how God hath carried on the work of grace *(viz. Repentance from dead Works and faith towards God, both of which they insist upon)* in his soule to that day." Then they all make their own confession of faith and describe the work of grace, on which they are questioned by the messengers from the neighboring churches.

The climax of the day comes when "they enter into a sacred and solemn Covenant, engagement, profession . . . whereby they protest and promise (by the help of Christ) to walk together as becomes a Church of God, in all duties of holinesse before the Lord, and in all brotherly love and faithfulness to each other, according unto God,

---

[8] Weld, *A Brief Narration of the Practices of the Churches in New-England* (London, 1651), 2.

with all producing their Covenant, agreed on before amongst themselves, then read it before the Assembly and then either subscribe their hands to it or testifie by word of mouth their agreement thereto."[9]

Finally, the representatives of the other churches offer the charter members of the church the right hand of fellowship, commend them to God, "and so prayers made, and praises given unto God, and a Psalme sung, the blessing is pronounced, and the Congregation dissolved."[10]

Apart from the democratic nature of the entire proceeding, what is most striking is the significance of the covenant that is the real charter of the new church. It has three important characteristics. Firstly, it is voluntary, arrived at after careful discussion and agreement by a small group of laity. Secondly, unlike a creed, it is more than a historical or mental commitment; it is an adherence of mind, heart, and will to follow Christ in all His ordinances in their purity. In the third place, it shows that every future member intended to be a witness to the transforming grace of God in Christ and thus a "visible saint," avoiding hypocrisy.

The Ordination of Church Officers

The earliest records of ordinations to the ministry come from John Cotton and Thomas Lechford. Lechford, in 1642, describes a New England ordination as follows:

---

[9] *Ibid.*, 2–3. In mentioning the covenant, Weld refers in the margin to John Cotton's *The Way of the Churches of Christ in New England* (London, 1645), 8, as his authority.
[10] *Ibid.*, 3.

Then they set another day [subsequent to the gathering of the church] for the ordination of said officers, and appoint some of themselves to impose hands upon their officers, which is done in a publique day of fasting and prayer. Where there are Ministers, or Elders before, they impose their hands upon the new Officers: but where there is none, there some of the chiefest men, two or three, of good report amongst them, though not in the Ministry, doe, by appointment of the said Church, lay hands upon them.[11]

Cotton's account, published three years later, is fuller, but corroborates Lechford's accuracy:

When therefore any of the Churches are destitute of any of these Officers, the Brethren of the Church look out from amongst themselves, such persons as are in some measure qualified. If the Church can finde out none such in their own body, they send to any other Church for fit supply, and each Church looketh at it as their dutie to be mutually helpfull one to another, in yeelding what supply they may, without too much prejudice to themselves. . . . Such being recommended to them for such a work, they take some time of tryall of them. . . . For every man of good gifts is not alwayes endowed with an honest and good heart; and every good heart is not fitted to close (so fully as were meet) with every good people: Every Key is not fit to open every Lock; nor every mans gift to edifie every people. . . . When the day [of ordination] is come, it is kept as a day of humiliation, with fasting, praying and preaching the Word, according to the patterne. Towards the close of the day, one of the Elders of the Church (if it have any) if not, one of

---

[11] *Plaine Dealing: or, Newes from New-England* (London, 1642), 3.

the graver Brethren of the Church, (appointed by
themselves to order the worke of the day) standeth
up and inquireth of the Church, If now . . . they
still continue in their purpose to elect such a one
for their Pastor, or Teacher, or Ruling Elder, whom
before they agreed upon. . . . He proceedeth to in-
quire into the approbation of the rest of the
Assembly. . . . Now seeing all is clear, he desireth
all the Brethren of that Church to declare their
Election of him with one accord, by lifting up their
hands; which being done, he desireth to know of
the partie chosen whether he doth accept of that
calling. . . . He then with the Presbytery [Elders]
of that Church (if it have any, if not two or three
others of the gravest Christians amongst the
Brethren of that Church, being deputed by the
body) doe in the name of the Lord Jesus ordaine
him unto that Office, with imposition of hands,
calling upon the Lord. . . . After this the Elders of
their Churches present, observing the presence of
God, both in the duties of that day performed by
the Officer chosen and ordained, and in the orderly
proceeding of the Church in his Election and
Ordination, one of them, in the name of all the
rest, doth give unto him the *right hand of fellowship*
in the sight of all the Assembly.[12]

This procedure would strike both Anglicans and
Presbyterians as extraordinary, for the former would require bishops to be the ordaining officers, and the latter
would insist upon ordination by a fraternity of ministers.
Puritans, having suffered persecution in England by
bishops, were not likely to approve of ordination by
bishops; while prizing the independence of each church,
they were not willing to undergo the corporate overlord-

---

[12] Cotton's *The Way of the Churches of Christ*, 39–41.

ship of presbytery, believing, with John Milton, that "new presbyter is but old priest writ large."

In view of the criticism of Presbyterian theologians, it was necessary to defend the Independent ecclesiology. This Thomas Hooker of Hartford did, in reply to Samuel Rutherford's *Due Right of Presbyteries*, which had criticized Cotton's *The Way of the Churches of Christ*, which was circulating in manuscript. This work of Hooker's was *A Survey of the Summe of Church-Discipline*, which was presented for the approval of a meeting of the ministers of all the New England colonies held at Cambridge, Massachusetts in 1645 to counter the attacks of Presbyterians and Baptists.[13] Hooker formulates an admirably concise and cogent statement of principles of Independent ecclesiology in the preface to his *Survey*. In it he makes a case for councils or "consociations" of churches to advise, approve, or admonish particular local churches. They may reprove an erring church, and renounce fellowship with it, but they have no judicial authority over it.

Hooker's definitions preserve the independence of each local church. For example, "Visible Saints are the only true and meet matter, whereof a visible Church should be gathered, and confoederation is the form." He even boldly asserts, "The Church as *Totum essentiale*, is, and may be, before Officers." In consequence, "ordination is not before election," and "there ought to be no

---

[13] The background is described in Williston Walker's *The Creeds and Platforms of Congregationalism*, 141. It should be noted that the first draft of Hooker's work was lost in a ship that foundered on the way to England, and an imperfect copy was posthumously published by his friends. However, the gist of his thought was included in the Cambridge Platform of 1645.

ordination of a Minister at large, Namely, such as would make him Pastour without a People." And so, "ordination is only a solemn installing of an Officer into the Office, unto which he was formerly called."[14]

Once the new church is constituted, it must find officers. In the earliest days it was customary to find them among the charter members. Weld states that if there are no suitable candidates for office among them, "they seek the Lord of the Harvest to direct them elsewhere," and indicates that this is unusual ("though usually those that joyn into a Church have one amongst them upon whom their eye is for such employment"[15]).

Who were these officers and what were their duties? Weld points out that the apostles, prophets, and evangelists of New Testament times were extraordinary officers at the origination of the Church and so have no successors in subsequent centuries. He adds that the ordinary officers are elders of two kinds, teaching and ruling. The teaching elders are also of two kinds, pastors and teachers. The duty of the pastor "is to bend himself to exhortation" and the office of the teacher "is to give himself to instruction in points of doctrine, explication of Scripture, confutation of errors, &c." The task of the ruling elder is "to order the Assemblies, to look to the life and conversation of the whole Church, and to visit from house to house, to see how all thrive in goodnesse, while the other give themselves to the Word and Doctrine." Weld adds that all of them conjointly govern the church and have to "prepare in private all matters for Church, and to survey the estates and ripen all such as are to be admitted in the

---

[14] Walker, *op. cit.*, 143–145.
[15] Weld, *op. cit.*, 3.

Church, before they produce them in publike, &c."[16]
Finally, the task of the deacons is to supervise the fi-
nances of the church in three ways. Their charge is to
supply the necessities of the indigent members "and
with a tender heart and careful hand supply them from
the Church-Treasury with such things as they need for
necessity, convenience, and comfort." They must also
see to the provisions for the ministry's sustenance and for
furnishing the Lord's Table with bread and wine on
Communion Sundays. In sum, the deacon's task is:

> Collect diligently
> To   Keep faithfully
> Distribute carefully

> the Churches treasure, that so hee may serve the
> Tables, which is the proper work; the Lords Table,
> Ministers Table, and the poors Table.[17]

There were also deaconesses, that is, church widows
"who may give themselves to works of mercy cheerfully," especially caring for the sick.[18] The varied work
of the officers of the church and their care for the souls
and the bodies of the members and their children
demonstrate that their communal responsibility as affirmed in their covenant was a profound reality, and not
mere lip service.

The Cambridge Platform of 1648 explains the duties of
the ministers in fuller detail after twenty years of experience in New England. Ministerial offices are defined:

---

[16] *Ibid.*
[17] *Ibid.*, 4.
[18] *Ibid.*

> The office of Pastor & Teacher, appears to be dis-
> tinct. The *Pastors* special work is, to attend to *exhor-
> tation:* & therein to Administer a word of *Wisdom:*
> the *Teacher* is to attend to *Doctrine*, & therein to
> Administer a word of *Knowledge:* & either of them
> to administer the *Seales* [sacraments] of that
> Covenant, unto the dispensation whereof the[y] are
> alike called: as also to execute the *Censures*, being
> but a kind of application of the word, the preaching
> of which, together with the application thereof
> they are alike charged withall.[19]

The Cambridge Platform also insists that ordination is not a permanent status enjoyed by a clerical caste. On the contrary, it is merely the "solemn putting of a man into his place & office in the Church wher-unto he had right before by election, being like the installing of a magistrate in the common wealth."[20] Consequently, "ordination is not to go before, but to follow election." If a minister is to serve another church, reordination is essential, and when this happens, "we know nothing to hinder, but *Imposition of hands* also in his *Ordination* ought to be used towards him again."[21] The Cambridge Platform asserts that at an ordination only the laying on of hands and prayer, after fasting, are necessary. The elders of the local church perform the act of ordination, and "in such Churches where there are no Elders, Imposition of hands in ordination is to be performed by some of the Brethren orderly chosen by the church therunto." This procedure is defended by claiming that the great responsibility is election, which is the substance of the office, so that the

---

[19] Walker, *op. cit.*, 211.
[20] Walker, *op. cit.*, 215.
[21] Walker, *op. cit.*, 217.

lesser action, ordination, need not require the presence of elders.

Great consideration was given by the whole group of elders to the responsibility of admitting new members, in order to maintain the continuity of "visible saints" in the local church. Hence investigation of the manner of life of applicants, as well as questioning them as to their understanding of the principal doctrines and ethical demands of Christian faith, and their experience of grace, were carefully carried out. Only in this way could the substantial purity of the Church be maintained and assurance provided of its fidelity to the ordinances of Christ, which was its justification for existing. But the Cambridge Platform insists that the examination is not to be conducted with severity: "Such *charity* & tenderness is to be used, as the weakest christian if sincere, may not be excluded, nor discouraged."[22]

"Censures" were also maintained to preserve the purity of the Church. Private offenses were dealt with by admonishment if the parties involved could not make up with mutual forgiveness. If the offense was public, more heinous, or even criminal, then excommunication follows, for the church is "to cast out the offender, from their holy communion, for the further mortifying of his sinn & the healing of his soule, in the day of the Lord Jesus."[23] The church should then refrain from all contact with such in spiritual matters and civil matters, apart from what natural and domestic relations require. The aim is to make the offending person feel ashamed, repent, and ultimately rejoin the fellowship of the religious

---

[22] Walker, *op. cit.*, 222.
[23] Walker, *op. cit.*, 229.

community.

The elders, as we have seen, were ordained after fasting, prayer, the laying on of hands, and the reception of the right hand of fellowship from the representative of the local church or churches who might be present by invitation. *Deacons*, however, were set apart for their office with less formality. John Cotton explained, "For our calling of Deacons, we hold it not necessary to ordaine them with like solemnitie, of fasting and prayers, as is used in the ordination of Elders."[24] In the case of the ordination of deacons, it meant that there were no visitors present from other churches, and preliminary fasting by the church members was not required as preparation. The same simplicity marked the ceremony when performed forty-five years later, as described by Judge Sewall:

> In the Afternoon Mr. Willard Ordained our Brother Theophilus Frary to the Office of a Deacon. Declared his Acceptance Jany 11th first and now again. Propounded it to the Congregation at Noon: Then in Even propounded if any of the Church or other had to object they might speak: Then took the Church's Vote, then called him up to the Pulpit, laid his Hand on's Head, and said I ordain Thee &c., gave Him his Charge, then Prayed, and sung the 2d part of the 84th Ps.[25]

It is significant that both ruling elders and deacons were ordained, and thus set apart by prayer and laying on of hands, namely, by the same ceremony that ordained

---

[24] *The Way of the Churches*, 42.
[25] *The Diary of Samuel Sewall* (ed. M. Halsey Thomas), I, 82–3, entry for November 8, 1685.

the ministers. This was the fullest expression of the priesthood of all believers hitherto achieved, even if later generations might be embarrassed by what Cotton Mather referred to perjoratively as "plebeian" ordinations, that is, ordinations by laymen.[26]

Ordinations Clericalized

As the seventeenth century wore on, and British Presbyterians such as Samuel Rutherford and Charles Herle embarrassed the American Puritans by claiming that the New Testament envisioned ordination as an act of presbytery (by fellow ministers), laymen gradually ceased to ordain ministers. Cotton Mather's embarrassment is clear in his attempt to gloss over the past by claiming that ordination by ministers early replaced ordination by laity. The latter custom, he incorrectly maintains, "has been so general, that setting aside a few *plebeian ordinations*, in the beginning of the world here among us, there have been rarely, any *ordinations* managed in our churches but by the *hands* of *presbyters*."[27] Mather's own view in the early eighteenth century was that of the majority, who claimed that "in the *imposition* of *hands*, there was their consecration to their ministry, and by this consecration they were owned, as admitted into the *order* of *pastors*, through the whole church of God."[28]

It is difficult to determine when clerical ordination began. However, there are clear instances of exceptions to plebeian ordination and even a demand that ordination in a prior church or even in another land should make re-

---

[26] *Magnalia Christi Americana*, II, Bk. v, 208.

[27] *Ibid.*

[28] *Ibid.*, 207–208.

ordination unnecessary. The beginning of the clericalization of ordination appears in the ordination in 1672 of
William Adams as minister of the Dedham Church. A
neighboring minister gave him the "charge"—that is, reminded him of his solemn responsibility to God and his
people—while two lay leaders of the church enacted the
laying on of hands, and another minister offered the right
hand of fellowship to the newly ordained. This was
clearly a mixed clerical and lay ordination, and therefore
transitional in character.[29]

The first instance recorded of a completely clerical-
ized ordination occurred in 1681 at Milton. The ordinand, Peter Thacher, reported the event in his diary:

> 1 June 1681. This day I was Ordained (though most
> unworthy) Pastour of the Church in Milton. My
> Text 2. Tim. 4. 5. Mr. [Increase] Mather Called
> the Votes, Old Mr. Eliot, Mr. Torry, Mr. Willard
> laid On Hands. Mr. Torry gave the Charge, Mr.
> Willard Gave the right hand of fellowshipe. We
> sung the 24 ps. Then I gave the blessing.[30]

Dissatisfaction with unclerical ordination seems to
have been fomenting since 1650, even though plebeian
ordinations continued until as late as 1661 at Norwich
and 1665 at Stratford (the famous "leather mitten" ordination which later Anglicans ridiculed).[31] John Bayly

---

[29] "Memoir of the Rev. William Adams," Massachusetts Historical
Society Collections, 4th series (1852), I, 20–21.

[30] Thacher, "Diary," MS I, 212 (typescript in the Massachusetts
Historical Society, Boston).

[31] See David D. Hall, The Faithful Shepherd: A History of the New
England Ministry in the Seventeenth Century (Chapel Hill:
University of North Carolina Press, 1972), 221.

came from England to Watertown in 1686, and, at his induction to the church on October 6, the ceremony was performed without any laying on of hands, implying that he regarded his previous ordination in England as valid and therefore not requiring renewal.[32] Judge Sewall's journal on this date records the laconic comment, "Mr. Bayly is ordain'd at Watertown, but not as Congregational Men are." William Brattle requested at his ordination at the Cambridge Church in 1696 that the ruling elder "should not lay hands on's head."[33] Benjamin Colman received an invitation to become pastor of a new church in Boston while he was in England, and took the most unusual step of being ordained by English Nonconformists in 1699.[34] These and similar actions indicated that the requirements for ordination approved by the Cambridge Platform were null and void in the third generation.

The developing sacerdotalism and sense of a separate caste of the New England ministry can be seen by comparing the ordination services of Cotton Mather in 1685, Samuel Sewall in 1713, and Samuel Cooper in 1746, all of which are amply documented.

Cotton Mather recorded in his diary that on the 13th of May, 1685, he preached and prayed a total of three hours before the vast Boston congregation gathered at the Second Church, and during the afternoon service his ordination took place, when his father, Increase Mather, had prayed and preached (on Acts 13:2), with the other

---

[32] Reported in William B. Sprague, *Annals of the American Pulpit; Or, Commemorative Notices of Distinguished American Clergymen of Various Denominations* (New York, 1857), I, 202.

[33] *Diary* (ed. M. Halsey Thomas), I, 222.

[34] *Ibid.*

two Boston ministers also laying hands on him (these were the Reverends Mr. Willard and Mr. Allen). The charge was delivered by his father, and the apostle to the Indians, the Reverend Mr. John Eliot, gave him the right hand of fellowship. Fortunately, the charge, which was written on a slip of paper and attached to the diary by wafers, has survived. It gives a vivid picture of the solemnity of the occasion and of the authority and duties of a minister, and for this reason warrants citation:

> Whereas you upon whom wee impose our Hands, are called to the Work of the Ministry, and to the Office of a Pastor in this Church of Christ, wee charge you before God and the Lord Jesus Christ and in the Presence of elect Angels, that you take heed to the Ministry which you have received in the Lord, to fulfill it, and that you feed the whole flock of God over which the Holy Ghost hath made you Overseer; that you study to shew yourself approved of God and a Workman that need not bee ashamed; that you give yourself to Reading and to Meditation, to Exhortation and to Doctrine; and that you endeavour to show yourself an Example of the Beleevers, in Faith, in Spirit, in Purity, in Charity, and in Conversation.
>
> And if you keep this Charge, wee pronounce unto you that the Lord of Hosts will give you a Place among His Holy Angels that stand by, and are Witnesses of this Dayes-Solemnity, and of your being thus solemnly sett apart to the special Service of God, and of Jesus Christ; And if you do thus, when the Lord Jesus shall appear, you shall appear with Him in glory. Hee, who is the cheef Shepherd will then give unto you a Crown of Glory which shall never fade away.[35]

---

[35] *The Diary of Cotton Mather* (ed. W. C. Ford), 2 vols. (Boston:

Judge Sewall, with paternal pride, reported Joseph Sewall's ordination to the ministry of the South Church, Boston, on September 16, 1713.[36] Cotton Mather commenced with prayer and Joseph Sewall then preached on the modest text 1 Corinthians 3:7: "So then neither is he that planteth anything, neither he that watereth; but God that giveth the increase." At the great assembly, nine churches sent representatives, and the rest may be cited in Sewall's summary:

> Twelve Ministers at the Table by the Pulpit. Mr. Pemberton made an August Speech, Shewing the Validity and Antiquity of New English Ordinations. Then having made his way, went on, ask'd as Customary, if any had to say against the Ordaining the person. Took the Churches Handy vote; Church sat in the Gallery. Then declar'd the Elders and Messengers had desired the Ministers of Boston to lay on Hands. . . . Dr. Increase Mather, Dr. Cotton Mather, Mr. Benjamin Wadsworth, Mr. Ebenezer Pemberton, and Mr. Benjamin Colman laid on Hands. Then Mr. Pemberton Pray'd, Ordain'd, and gave the Charge Excellently. Then Dr. Increase Mather made a notable Speech, gave the Right Hand of Fellowship, and pray'd. Mr. Pemberton directed the three and Twentieth Psalm to be sung. The person now Ordain'd dismiss'd the Congregation with Blessing.[37]

There is no mention of any layman taking part; the entire congregation is herded in the gallery, while a solid

---

[36] *The Diary of Samuel Sewall* (ed. M. Halsey Thomas), I, 726.
[37] *Ibid.*

phalanx of clergy dominates from the table beneath the pulpit. The clergy are a separate caste.

We are fortunate in having all the documents necessary for reconstructing the service on May 21, 1746, when Samuel Cooper was ordained to the pastoral office in Brattle Street Church in Boston.[38] Mr. Sewall's charge fills three pages, and it must suffice to cite the beginning and end of it, with a summary of the central part. It begins as follows:

> Wheras you on whom we now lay our Hands, have received a Call to the Work of the Evangelical Ministry, and to the Pastoral Office in this Church, and have accepted the same:
>
> We do in the name of Christ and by his Authority, Ordain you to be a Minister of the everlasting Gospel, and a Pastor to the Flock in this Place; to take Part of this Ministry with that aged Servant of GOD, with whom your late Father served as a Son with a Father in the Gospel. And we charge you before GOD, and the LORD JESUS CHRIST, who shall judge the quick and the Dead, at his Appearing and his Kingdom; that you fulfill this Ministry which you have received of the LORD. Take heed thy self, and to all the Flock, over which the HOLY GHOST maketh you an Overseer, to feed the Church of GOD, which he hath purchased with his own Blood. For this End give thyself continually to Prayer, and to the

---

[38] The full title and description of this document is: *One Chosen of God, and called to the Work of the Ministry, willingly offering himself: A Sermon preached at the Ordination of the Reverend Mr. Samuel Cooper to the Pastoral Office in the Church of Christ in Brattle-Street, Boston, May 21, 1746. By Benjamin Colman, D.D., Senior Pastor; Aet. 73. to which are added The Charge then given by the Rev. Dr. Sewall and the Right Hand of Fellowship by the Rev. Mr. Prince* (Boston, 1746).

Ministry of the Word.[39]

The duties are then spelled out, and include praying for all men, preaching the Word, blessing the flock, administering the sacraments of baptism and the Lord's Supper, dispensing the discipline of the church, knowing the state of the flock, attending to reading, letting no man despise his youth, being an example to the believers, and, finally, "Endure Hardness as a good Soldier of JESUS CHRIST."[40]

The conclusion of the charge is entirely a mosaic of New Testament instructions, deriving from the Epistles of Saint Paul, which had by now become almost a formula[41] at ordinations in New England:

> And now, We again say unto you, *Feed the Flock of God*, taking the Oversight thereof, not by Constraint, but willingly; not for filthy Lucre, but of a ready Mind, neither lording it over GOD's Heritage, but being an Example to the Flock. And when the chief Shepherd shall appear, you shall receive a Crown of Glory that fadeth not away.[42]

---

[39] *Op. cit.*, 28.

[40] *Op. cit.*, 28–30. The summary is almost entirely in the words of the original.

[41] It is found in almost identical terms in the charge given by Dr. Increase Mather in the ordination of the Reverend William Waldron in 1722 and included in Cotton Mather's *Love Triumphant, a Sermon at the Gathering of a New Church, and the ORDAINING of their PASTOR in the North Part of BOSTON, May 23, 1722, with Copies of Other Things Offered in the Publick Actions of That Solemn Occasion* (Boston, 1722), 33–35.

[42] *One Chosen of God*, 30.

The offering of the right hand of fellowship by the Reverend Mr. Prince was also accompanied by a speech, in customary fashion. This began by expressing the approbation of the ordination on the part of the ministers and messengers of the neighboring churches. It continued by expressing the brotherly relationship of these ministers and the promise "we will be suitably concerned for you, mindful of you, and ready to help you with our Prayers, Advices, Admonitions, and all other Expressions of a Brotherly Charity, Concern, and Watchfulness, as it becometh us to yield to a neighbouring Minister of CHRIST."[43] Prince then said this was an opportunity also to manifest the sisterly relationship subsisting between this church and others in the vicinity of the same order, "whereby we avoid the style of *Independency* among all that know us, and preserve the more desireable Name of *Congregational* Churches . . . for our mutual Safety, Strength, and Benefit."[44]

It is evident that the criticism of Presbyterians, and the greater impressiveness of Episcopal ordinations in England, not forgetting the growing civility, elegance, wealth, and tolerance of the expanding city of Boston, all contributed to the greater solemnity and elegance of the ordination services at the midpoint of the eighteenth century. The simplicity, sincerity, and plebeian character of the early ordinations of those who risked their lives to cross a dangerous sea to live in a wilderness inevitably contrasts with the professionalism and elegance of the settled and relatively affluent ministers of a century later. The earlier language was functional; the later lan-

---

[43] *Ibid.*

[44] *Op. cit.*, 31–32.

guage is formulaic, and almost as liturgical as that of the Book of Common Prayer which their ancestors repudiated, but much less concise.

Explanations for the growing sacerdotalism of the Puritan clergy must also allow for the fear of the second-generation ministers that the supposed decline of the piety of their congregations and the obvious clerical-lay divisions of these days were due to a lessening of respect for God's Word and His ambassadors. They therefore redefined their office "as devolving as much from apostolic succession as from the call of a particular congregation."[45] The growing power of the ministry was exhibited in three ways. Firstly, as mentioned previously, ministers were ordained exclusively by other ministers, instead of by their own congregations. Next, they exercised greater control in the admission to church membership, since the Reformed Synod permitted prospective church members to relate their testimony of saving grace to the ministers instead of to the membership of the local church. Thirdly, they not only administered the sacraments with greater solemnity, but were given the right to withhold both baptism and the Lord's Supper from feuding congregations until peace was restored. As a result, ordination, in becoming professional, had additionally become portentous and even officious.

---

[45] Harry S. Stout, *The New England Soul: Preaching and Religious Culture in New England* (New York: Oxford University Press, 1986), 107.

10

Architecture

The name the Puritans gave to their sanctuaries—that of "meetinghouse"—was profoundly meaningful. The term was first used by Winthrop in his journal entry for March 19, 1631/2, in reference to a building designed for worship that had been constructed in Dorchester, Massachusetts. The term was appropriate for two reasons. For the Puritans, a "church" meant a community of Christians, the Body of Christ, and never a building, as it had for the Anglicans from whom they dissented. One of the pioneer ministers, Richard Mather, asserted that "there is no just ground from the Scriptures to apply such a trope as church for a public assembly."[1] The meetinghouse was chiefly the place where they met God.

In addition to its theological significance, the meetinghouse functioned as a political center where town meetings were held by the community, and—in the earliest days—also as a military bastion where gunpowder was stored and from which the sentries could espy an approaching enemy from their turret on the roof. So it was a meetinghouse in both sacred and secular senses. This element of etymology is expressed in an early eighteenth-century document that claims:

---

[1] Cited in Noah Porter, *The New England Meeting House* (New Haven, Conn.: Yale University Press, 1953), 5.

> The *Meeting House* was, as its name indicates, the
> place where all public meetings were held, Builded
> and owned by the town, it was used on Sabbaths and
> "Lecture Days" for public devotional services; it
> was the political center of the community, where
> they held their own meetings, elections, and other
> public gatherings, and the "alarm post" to which
> they rallied when threatened by Indian attack, or
> when duly warned to appear, fully armed and
> equipped, to meet some emergency of "His
> Majesty's service."[2]

H. R. Stiles insists that the buildings possessed none of
the inherent sacredness of the edifices where their fore-
fathers had worshipped in England, for they were dissenters and their places of worship in England were
mere "conventicles" and "as such were simply conve-
niences for all public town purposes."[3]

The Origins of the Meetinghouse

It is difficult to determine the origins of the New
England Puritan meetinghouse for two reasons. One is
that the records of so many of them have disappeared, and
there is only one very early example of such a meetinghouse, considerably restored, still remaining in New

---

[2] Sherman W. Adams, *The History of Ancient Wethersfield,
Connecticut* (1908), II, 219. It is a citation from a document edited
by H. R. Stiles. However, it should be noted that the separation
between church and state was marked as early as the 1650s in Boston
as symbolized by the removal of the Commonwealth government
from Boston's meetinghouse, where the General Court and town
meetings had convened, to a newly built town house. See Darrett B.
Rutman, *Winthrop's Boston: Portrait of a Puritan Town, 1630–1649*
(Chapel Hill: University of North Carolina Press, 1965), 276.

[3] *History of Ancient Wethersfield*, II, 219.

England, the "Ship Meeting House" at Hingham, Massachusetts. A second reason is that we do not know which of the possible Protestant sanctuaries in Europe may have influenced the Puritans in New England. Had any of them seen the great Huguenot Protestant temple at Charenton, built in 1623, with its high pulpit and its two vast galleries admirably designed for hearing the preaching of God's Word? Did they copy the whitewashed simplicity of the Dutch Reformed churches in Holland, where some of them had sought refuge from persecution before joining the Great Migration to New England? Was there any influence on them, as Marian Cord Donnelly suggests,[4] from the shape, function, and location of the market-halls of England, or even from a very few simple English churches? Or were they simply domestic buildings writ large, deliberately refusing to imitate the Anglican churches? Certainly, they employed the device of a pulpit against the long wall to gain maximum audition, but that was a device used in many countries that became officially Protestant and adapted formerly Catholic fanes by such alterations. Certainly, Anglican churches were used for other than liturgical gatherings on occasion. Certainly, the dual use of market-halls for political and mercantile purposes, with their hip roofs and gables, may well have had an impact on the making of American meetinghouses. But none of these influences can be proved, and their cumulative impact is very unlikely, because there was virtually no Puritan building in England during the Protectorate and the Commonwealth, when Puritans took over the Anglican churches for their

---

[4] *The New England Meeting Houses of the Seventeenth Century* (Middletown, Conn.: Wesleyan University Press, 1948), 7, 107f.

use, often with one congregation in the nave and sometimes another in the chancel of the larger churches; and the Thirty Years War in Europe virtually brought all Protestant building to a standstill. It is highly probable, therefore, that the New England Puritan meetinghouse in all its austerity, yet admirably functional, was an authentic, native product later to be copied by English Dissenters.

The Development of Meetinghouses

Little is known about the earliest meetinghouses. At the outset the pioneers may simply have met in houses, possibly in the houses of their ministers. The next stage would then be to build temporary meetinghouses of sawn planks, perhaps with a thatched roof and probably surrounded with a defensive palisade. Such houses were constructed strongly enough to make them secure from potential Indian attacks, and had the further advantage that they were conveniently created from the adjacent forests. These rude houses of worship probably lacked pulpits, and rough benches were used for seating. The New London town records show that on July 8, 1652, "O[bidiah] B[ruen] lent the town for thatching meeting house Hugh Calkin pd. Chaple 00-03-06; Ralph Parker pd. Chaple 00-05-06."[5] J. Frederick Kelly guesses that "a dim light struggled through small windows covered with cloth or oiled paper, for glass was too scarce and costly to be used at first."[6] These first primitive buildings were not intended to last; they were only to serve temporarily

---

[5] J. Frederick Kelly, *Early Connecticut Meeting Houses* (New York: Columbia University Press, 1948), I, xxx.

[6] *Ibid.*, 7.

until more suitable and substantial meetinghouses could be constructed. For example, Hartford's first rough meetinghouse was used only for the space of four years.

The first period meetinghouses, according to the time frame adopted by Marian Cord Donnelly, were built between 1630 and 1642 and coincided with the Great Migration. Forty of them were built, including 29 in Massachusetts, 6 in Connecticut and Long Island; four towns replaced their meetinghouses with second buildings.[7] While the majority of these early edifices were square, like the Cambridge one to which reference is made on December 24, 1632, the neighboring meetinghouse at Roxbury was almost certainly rectangular.[8] The dimensions of the Dedham meetinghouse, the earliest to be known, and which was built in 1638, show that the first meetinghouses were small. Dedham was 36 feet long, 20 feet wide, 12 feet high, and it was thatched. It was extended in 1646; a turret to accommodate a bell was added in 1651, and a gallery was inserted in 1658. The first meetinghouse was replaced by a second in 1672. Marian Donnelly's conjectural diagram of the Dedham meetinghouse exterior shows a central door, with double casement diamonded windows on either side, and a thatched roof. Her conjectural diagram for the Sudbury meetinghouse erected in 1643 looks like the Dedham edifice.

These buildings were highly functional, and where they were rectangular the pulpit was probably built against the north wall, with the door facing the clement south, and with a middle aisle or alley that divided the sexes; the seating was probably benches with occasional

---

[7] Donnelly, *The New England Meeting Houses*, 13f.
[8] *Ibid.*, 44.

chairs. There may have been a Communion table in front
of the pulpit. The dominant effect was of convenience,
simplicity, and domesticity, with no concessions to either numinosity or symbolism. These triple-purpose
buildings were thoroughly utilitarian and functional.

Meetinghouses of the Middle Period were erected
between 1643 and 1660, during the most promising period
for rising Puritans, in both old and New England, when
the religious life of the American settlers was eagerly
watched in old England, and when, as we have noted,
three American ministers were invited to serve in the
national and reforming Westminster Assembly in England. Forty-one meetinghouses were built during this
time, of which 29 were for new congregations and 12
were for replacement of old structures. Twenty-seven
were erected in Massachusetts, 6 in Connecticut, 4 on
Long Island, 3 in New Hampshire, and 1 in Maine.[9]
Where the dimensions of these buildings are known, 5
were square and 7 rectangular, and 4 others were probably rectangular. It is significant that they were never
cruciform, nor oriented like Anglican or Roman Catholic
churches. By 1660 there were at least 80 meetinghouses
in New England, 16 with galleries, of which only 4—
Dorchester, Ipswich, Medfield, and Newbury, Massachusetts—appear to have had them from the start.[10]

What were these meetinghouses like? Marian
Donnelly provides a conjectural diagram of the second
meetinghouse in Sudbury, Massachusetts. This was 40
feet long, 24 feet wide, and 24 feet high, and was obviously built to accommodate a larger congregation than the

[9] *Ibid.*, 45.
[10] *Ibid.*

first edifice. Its roof was almost certainly shingled instead of thatched, and it was gabled. It had two doors on one long side, and probably also a pulpit on the opposite side. Two tiers of windows, with diamond panes, let in the light. But there was also another type of meetinghouse in this middle period. It was a square building with a pyramidal hip roof which was surmounted by a raised platform from which projected a turret and enclosed bell. Hartford, Connecticut, had the first known example of this type in 1640, but similar edifices were built in Cambridge, Massachusetts, in 1650, Watertown, Massachusetts, in 1656, and Portsmouth, New Hampshire, in 1657.[11]

The Late Period, according to Donnelly's chronology, is from 1661 to 1700. During this time, 122 meetinghouses were built, of which 52 were new and 58 were second buildings on their sites, while 11 were the third, and 1 was the fourth. Seventy were built in Massachusetts, 37 in Connecticut, 5 in Maine, 5 on Long Island, 3 in New Hampshire, and 2 in Rhode Island. Where definite dimensions are available, 39 were definitely and 6 probably rectangular, whereas 14 were definitely square in plan with 1 possibly so.[12]

This was not a confident period, and the fortunes of the Bible state seemed in decline. The Half-Way Covenant of 1662 allowed parents who were baptized themselves (although they had not received saving grace and could not become full members of the church and attend celebrations of the Lord's Supper) to have their children baptized. There was less fervor in spirituality,

---

[11] *Ibid.*, 46.

[12] *Ibid.*, 64–65.

and ministers preached jeremiads to try to revive piety. The political control by the clergy was also weakening, for the Connecticut and New Haven colonies were united in 1662 under a royal charter with freedom for other forms of churchmanship to establish themselves, and Massachusetts was requested to extend the franchise outside membership of the Congregational church.

The population increased and so there was a demand for larger meetinghouses, and better construction. Almost all these meetinghouses had entrance doors on the south side with the pulpit on the opposite northern side. The abandonment of the Anglican orientation of worship, with the altar at the narrow east end, provided space on the east side where extra pews and galleries might be built, and where the acoustics were better. Galleries were part of the original plan of 25 meetinghouses in this period, and they were added in 21 other cases. Porches approached by stairs improved the meetinghouses of Newbury, Massachusetts, in 1661, the Third Church of Boston in 1669, and of Stratford, Connecticut, in 1680. Eight meetinghouses had extra gables or dormer windows added to them, and twenty others had bell or watch turrets built on their roofs. The larger meetinghouses were distinguished by their hip roofs, with crowning turret and balustrade.[13] The greatly increased size of the meetinghouses of this period was their dominant characteristic.

The largest meetinghouse in seventeenth-century New England was the Third Church of Boston, known as the Old South Church and built of red brick. This was erected in 1669 and demolished in 1729. It was 75 feet

---

[13] *Ibid.*, 65–66.

long, and almost 51 feet wide, excluding the porches on the south, east, and west sides. The report of its demolition in the *Boston Weekly News-Letter* gives a vivid idea of its size and even of its comparative elegance:

> Friday the 28th of Feb. last was kept as a Day of Fasting & Prayer by the South Church & Congregation in this Town, upon occasion of taking down their Old Meeting-House & Building a New, One of Brick which is to stand in the same place. The last Lord's Day the second of this Instant, was the last time of Meeting in their Old House, which has stood for Three-Score Years the last January, since 'twas raised. On the Monday, the Workmen took down the Windows, the Pews, the Pulpit and the Seats both below and in the Galleries. On the Tuesday in the Forenoon, they took down the Belfry, the Porches, the Stairs and the Galleries themselves. In the Afternoon they drew off the Boards at both Ends and laid it open: and about Five a Clock, They turned over the whole remaining Part of the Building at one Draught into the Yard on the North side; in so doing it fell all to pieces.[14]

The long side of the church had three gables and boasted on its roof a huge central turret, an open structure that rested on four posts, with a pyramid at each corner, all surmounted by a weathercock. In addition, the roof and the three porches were covered with lead.

The only surviving, though considerably restored and extended, meetinghouse from this period is the second edifice of Hingham, Massachusetts, erected in 1681. It is supposed that its sobriquet, the "Old Ship," is derived from the timbers of the loft, which resemble an inverted

---

[14] Issue of March 6, 1729.

ship and which may have been put together by local ships' carpenters. Originally it was 55 feet long, 45 feet wide, 21 feet high, and covered by a steep four-sided hip roof surmounted by a cupola. It had galleries on one side and at both ends, and the pulpit was on the north wall. Marian Donnelly's conjectural diagram discloses the south wall with doors at each end, two tiers of diamond-paned windows, an extra dormer window, and a conical-topped turret with weathervane enclosed in a balustrade.[15]

The fourth period, the eighteenth century, will see the gradual development of increasing elegance and even opulence until, at its end, the meetinghouse will become a Congregational church, with the return to a quasi-Anglican style, marked by towers and spires at the narrow end, with the pulpit (highly ornamented by carving and occasionally in goblet shape) on the opposite narrow end. The beginning of this change can be seen in the architecture of the Brattle Street Church in Boston which was erected in 1699. Several factors accounted for the change. Among them was the loss of confidence in the Calvinistic theology which reinforced the covenant conception of the church, as Arminianism stressing human endeavor increasingly took over, and a growing rationalism weakened orthodox piety. Denominational pluralism, with the arrival of Episcopalians, Baptists, and Presbyterians—all allowed to build their own churches—undercut the establishment of Puritan orthodoxy and orthopraxis. The growth of population meant that New England was no longer the frontier of a wilderness. The wealthy members of the congregations demanded dignity,

---

[15] *Op. cit.*, Figure 25.

comfort, and elegance in their ecclesiastical edifices in the larger towns. And, finally, English architectural manuals showing the influence of Sir Christopher Wren (in his own "Wrenaissance" after the Great Fire) had a profound impact on American design which appealed to those in the Puritan tradition because they were designs of "auditory churches."[16] It is significant that the designs of Inigo Jones and of Gibbs were published in 1727, Halfpenny's work on the Five Orders in 1736, and Ware's volume on Palladian architecture in 1755. These offered glimpses of classical work in pilasters and paneling, as well as round-headed and clustered windows and porticoes, thus greatly expanding the decorative vocabulary of builders of meetinghouses. Another important factor helping to explain the transition from meetinghouse to Congregational church is that the development coincided approximately with the official separation of church and state in New England. As a consequence, this encouraged the development of characteristically ecclesiastical architecture instead of dual-use buildings.[17] There was no longer any sense of the "gathered church" whose members had covenanted to live as interdependent communities of "visible saints." Therefore the old domesticated simplicity and unornamented austerity and functionalism disappeared completely by 1800.

---

[16] For the analysis of the reasons for the demise of strictly Puritan architecture, see Richard C. Austin's unpublished typescript, "The Meetinghouse of Colonial New England as an Expression of Puritan Theology," 114f. This Bachelor of Divinity thesis submitted to Union Theological Seminary in 1959 deserves publication. It can be found in Union Seminary Library in New York City.

[17] I owe this suggestion to a former student, the Reverend Brett P. Morgan.

How one of the new elegant meetinghouses struck the imagination of a gifted child can be seen in the nostalgic reminiscences of Harriet Beecher Stowe of worshipping (probably in about 1825) in Litchfield, Connecticut's second meetinghouse, built in 1762:

> To my childish eye, our old meetinghouse was an awe-inspiring thing. To me it seemed fashioned very nearly on the model of Noah's Ark and Solomon's Temple. . . . Its double row of windows; its doors with great wooden quirls over them; its belfry, projecting out at the east end; its steeple and bell; all inspired as much sense of the sublime as Strasburg Cathedral itself; and the inside was not a whit less imposing. How magnificent, to my eye, seemed the turnip-like canopy that hung over the minister's head, hooked by a long iron rod to the wall above! And how apprehensively did I consider the question what would become of him [her distinguished father, Lyman Beecher] if it should fall! How did I wonder at the panels on either side of the pulpit, in each of which was carved and painted a flaming red tulip, with its leaves projecting out at right angles, and then at the grapevine, in bas relief, on the front, with exactly triangular bunches of grapes alternating at exact intervals with exactly triangular leaves. The area of the house was divided into large square pews, boxed up with a kind of baluster work. . . . But the glory of our meetinghouse was the singers' seat, that empyrean of those who rejoiced in the mysterious act of fa-sol-la-ing. There they sat in the gallery that lined three sides of the house, treble, counter, tenor and bass, each with its appropriate leader and supporters.[10]

---

[10] *Harriet Beecher Stowe: The Story of My Life*, by her son, Edward Stowe, and her grandson, Lyman Beecher Stowe (Boston: Houghton

The eighteenth-century meetinghouses were much larger, in order to accommodate the growing population and the renewal and extension of religious life brought about by the Great Awakening. Galleries were built as a matter of course from the start, and these involved piercing the walls with two tiers of windows. The latter were no longer of the casement type with diamond panes, but were larger and double-hung with rectangular lights of glass. In some cases Palladian windows were erected behind the pulpit or over the main door on the south wall. Galleries necessitated the appearance of the high pulpit, overhung with a canopied sounding board. The pulpit itself was paneled and often carved, and, as in Sandown meetinghouse in New Hampshire, was goblet-shaped, with an impressive stairway leading up to it. The square plan of edifices disappeared and was replaced by an oblong plan. When there was a steeple it was placed on one long end of the building, with its tower serving as a vestibule for a side entrance. All the details exhibit what J. Frederick Kelly calls "Georgian robustness."[19]

The Location and Interior Arrangements

Functionally, symbolically, as well as physically, the meetinghouse often stood near the center of the Puritan township, usually on rising ground or on a knoll.[20] It was commonly oriented toward the south, where the door most frequently used would be protected from the wind.

Mifflin, 1911), 28–30. The book uses the autobiographical *Memoirs of Harriet Beecher Stowe.*

[19] *Op. cit.*, I, xxxi.

[20] Austin, *op. cit.*, 53. Exceptions were frequent, as pointed out in Jack Greene and J. R. Pole, eds. *Colonial British America*, 92.

Among the *Winthrop Papers*, and dated *circa* 1635, there is an anonymous "Essay on the ordering of towns" which declares: "First, Suppose the Towne Square 6 miles every waye. The Howses orderly placed about the midst, especially the Meeting house the which we will suppose to be the Centor of the wholl Circonference."[21]

Anthony Garvan observes that the first settlers in their town planning reserved a few central acres in the village for the meetinghouse and the minister's house. Thus the yard of the meetinghouse might either face the green and commons, stand at the junction of the four squares of the town, or just face the commons.[22] The meetinghouse was the central focus of the community for religious and political reasons, as can be seen, for example, in an early town plan of New Haven, Connecticut.[23]

The erection of the meetinghouses was a community endeavor. The first meetinghouses were built from the materials at hand. For example, the town records of Longmeadow, Massachusetts, reflect this fact in the following entry: "Voated: that the meetinghouse should be built Thirty Eight foots square, if the Timber that is already gotten will allow it, or If the Timber be too scant to make it sumthing less."[24] When the town voted to build a meetinghouse, a tax was levied on all the inhabitants of the town, as when the second meetinghouse at Hingham, Massachusetts, was erected in 1681; 143 persons con-

---

[21] *Winthrop Papers*, III, 181–182, cited by Donnelly, *op. cit.*, 17.

[22] *Architecture and Town Planning in Colonial Connecticut* (New Haven, Conn.: Yale University Press, 1951), 46.

[23] This appears as Figure 19 in Donnelly, *op. cit.*

[24] Cited in Ola E. Winslow, *Meetinghouse Hill, 1630–1783* (New York: Macmillan, 1952), 53.

tributed a total of 430 pounds sterling. The tax list indicates that the wealthy and the poor paid according to their means.[25] The raising of the frame and roof of the meetinghouse was a joyful event for the entire community, the men stretching their muscles and the women seeing to the food and drink. Some indication of the jollity on these occasions is afforded by an anecdote reported by Eva Speare. At the raising of Plymouth's meetinghouse, when the women of the town begged for a steeple to be built, Colonel David Webster stood on his head on the ridge pole and, elevating his six-foot length into the air, shouted, "I will be your steeple."[26]

If skill and tact were required for town planning, they were not less necessary for what was termed "dignifying the seats"—that is, in the allocation of the seating according to status. This was the delicate task of a committee appointed for the purpose. According to Stiles:

> the estimation in which a man or a woman was held in the community wherein he dwelt, was very clearly shown by the seat which was assigned to him or her in the meeting-house. The completest schedule of this process . . . which we have found among any New England town records, is that formulated in the instructions given to a Wethersfield seating committee, in March 1717, wherein they were directed to seat the people according to the following "grounds of advancement," viz.: *Age; dignity of descent; place of public trust; pious disposition;*

[25] Edmund W. Sinnott, *Meetinghouse and Church in Early New England* (New York: McGraw-Hill, 1963), 32.

[26] *Colonial Meetinghouses of New Hampshire* (State of New Hampshire: Daughters of Colonial Wars, 1938), 29.

estate; peculiar serviceableness of any kind.[27]

The complexity of determining such matters is illustrated by the fact that the Waterbury, Connecticut, second meetinghouse of 1729 contained twenty-six square pews that were awarded thirteen grades or "dignities."[28] The most prestigious pews were those nearest to the pulpit, and the least prestigious those in the remoter parts of the galleries, where children, blacks, and, in rare cases, Indians sat. The men usually sat in the section of seats on the minister's right as he faced the congregation, while the women sat in the section on his left. The men and women were thus separated by a wide central aisle known as the broad or great alley. It was a great innovation when the committee arranging the seating for the new meetinghouse in Guilford, Connecticut, was instructed on November 23, 1713, "that the men & women sit together in the meeting house in the pews."[29] According to Leonard Bacon, children followed their parents to the door of the meetinghouse, but were not allowed to sit with them, being placed under the supervision of a tithing-man. The young unmarried men sat in one gallery and the young unmarried women in an opposite gallery. Soldiers, however, sat on both sides of the gallery near the door.

Both furniture and arrangements were even simpler in the earliest meetinghouses, remaining so in the remote rustic locations. Leonard Bacon, guessing about the first meetinghouse in New Haven, wrote: "Immediately be-

---

[27] Adams, *op. cit.*, I, 222.

[28] Kelly, *op. cit.*, I, xxviii.

[29] *Ibid.*, 172.

fore the pulpit, and facing the congregation was an elevated seat for the ruling elder; and before that, somewhat
lower, was a seat for the deacons behind the communion-
table. On the floor of the house there were neither pews
nor slips, but plain seats."[30] He added that there were 9
seats on either side of the center alley and each could accommodate 6 persons, together with 5 cross seats and another shorter than these 5; along each wall between the
cross seats and the side door were 5 more seats, and 6 beyond the side door. We may guess that the furniture in
New Haven's meetinghouse in 1655 was not very different, because on February 11th of that year it was "agreed
that (because there wants seats for some, and that the
Allies [Alleys] are so filled with blockes, stooles, and
chaires, that it hinders a free passage) low benches shall
be made at the ends of the seates, on both sides of the
Allies, for young persons to sitt on."[31]

By 1681 when the Hingham Old Ship meetinghouse
was built, the seating arrangements were more compli-
cated. Edmund Sinnott enables us to visualize the occu-
pants of the pews:

> On the main floor of the meetinghouse there
> were two rows of seven benches on each side of the
> alley, nine or ten persons being assigned to each
> bench, and nine shorter seats on the north side of
> the house, doubtless at right angles to the others.
> At the head of the women's benches, apparently
> adjacent to the pulpit, was the single pew, which

---

[30] *Ibid.*, xxviii, citing Bacon's *Thirteen Historical Discourses, on the
Completion of Two Hundred Years from the Beginning of the First Church
in New Haven* (New Haven, Conn.: Durrie & Beck, 1839), 48f.
[31] Kelly, *op. cit.*, II, 5.

was assigned to Mrs. Peter Hobart, the widow of
Hingham's first pastor, and to Mrs. John Norton,
wife of the second.

Both on the floor and in the gallery the front
benches, or "foreseats" were especially esteemed,
and it therefore is interesting to observe that
wealth was not the only basis for their assignment.
Thus, in the floor foreseat we find, to be sure, the
heaviest taxpayer, Daniel Cushing, and the next
heaviest, William Hearsey, and two other men of
means, Nathaniel Baker, and Thomas Lincoln,
"husbandmen"; but here, too, sat Captain Joshua
Hobart, Edmund Hobart, Thomas Hobart, and
Doctor John Cutler, all of whom stood relatively
low on the tax roll and were honored for other
reasons, the last perhaps because of his
profession.[32]

It was not until the eighteenth century that box pews, or
"sleep pens," were introduced into the meetinghouses.
Some of them were equipped with writing ledges so that
the fathers of families might take notes of the sermons and
catechize the children and servants as to their understanding of and attentiveness to the preaching.

It is a common but erroneous opinion that the hardy
Puritans did without any form of heating in their meetinghouses, even in the severest winter. Donnelly points
out that the contract for the enlargement of the meetinghouse in Salem, Massachusetts, as early as 1638 specified
"One Catted Chimney of 12 foote long, and 4 foote in
height above the top of the building."[33] She also adduces

---

[32] *Op. cit.*, 33.

[33] *Op. cit.*, 16, citing the town records of Salem, Massachusetts, 3
vols., published by the Essex Institute Press, 1868–1934, I, 81.

evidence that later at Southampton in New York State each family was instructed "by turn lykewise make a fire in the meeting house upon each Sabathe daye, and to give notice to the next whose turn yt is."[34] There is also a record that the Killingworth, Connecticut, founding congregation voted to build a meetinghouse "with a Doble Chimney at one end."[35] Where there was no chimney or stove in the meetinghouse, women sometimes carried heated stones in their muffs, while the men often drew bags over their feet to warm them. In some cases members of the congregation used portable stoves. But where none of these heating devices were available, worshippers in winter must have been glad to warm themselves at the fireplace of the parsonage or neighboring tavern at the noon hour between services.[36]

Throughout the evolution of the New England meetinghouse, the dominance of the pulpit remained constant. Placing it against the middle of the long side of the room, generally on the north, made it possible for those furthest away from the pulpit to hear the proclamation of the Word of God clearly. This was not the case when, in the late eighteenth century, the pulpit, in Anglican fashion, was placed on one of the shorter ends of the rectangle. With the advent of galleries, the pulpit was even more elevated. For example, in the Sandown meetinghouse in New Hampshire, the Bible in the pulpit remained two feet above the level of the base of the gallery, so that the preacher's head was some 6 or 7 feet above the heads of

---

[34] *Ibid.*, I. 37 citing *The First Book of Records of the Town of Southampton* (Sag Harbor, N. Y., 1874).

[35] Kelly, *op. cit.*, I, 247.

[36] *Ibid.*, xxviii.

the people sitting below him on the ground floor, and 4 1/2 feet to 6 1/2 feet below the heads of the folk in the gallery. He could be seen and heard by all, especially as there was a sounding board above him. Where there was a minimum of decoration in the meetinghouses, it was concentrated on the pulpit, as in the example of Litchfield referred to by Harriet Beecher Stowe, in which unsymbolic tulips were combined with symbolic bunches of grapes. Some pulpits had three levels, but, more commonly, they had two. The preacher occupied the highest level, while the second level would be used for presiding at civil occasions or religious catechizing, and if there were three levels, the third and lowest would accommodate the clerk who took notes from the sermons or the precentor who lined out the metrical psalms.

A simple Communion table was placed in the early meetinghouses in front of the pulpit. John Cotton insists that the Lord's Supper is a solemn service and the privilege of the committed Christian, and that he, as presiding minister, blesses the bread (as later the wine) and "he taketh it himselfe, and giveth it to all that sit at Table with him, and from the Table it is reached by the *Deacons* to the people sitting in the next seates about them, the Minister sitting in his place at the Table."[37] This citation makes it clear that the Communion table was an important article of furniture in the earliest meetinghouses. It clearly diminished in importance in the eighteenth-century meetinghouses, where it shrank often into a flap or shelf from which the minister served the deacons and

---

[37] *The Way of the Churches of Christ in New England* (London, 1645), 68.

they the members of the church. In the Sandown meetinghouse, there is a most elegant goblet-shaped pulpit
with impressive stairs, but a hinged board on the front of
the pulpit has to do for a Communion table, clearly indicating that the chief sacrament has been downgraded into
an occasional ordinance rarely celebrated for the few
church members. Nor is this a unique case. In an address
given on the 250th anniversary of the foundation of the
Congregational church of Milford, Connecticut, the
Reverend J. A. Biddle pointed out that the second grand
meetinghouse of 1728 was exceedingly plain within, and
that in front of the pulpit stood the deacons' seat, and "to
this seat was attached a leaf used for a communion
table."[38] The reduction of the Communion table to a
mere hinged shelf or leaf was almost certainly accompanied by a theological reduction of its significance. The
Communion service in Cotton's days expressed virtualism, the conviction that Christ was spiritually present in
the ordinance. The reductionist theology was better described as memorialism, the mere recollection of a crucified Christ, rather than the presence of the once crucified and now risen Lord. A similar diminution of the
meaning of baptism is evident in the early rejection of
stone fonts such as were used in the Church of England,
and the provision of a pewter or silver basin that was set
in an insignificant ring attached to the pulpit.[39] Furthermore, baptism could not be as meaningful a symbol of
initiation into the Christian community if conversion (or
an experience of saving grace) became the prime
additional requirement for church membership, along

---

[38] Kelly, *op. cit.*, I, xxxiii, cites this address.
[39] *Ibid.*, xli.

with doctrinal understanding and a righteous life. Thus the very architecture itself indicated a growth in worldliness and a lessening of piety.

It is hardly surprising that complaints were increasingly made not only about the diminished attendance at the Lord's Supper, but also about those who slept during sermons. Furthermore, the boisterous behavior of boys in church was an early disruption of worship necessitating the appointment of an officer whose sole responsibility was to maintain quiet during the services. This was the tithing-man. In 1721 the Plainfield, Connecticut, meetinghouse was disturbed by disorderliness in the back seats. As a result a tithing-man was stationed in the gallery to supervise the conduct of the young people below and to prevent them from damaging the meetinghouse "by opening the windows or any wise damnifying the glass and if any (him or her) did profane the Sabbath by laughing or behaving unseemly, he should call him or her by name and so reprove them therefor."[40] His other task was to awaken sleeping members of the congregation. For this purpose he wielded a long rod with a knob at the end with which he poked offenders. In Vermont the weapon was ten feet long, with a heavy knob applied to male sleepers, but the other end had a fox's or a hare's tail for gentler use with sleeping women. One tithing-man in Vermont who attacked a sleeping man ferociously was admonished by the elders of the meetinghouse and told to use "more discretion and less haist." Other sleepers alarmed the congregation by their rude awakening from nightmares.[41]

---

[40] *Ibid.*, II, 132.

[41] Elise Lathrop, *Old New England Churches* (Rutland, Vt.: Tuttle

One other unusual officer in the meetinghouse deserves consideration. He was the man responsible for
calling the congregation to worship on the Sabbath by
drum, or trumpet, or bell, and in time he was given a
balustraded turret on the roof of the meetinghouse from
which to sound his summons. He could, of course, also
sound the alarm in any secular emergency, as, for example, when Indians were on the rampage. The summons to
worship for the New Haven, Connecticut, meetinghouse
came from a turret above the building sounded by a
drummer from 1640 to 1681, when the drum was replaced
by a bell in a belfry.[42] In Windsor in the same state in
1656, the call to worship issued from a drum and a trumpet.[43]

The Theological Implications of the Architecture

It would be easy to escape the theological implica-
tions of the architecture of the meetinghouse by merely
insisting on its plainness and austerity, and by pointing
out that its only essentials throughout its history were
three: pulpit, Communion table, and seating. That would
be true as far as it goes, but the point is that it does not go
far enough. The plainness was not only found in the architecture, but also in the style of the sermons, so that the
glory would be given to God by obedience and not by
vaunting pride in human invention or ornamentation. It
is not enough to say with Anthony Garvan that the
Puritans devised an "architecture of negation" based on
departing as far from Roman Catholic architecture, sym-

Publishing, 1938), 159.
[42] Kelly, *op. cit.*, II, 7.
[43] *Ibid.*, 303.

bolism, and ceremonial as they could, but also based on adding nothing in decoration that was not explicitly demanded by the Westminster Directory, which, as he points out, was to be used in Anglican churches taken over by Independent or Presbyterian Puritans. Garvan adds, however, that the meetinghouses of New England were not fashioned as a casual or unthinking response to the American wilderness, but were the result of "a full-fledged Protestant aesthetic."[44] It was also the result of a century of planning in Europe. The plain style, in Richard C. Austin's view, included a nonliturgical floor plan, a movable Communion table, galleries with unstained windows, and the two-story facade, as well as the low ceiling and elaborate pulpit. Protestants therefore had their chance to start afresh in New England, where there were no church edifices before the Great Migration, apart from those of the Plymouth pilgrims.[45]

The aesthetic of Puritan architecture was theologically controlled. It is therefore far too negative to assert, as Harry S. Stout does, that "the buildings meant nothing because the church—the gathered body of believers—meant everything."[46] Chief among Puritan considerations was the insistence on biblical obedience, making the pulpit the throne of God's Word in Scripture. That is why the high pulpit dominated the meetinghouse throughout its history, and why the Bible resting on a red or green velvet cushion was the focal point. Here the

---

[44] "The Protestant Plain Style before 1630," *Journal of the Society of Architectural Historians*, IX (1950), 13.

[45] Austin, *op. cit.*, Chapter II.

[46] *The New England Soul: Preaching and Religious Culture in New England* (New York: Oxford University Press, 1986), 14.

message of God was expounded on the Lord's day to the Lord's elect and covenanted people. The central position of the pulpit and Bible demonstrate that the people of God are created by listening to the revelation of God confirmed in their hearts by the Holy Spirit. While preaching was important in the Church of England, Holy Communion was even more important, which is why the altar was central and the lectern and pulpit placed on the side in Anglican churches. Puritans wished to express the primacy of the Word over the sacraments of the Word.

In the second place, the Puritans laid great stress on being people of the covenant of grace, ratified by the life, sacrificial death, resurrection, and ascension of Jesus Christ and confirmed by the fulfillment of His promise to send the Holy Spirit to His chosen people. The sacraments were the signs of this covenant relationship, which was extended to the children of the faithful at baptism and renewed for adults at every Lord's Supper. God's family needed a house like any other, except one that was larger. Hence the architecture was naturally domestic, for it was not supposed that this was a temple in which God dwelt. Moreover, the ample illumination, rather than any "dim, religious light," issuing from the clear, unstained glass of the windows, enabled the covenanted people to see one another and rejoice in their interdependence as Christians committed to mutual support. In addition, it was often a window with a rounded top—and often the only one in the meetinghouse—that combined with the rounded base of the pulpit itself to create an oval frame for the preacher and the Bible, thus forming a perfect focus.[47]

In the third place, the creation in the eighteenth century of box pews, or "sleep pens," to accommodate the leading families along the warmer walls of the meetinghouse where dignity and comfort were dominant, as well as the rivalry of towns in building church-like edifices with steeples at the narrow end and pulpits at the other narrow end—so that acoustics became less important—signaled the serious decline of piety. In imitating Anglican fashions, elegance, and decoration, the successors of the Puritans betrayed their ancestors and their heritage.

One can only conclude that they had forgotten the warnings of James Ussher, the Puritan Irish archbishop, and of their own historian, Dr. Cotton Mather. Both warnings are contained in the latter's *Magnalia Christi Americana*—"The Great Accomplishments of Christ in America." Ussher recalls, "In times of persecution, the Godly did often meet in barns and such obscure places, which were indeed public because of the Church of God there; as wherever the Prince is, there is the Court, tho' it were in a poor Cottage." Cotton Mather added:

> There is now no place which renders the worship of God more acceptable for its being performed there. To prepare and repair places for the public worship . . . is but an act of obedience to him who requires worship from us . . . but the setting of these places off with a theatrical gaudiness does not savor of the spirit of a true Christian society.[48]

---

[47] A point made by Austin, *op. cit.*, 64.

[48] *Op. cit.*, (London, 1702), Bk. v, 54.

In 1726 Cotton Mather boasted that almost every town in New England "can say, We have a modest and handsome house for the worship of God, not set off with gaudy, pompous, theatrical fineries, but suited unto the simplicity of Christian worship."[49] Presumably, as they grew more handsome and more elegant, as they certainly did, they grew less simple, less austere, and less Puritan in character.

From the standpoint of a much later and ecumenical age, we can assume that the danger of the Laudian Anglican church was that the reverence for beauty might be a substitute for ethical duty, and that the danger in Puritan architecture was that colorblindness and poverty of the imagination might be confused with simplicity and austerity so that the *tabula Domini* could become a *tabula rasa*.

---

[49] *Ratio Disciplinae Fratrum Nov.-Anglorum* (Boston, 1726), 5.

11

Conclusion:
A Triple Analytical Perspective

It is good to conclude a study of this kind by broadening the horizons, and by viewing American Puritan worship in a triple perspective: retrospective, comparative, and evaluative. The first perspective will involve a retrospective look at significant changes in the history and its causes. The second perspective will be a transatlantic comparison of Puritan worship during the same period in both old and New England. The third perspective will be a broad, analytical assessment of the strengths and weaknesses of Puritan worship.

In detailing the changes in public worship, the major source of information is Cotton Mather's *Ratio disciplinae fratrum Nov.-Anglorum* (1726). It bears a highly significant subtitle: *A Faithful Account of the Discipline Practised in the Churches of New England. With Interspersed and Instructive Reflections on the Discipline of the Primitive Churches.*[1] Its value likes in the orthodox conservatism of its learned author, who, in his day, was the most prominent clergyman in the Massachusetts Bay Colony, as well as being the Colony's proud historian, and a Fellow of the Royal Society of London. In many cases his statements about

---

[1] Cotton Mather's *Ratio disciplinae* was published in Boston.

developments will be checked from other primary
sources, especially if they belong to the more liberal
group in the Brattle Street Church in Boston, or to the pioneer of liberal measures in Northampton, Solomon
Stoddard.

Changes in the Regular Lord's Day Worship

In Cotton's day it was obligatory to provide a running
commentary on any passage of Scripture. There were no
lessons without exposition. This was understandable
when *lectio continua* was customary, and preachers, instead of taking themes from the Bible, preached through
whole books of the Bible in series. It was also natural
when several churches at the outset had two ministers,
one a teacher and the other a pastor, that the necessity of
exposition should always be insisted upon, and especially
when the novelty of Puritanism's divergences from
Anglicanism required biblical justification as its authority. On the other hand, while the newer homiletical
method of taking a text rather than a chapter of the Bible
could lead to the use of a text as a pretext, it had the com-
pensating advantage of allowing a preacher to take a central theme and illustrate it from many sections of the
Scriptures. It may additionally have led to the production of shorter sermons. However, the novelty—for
which there was good Anglican precedent—according to
Cotton Mather, "has not been so generally taken up as
many have wished for."[2]

---

[2] Op. cit., 64. Yet Mather admits that lections without commentary
are read "in many of our churches." He objects to it because there
is no clear tradition of it in Puritan churches, because it is not a pastor's task, and because many sermons already include much

In early days it was rare for a preacher to take sermon notes with him into the pulpit. He was expected to be fluent extemporaneously in both prayers and sermons. In the early eighteenth century, however, sermon notes could be used provided that the preacher was not glued to them. Cotton Mather says the general practice is "that the Preachers would keep to such a *Middle Way* in it, as not thereby to lose or blunt, the Vivacity of their Delivery; but, as it has been sometimes express'd, *Cast* their Eye upon the *Quiver*, for the Arrow to be fetched from thence, and yet not keep it entirely *fixed* on the *Quiver*, all the while the Arrow is delivering."[3]

The Lord's Prayer was considered by the first American Puritans as a model or pattern for prayers, rather than a prayer to be repeated at each gathering for worship, as in the Roman Catholic or Anglican manner. It was possibly first used as a set prayer in the Brattle Street Church in 1699, but it was not a required item as listed in the famous *Manifesto* issued by that church.[4] In

---

Scripture, and also because many passages of the Bible are unsuitable for public reading. He does, however, point out that John Cotton approved of bare lections, basing his judgment on Deuteronomy 31:11–13 and 27:14–26.

[3] *Op. cit.*, 61. Cotton Mather went more fully into this matter in *Manductio ad Ministerium* (Boston, 1726). There he argued that ministers who bring notes into the pulpit are rightly challenged by their listeners: "How can you demand of them to Remember much of what you bring to them: when you Remember nothing of it yourself?" (p. 106). He insists upon vivacity and earnestness as important attributes of the preacher.

[4] Samuel Kirkland Lothrop, a minister of Brattle Street Church, Boston, and the author of *A History of the Church in Brattle Street, Boston* (Boston, 1851), 51, relates: "I have also received it by tradition from my predecessor, that the minister of this church was

any case, Cotton Mather does not mention the use of the Lord's Prayer in the worship of his day, but he provides a strong defense of unliturgical prayer, insisting that

> the *Pastors* reckon, that the Representation of their Peoples Condition in Prayers, with fit *Expressions of their own choosing*, is a necessary *Gift* and *Work* of the Evangelical Ministry. . . . Our Pastors by *blowing up the Flame* of the *Gift*, attain to such Measures of it, that their Flocks apprehend a *Liturgy* would be a sensible Injury unto them.[5]

After a century there was a considerable improvement in the quality of the music in the churches. Although they were slower than their Nonconformist cousins in England to follow Isaac Watts in making the transition from psalmody to hymnody (as Watts put it, "to teach my author [David] to speak like a Christian"[6]), the handful of tunes provided by *The Bay Psalm Book* were added to in the course of time, and some churches even provided psalm books to prevent the dulling practice of

---

expected or required to repeat the Lord's Prayer once in some part of the service every Sunday, and accordingly I have always observed this rule, though I have not found any authority for it but tradition, which, as it came to me, so I suppose, has been handed down from pastor to pastor." The famous Brattle Street *Manifesto*, issued at the formation of the church in 1699, is reprinted on pp. 20-26 of this history, as also in Alden T. Vaughan, ed. *The Puritan Tradition in America, 1620–1730* (New York: Harper & Row, 1972), 329–333.

[5] *Ratio disciplinae*, 46–47.

[6] This citation appears in Watt's *The Psalms of David Imitated in the Language of the New Testament and Applied to the Christian State and Worship* (London, 1719). See Watts' *Complete Works*, ed. Burder (London, 1810), IV, 119.

lining out, which destroyed both sense and harmony.[7] It appears that a reformation in church music took place in the churches of New England dating from about 1720 in which the clergy took the lead. Singing schools were established and from these issued church choirs.[8] The first Puritans considered that church choirs filched the congregation's privilege to sing God's praises with heart and voice.

Changes in the Celebration of the Sacraments

In the actual celebration of the sacraments of baptism and the Lord's Supper the changes were few, but there were important developments in the liberalizing of admission to them, as also in the preparation for the reception of the Lord's Supper, and there was an increased appreciation of the dramatic and prophetic symbolism exhibited in both sacraments.

Curiously, the only change in the ceremonial of the Lord's Supper is a regression rather than an improvement. The two prophetic signs are the fraction of the bread, as a vivid reminder that Christ's body was broken

---

[7] Cotton Mather, *Ratio disciplinae*, 52–53. See also the work of Peter Thacher and of John and Samuel Danforth published in 1723, *An Essay Preached by Several Ministers . . . as to . . . Cases of Conscience Concerning the Singing of Psalms in the Publike Worship of God . . .*, which was communicated to a council of churches on January 30, 1722/3, as an indication of the renaissance of music in Puritan worship.

[8] Ezra Hoyt Byington, *The Puritan in England and New England*, 4th ed., (New York: Franklin, 1972), 151–152. The tunes were borrowed from Ravenscroft and the favorites were Litchfield, Canterbury, York, Windsor, Cambridge, St. David's, Martyrs, Hackney, and, of course, the Old Hundredth.

on the Cross, and the libation or pouring out of the wine, which is a second signal of the Redeemer's life blood poured out in atonement for the sins of the world. Both fraction and libation were firmly insisted upon by John Cotton. The fraction could not be omitted because of the dominical declaration, "This is my body which is broken for you,"[9] quite apart from the fact that the primitive Church, as reported in the Acts of the Apostles, called the Communion service "the breaking of bread."[10] John Cotton explains the reasons for the fraction as well as the libation: "In the Lords Supper the receiving of the bread broken, and the wine poured out, is a sign and seal of my receiving the body of Christ broken for me and of his bloud shed for me."[11] Curiously enough, Cotton Mather, who is most anxious to maintain the earliest Puritan tradition, deviates from it in asserting that there is no authority for the act of libation, rudely negating the action thus: "*Though the Pouring out of the Wine* is not properly one of the *Sacramental Actions*, and if there stand any *Tankards* on the *Table* ready filled, it is accordingly omitted *there*; . . ."[12]

There is no consistency found in the frequency with which the Lord's Supper was celebrated, and one has the impression that it depended very much on the interest of

---

[9] 1 Corinthians 11:24, according to many ancient authorities, but even if it is translated as, "This is my body which is for you," the preceding words indicate that the *klasmos* or breaking of the bread was performed by Jesus as an illustrative and prophetic gesture.

[10] Acts 2:42, 46.

[11] *Spiritual Milk for Babes in Either England*, 14, in the Boston edition of 1668, originally published in London in 1646.

[12] *Ratio disciplinae*, 100.

the minister. In the 1630s the Lord's Supper was held each month ("once a moneth at least," says John Cotton[13]), as the highest privilege of the covenanted members of the church. By Cotton Mather's time there was no pattern at all. He reports as follows:

> The Churches like the *Primitive*, have no Times universally stated for their Celebration of the Eucharist. Some have it once in *Four* Weeks, some in Six, some in Eight, and some, the *first Lord's Day* in every *Kalender* Month; and some, the *last:* Some in the close of the *Afternoon:* but most in the close of the *Forenoon*. And the *Pastors* likewise reserve themselves a Liberty of *Altering* the Times as they judge for the *Emergencies*.[14]

There was, however, concern for adequate preparation for receiving Communion. Cotton Mather describes these in some detail:

> In most places there are held private *Meetings* of the Christians, on some Day of the Week, Preparatory to the Communion; and it is a frequent thing for the Pastor to be present at some or other of them; or else perhaps to hold a *Publick Lecture*.[15]

We have already indicated that there was a lengthy struggle to liberalize the admission to both sacraments. The first sign of easier access to the sacrament of baptism occurred in the Half-Way Covenant, in which baptized

---

[13] *The Way of the Churches of Christ in New England* (London, 1645), 68.

[14] *Ratio disciplinae*, 95.

[15] *Ibid.*, 97.

parents, well-informed about the Christian faith, and living an honorable life, although they had not been converted, were allowed to present their children for baptism. It was hoped that such children would themselves eventually come to a saving knowledge of Christ, make a satisfactory account of this experience before the church meeting, take the covenant, and then be welcomed at the Lord's Table. This, however, happened all too rarely, and the relatively liberal ministers, embarrassed at the minimal percentage of those who passed the hurdles from baptism to Lord's Supper, insisted on removing those hurdles, except for a knowledge of Christian principles and living a decent life without scandal. The radical innovator was Solomon Stoddard, who argued that only God knew who was a genuine Christian, not the minister nor the local congregation, so that there was no infallible way to keep hypocrites from the Lord's Table, and in fact the hurdles were keeping many decent Christians away from Communion because they disliked having to make a public "relation" or narration of their experience of grace. Furthermore, he insisted that the Communion itself was a moving means of grace which might well succeed in being a "converting ordinance."

Stoddard had proposed this step in a controversial sermon in 1677 and had defended this view before the Reforming Synod of 1679. It was attacked by Increase Mather in a sermon before the Massachusetts General Court in 1677 as well as in the synod. Increase Mather's view was that to accept Stoddard's proposal was to lose New England's traditional restriction of the Lord's Supper to visible saints. Stoddard's most elaborate defense of his theory appeared in his *Appeal to the Learned*. Here he affirmed:

> This Ordinance [the Lord's Supper] has a proper tendency in its own nature to Convert men. Herein men may learn the necessity & sufficiency of the Death of Christ in order to Pardon. Here is an affecting offer of Christ crucifyed; here is a Sealing of the Covenant, that if men come to Christ, they shall be saved, which is a great means to convince of safety in coming to Christ.
>
> All Ordinances are for the Saving good of those that they are to be administered unto. This Ordinance is according to Institution to be applyed to visible Saints, though Unconverted, therefore it is for their Saving good, and consequently for their Conversion.[16]

By 1690 Stoddard was having influence even upon his critics, for in that year Cotton Mather's *Companion for Communicants* allowed that assurance was not absolutely necessary for attendance at the Lord's Table, and the intending communicant had only to write a note to the minister or privately inform him of the impact preaching and reading the Bible had made on his soul, so that even such a bruised reed could expect to be accepted by Christ. By 1726 Mather acknowledged the varying attitudes of different churches in admission to Communion. Some pastors, he declares, believe that any test before admission is quite without New Testament authority, whereas others affirm with equal rigor "that nothing short of a Probable and Credible Profession of a *Justifying Faith*, qualifies for the *Eucharist;* where the Benefits of that Faith are sealed unto us." Mather himself belongs to the second group, and believes that "experimental piety" is

---

[16] *Op. cit.*, 25. For the founding fathers, "visible saints, though unconverted" would be perceived as a flat contradiction.

also to be examined.[17] It is disappointing to report that lowering the hurdles did not result in a larger attendance at the Lord's Supper even in Stoddard's own church, and it seems that many were wholly indifferent to the Supper, while others were too eager to restrict it to the elect and may have confused them with the elite.

The lowering of the hurdles to membership had been going on for a much longer time than was indicated by the Mather-Stoddard debates, although they undoubtedly hastened the process. Before the 1680s women who were candidates for full membership could either be examined in private by the minister or have their relations read. In 1678 the Boston Third Church allowed bashful men to offer private testimony about the state of their souls and voted in 1685 to exclude the wider membership from discussing their qualifications for membership. In the same year the Charlestown Church voted that "men's relations (their own pronouncing theirs having been constantly found inconvenient) be for the future read." Although these were important changes in procedure, they were pointers, according to David D. Hall, to the abolition of the category of full communion, the very step that Solomon Stoddard had already taken.[18]

Apart from all the considerable discussion, and the better instruction on the preparation for and the meaning and value of the Communion that was provided by a host of treatises both English and American, it appears that the

---

[17] *Ratio disciplinae*, 95.

[18] *The Faithful Shepherd: A History of the New England Ministry in the Seventeenth Century* (Chapel Hill: University of North Carolina Press, 1972), 205–206. Hall notes the procedural changes in detail and supplies the historical undergirding.

Lord's Supper was celebrated very much as it had always been in New England, but that perhaps Calvin's sons had won the debate over the sons of Zwingli, and that memorialism (or, as Gregory Dix termed it, "the doctrine of the real absence") was less common than virtualism—a conviction of the real spiritual presence of Christ at His own Table.

What is even more impressive, however, is the change in the character of sacramental spirituality late in the seventeenth century. Previously this had been excessively subjective and introspective and its exponents seemed suspicious of the possibility of any communication of the infinite and invisible God with the finite and visible creation. This new approach E. Brooks Holifield terms "the piety of sensation," and he rightly emphasizes the confluence of many factors conducive to its development. He argues that "it is revealing that the expanding interest in natural theology, the new meditative practices, hermeneutical developments, and sacramental piety all converged towards a common ideal: the rehabilitation of the visible."[19] No New England ministers visualized the symbolic significance of the Lord's Supper more vividly than Edward Taylor and Samuel Willard.

Changes in the Occasional Services

The most dramatic changes did not take place in the regular or sacramental services, but in the occasional ones, such as ordination, marriages, and funerals.

The ordinations are evidence of a developing profes-

---

[19] *The Covenant Sealed: Puritan Sacramental Theology, 1570–1720* (New Haven, Conn.: Yale University Press, 1974), 137.

sionalism in the pastors which led to an almost complete clericalization of the leadership. The earliest Puritan churches in New England regarded the election or choice of a man as minister by a local church to be more important than ordination, and election was an exclusively lay act. So much was this the case that ministers were required to be re-ordained in accepting a new pastorate. Thomas Hooker had clearly formulated these principles in two of his statements. One is: "*Ordination* doth depend upon the peoples lawfull *Election*, as an Effect upon the *Cause*, by virtue of which it is fully Administered." The second is: "There ought to be no Ordination of a Minister at large, *Namely such as should make him Pastour without a People.*"[20]

Ordinations grew increasingly more formal and the roles of the principal participants in them became exclusively clerical, as can be seen in Peter Thacher's ordination at Milton Church in 1681. This was carried out according to a strict fourfold procedure. Following the vote to proceed to ordination, four ministers laid their hands on the ordinand, while one of them invoked the Holy Spirit in prayer, then the charge reminding the ordinand of his responsibilities was delivered by the Reverend Mr. Torry, and the right hand of fellowship, symbolizing recognition by the neighboring churches, was given by the Reverend Mr. Willard. The final blessing was given by the new minister.[21] This entire reversal of the earliest procedure was continued thereafter, with the only lay

[20] *A Survey of the Summe of Church Discipline*, Part 2, 41 and 66. These positions were affirmed in the Cambridge Platform of 1645.
[21] See Thacher's "Diary," MS. I, 212 (typescript of the Massachusetts Historical Society, Boston).

contribution to the rite being the vote of the church members. As Charles Hambrick-Stowe points out, such clericalization of the ordination rite made local congregations reluctant to ordain candidates for the ministry, and in some cases trial ministries lasted for years.[22]

One small but significant change was the relieving of the ordinand from "preaching himself in" at the ordination service which was a very exhausting emotional experience. Happily, the service was abbreviated in the course of time. Cotton Mather wrote: "The speeches on these Occasions are now usually *Concise* and *Short*. But formerly they were sometimes *Ample* and *Copious*."[23] As one thinks of Mather's own ordination ceremony in 1685, in which he had that morning, prior to the rite, preached and prayed for a total of three hours, and the other Boston ministers had indulged in a marathon of competitive sacred oratory, it is easy to believe that brevity is the soul of wit, and was desperately needed.[24]

Growing clericalization inevitably led to ministers taking a larger part in the rites of marriage and the burial of the dead. In the former case they replaced the magistrates, and in the latter enlarged their former minimal (and sometimes mute) role.

Marriage services which were formerly conducted in the courthouse or the home were later held in the meetinghouse or the home, but they were always performed

---

[22] *The Practice of Piety: Puritan Devotional Disciplines in Seventeenth-Century New England* (Chapel Hill: University of North Carolina Press, 1982), 129.

[23] *Ratio disciplinae*, 33.

[24] *The Diary of Cotton Mather*, (New York: Fredrick Ungar, 1911) 99f.

by the minister. Cotton Mather observes that at the first
settlement of the English colonies in North America,
"*Marriage* was ever celebrated by the *Civil Magistrate;*
who not only gave the Marriage Covenant unto the
Parties, but also made the *Prayers* proper for the Occasion." He adds, with professional concern, "However, if
a *Minister* were present, he was desired usually to make at
least one of the Prayers." In his pompous way, Mather
avers also that "it is most proper" for the ministers to offer the "*Prayers* of *Benediction* on the *Marriage.*"[25]

The most striking change of all took place in the burial
service. Originally there was merely a silent following of
the coffin on foot to the cemetery for the burial, without
even a prayer to speed the soul on its way or to comfort
the mourners. This is explicable perhaps only by a de-
terministic theology that implied that the fate of the deceased was already divinely decided upon so that prayers
were otiose.

Both the ritual and the ceremonial of funerals became
greatly elaborated. "In many Towns of *New-England,*"
wrote Cotton Mather, "the Ministers make agreeable
Prayers with the People come together at the *House* to attend the *FUNERAL of the Dead.* And in some, the
Ministers make a short *Speech* at the *Grave.* But in other
places both of these Things are wholly omitted."[26] The
first time prayer was offered in the home of a mourning
family was in 1685, and the first spoken eulogy was
recorded in 1701.[27] Cotton Mather's brief account, however, gives no indication of the vast development in the

---

[25] *Ratio disciplinae*, 111–112.
[26] *Op. cit.*, 117.
[27] Sewall's *Diary* (ed. M. Halsey Thomas), I, 449.

ceremonial preparations or accouterments of funerals. Nor does he mention that it became customary to return to the home of the deceased for a feast.[28]

The whole attitude toward the final rite of passage changed in radical fashion. Larzer Ziff rightly categorized it as a transition from the monitory to the sentimental, from a reminder of the vanity of this world to a degree of self-indulgence in religious devotion with a place for comfort.[29]

Although the first Puritan settlers had objected strongly to the character of Anglican funeral rites in which every deceased person was committed to the grave "in sure and certain hope of resurrection to everlasting life," however scandalous that life had been, and repudiated all encomiastic references, their early eighteenth-century successors disregarded such considerations. Eulogies were a common part of the sermon, devoted to the memory of the deceased and printed at the cost of the family, and the sermon was preached on the night of the funeral. Moreover, gloves and rings were sent to relatives and friends of the deceased who attended the funeral wearing such, as well as mourning scarves and cloaks; these attendees took turns in carrying the coffin to the grave, except when plumed horses were used to draw the hearse, as was the case in some wealthier funerals.[30]

The new sensibility was marked by the provision of family tombs, as by the images carved on the gravestones

---

[28] David E. Stannard, *The Puritan Way of Death* (New York: Oxford University Press, 1977), 113*f.*

[29] *Puritanism in America: New Culture in a New World* (New York: Viking Press, 1973), 253.

[30] Stannard, op. cit., 113*f.*

where death symbols gave way to signs of immortality. In short, the early New England burials became fully-fledged funerals within a century.

Some Causes of the Changes

What were the causes for these changes in the rites and ceremonies of Puritan worship in New England? As we have seen, one was the increasing professionalism that was developing among the ministers themselves. Perhaps it was inevitable that they should seem to be imitating their Anglican counterparts across the Atlantic in the more civil rituals of marriages and funerals, since the Puritan ministers were the "established" clergy of the New England colonies. An allied factor was the increasingly felt need for a growing connectionalism in church polity which was accelerated in the last decade of the seventeenth century by the temporary union of Congregationalists and Presbyterians in England. This had been seen much earlier in the consociation of churches in a more disciplined order in the Hartford Colony under the influence of Thomas Hooker. It was, however, to become more widespread in the formalization of ordinations in which ministerial neighbors of the church of the ordinand played leading roles and in the demand for and establishment of synods in which joint doctrinal and pragmatic platforms could be prepared to deal with common problems. All this tended to alienate the clergy from the laity as they developed into a superior and almost sacerdotal caste.

Another factor causing change was the increasing toleration demanded for other forms of church order than Independents in New England. After the restoration of the monarchy in England in 1660, the Episcopalians in

North America had to be tolerated and, after the Glorious Revolution of 1688, the Baptists and Quakers also. Indeed, there may have developed an imitation of the Episcopalians in a more formal ritual and a more elaborate ceremonial for marriages and funerals.

A third cause for change was making the sacraments more readily available to the congregations at large because so small a percentage of those baptized ever became communicants. Already in 1699 the followers of the new Brattle Street Church in Boston, the fourth Congregational church in that city, liberalized the approach to the sacraments. They declared in their founding *Manifesto*: "We allow of baptism to those who profess their faith in Christ and obedience to Him, and to the children of such, yet we dare not refuse it to any child offered to us by any professed Christian upon his engagement to see it educated, if God give it life, and ability, in the Christian religion."[31] Furthermore, admission or refusal was left entirely in the hands of the pastor. The same church declined the requirement of any public or private relation of conversion for admittance to the Lord's Supper:

> But we assume not to impose upon any a public relation of their experiences; however if anyone think himself bound in conscience to make such a relation, let him do it. For we conceive it sufficient if the pastor publicly declare himself satisfied in the person offered to our communion, and seasonably propound him.[32]

By 1718, when Thomas Prince was ordained to the

---

[31] *The Puritan Tradition in America*, ed. Alden T. Vaughan, 331.
[32] *Ibid.*

South Church in Boston, he preached a sermon that
sounded the alarm as to the disparity between the large
number baptized and the paucity of those who were
admitted to the Lord's Supper. Only 14 percent surmounted the hurdles surrounding the Lord's Table. He
claimed:

> . . . it appears from the Records that the Church
> was founded on the 12 of May 1669; And since that
> Time which is not yet Fifty Years, to Seven
> Hundred Communicants & near as many more that
> have Own'd the Covenant, there have been about
> Five Thousand Baptized Persons.[33]

The more significant fact in relation to leakage is that
many members of the community of a given town were
not even baptized, far less communicants. Kenneth
Lockridge's studies of the town records of Dedham are
illuminating. He found that 80 percent of the children
born between 1644 and 1653 were baptized, but that only
40 percent of the infants born between 1651 and 1664
were baptized, and that church membership had declined to 56 percent of the male ratepayers by 1661.[34]
Clearly this worsening situation called either for the
preaching of more converting sermons or for the relaxing
of the standards of admission to both sacraments. The
conservative ministers demanded the former strategy,

---

[33] *A Sermon Delivered by Thomas Prince, M.A. on Wednesday October
1, 1718 at His Ordination to the Pastoral Charge of the South Church in
Boston* (Boston, 1718), 3.
[34] Lockridge's essay, "The History of a Puritan Church, 1637-
1736," is contained in Alden Vaughan and Francis J. Bremer, eds.
Puritan New England (New York: St. Martin's Press, 1977), 97f.

and the liberal ministers the latter strategy.

Another cause of change was the increasing sophistication developing in Boston and its growing cosmopolitanism as a seaport, and its imitation by other towns with growing populations. This can be seen in various manifestations, such as in Judge Sewall rebuking his daughter for receiving the Communion elements with gloved hands and his dislike of his minister Cotton Mather wearing a periwig, or in the development of more elegant church architecture and fittings, with Palladian windows, triple galleries, and boxed, paneled and curtained pews, together with towers and steeples on the exterior of the meetinghouses. In addition, in prayers and sermons, there was a greater courtesy toward God and humanity in manner and more polished elegance in language.

At the same time there was a significant theological change. At the end of the seventeenth century, Arminianism was creeping in to allow not only a greater percentage than Shepard's one in a thousand who might hope for salvation, but also a place for greater collaboration with the deity, technically known as synergism. Contemporary with this development was a recognition of the evidence of the divine impact on the natural world, and God was seen to be more immanent than transcendent. All this inner change presaged and demanded an external rationalization and sophistication of behavior.

Furthermore, there was a new and important difference in the relation of the New England religious community to its English counterpart of the same faith and polity. When the Puritans first came to these shores in a revolutionary era, they were acutely conscious of demonstrating the new holy commonwealth (either a New Jerusalem or at least a New Canaan) in North

America as comprised of a community of visible saints.
Cotton's accounts of the development of nascent Puritanism, unfettered by monarch, prelate, or even new
presbyter, were eagerly read in England as the wave of
the future.

However, only a generation later this country was no
longer the cynosure of English eyes, because history had
bypassed New England, and victorious Puritanism in
England had become by 1662 persecuted Nonconformity. The great expectations aroused by "the errand into
the wilderness" had ended in a bleak house: the land of
promise had become only a province, and a distant one at
that, of Great Britain. In consequence, according to
Daniel Boorstin, ultimately the heirs of the original
Puritans had moved from Providence to pride and from
mystery to mastery.[35] Alan Simpson sensed the consequent disillusionment that set in vividly:

> There is less and less to sustain their sense of the
> New World as a beacon for the Old when the
> progress of events in England reduced the New
> England Way first to a backwater of the Puritan
> spirit and later to a provincial anachronism.[36]

Moreover, the inhospitable conditions of the first two
generations developed a type of character for religious

---

[35] *Puritanism and the American Experience*, ed. Michael McGiffert
(Reading, Mass.: Addison-Wesley, 1969), 109. Boorstin's essay
demonstrates how the very success of original Puritanism led to its
undoing, as the God-directed became self-sufficient, and thrift and
hard work combined to produce commercial success and worldliness.
[36] *Puritanism in Old and New England* (Chicago: University of
Chicago Press, 1955), 34.

purposes which was hardworking, enthusiastic, honest, and thrifty and which was bound to become a worldly success. In the course of time the revolutionary enthusiasm of the first generation stratified into a Puritan tradition in which the chief changes were in appearance, not in essence, in ceremonialism, not in the ritual or structure of worship, but even so there was, as a result of all the causes we have enumerated, a difference in attitude and spirit. It was cooler, more rational, less otherworldly, and one senses that the Puritan was becoming more of a Yankee.

Puritan Worship in Old and New England Compared

We stated in the beginning that it would be interesting to see if there were any significant differences between the two transatlantic varieties of Puritan worship. In fact there were several such differences.

The most striking innovation in American Puritan worship and the consequence of a desperate idealistic attempt to maintain a church of visible saints against all original sin and human depravity was the requirement of a narrative or relation of the experience of conversion before admission to the owning of the covenant of the church and hence to the chief sacrament, the Lord's Supper. It was both the glory and agony of the American Puritan churches. Edmund Morgan seems to have proven his contention that the test of saving faith (already evident in the Separatist Henry Ainsworth) was first applied rigidly among the non-Separating Puritans of Massachusetts and thence spread via the Plymouth, Connecticut, and New Haven colonies back to

England.[37] This took place about 1634, was debated violently from 1677 to the 1720s, and was reinstituted by Solomon Stoddard's grandson and former assistant at Northampton, the eminent theologian and evangelist Jonathan Edwards, for all candidates for membership in 1748. It was also defended by Edwards in his *A Humble Inquiry into the Rules of the Word of God, Concerning the Qualifications Requisite to a Complete Standing and Full Communion in the Visible Christian Church* (Boston, 1749). This gave a notable propulsion toward conversionist preaching and revivalism that has been characteristic of the development of popular American Protestantism in the nineteenth and twentieth centuries. That is an index of the importance of this innovation.

This innovation was exported to England, but it appears that it was both shorter-lived and less stringently applied there than in New England. There was less uniformity in England and less compulsion. Moreover, if the relations reported by Rogers in Dublin were typical of transatlantic Puritan requirements, they expressed greater assurance of salvation than the narrations reported by Shepard in New England. Indeed, the latter frequently expressed anxiety, uncertainty, doubt, inconclusiveness, and fear of hypocrisy.[38] The members of the Independent churches in England could express their convictions about the work of grace in subsequent church

---

[37] *Visible Saints: The History of a Puritan Idea* (New York: New York University Press, 1963; rpt. Ithaca, N.Y.: Cornell University Press, 1965), 66.

[38] Patricia Caldwell, *The Puritan Conversion Narrative: The Beginnings of American Expression* (Cambridge, England: Cambridge University Press, 1983), 78, 122–123.

meetings. Such an opportunity was effectively excluded in New England after its abuse by the Antinomians, and, according to Patricia Caldwell, this meant that the New England conversion narrative "takes on a special, even mysterious importance, not only because New England was its birthplace, but also because it was confined to that one special moment when the believer sought union with the church."[39]

There was also a second important difference between English and American Puritanism. In the mid-seventeenth century both countries were buoyed up with millenarianism but that hope was quickly crushed in England by the restoration of the monarchy and the renewed domination of the Church of England. Millenarianism lived on in a modified manner in New England for a further century in the foundation and development of the United States of America.[40]

It had impelled the original errand into the wilderness, as the voyaging Puritans conceived themselves to be the New Israel, journeying from the Egypt of sin, crossing the Red Sea of baptism, and wandering through the wilderness in the Canaan of New England. In a second and peculiar historical sense, their journey had a unique meaning for them because they had left a sinful land, crossing the stormy and faith-testing Atlantic, to gain a new life in fidelity to God's ordinances, and were struggling to maintain that life as visible saints in the wilder-

---

[39] *Op. cit.*, 79.

[40] This view is carefully developed by Mason I. Lowance, Jr. in *The Language of Canaan: Metaphor and Symbol in New England from the Puritans to the Transcendentalists* (Cambridge, Mass.: Harvard University Press, 1980).

ness—in the hope of living with the saints in a glorious thousand-year rule on earth. In the vivid words of Sacvan Bercovitch, "Their summons from Egypt was an evangelical call, their Atlantic crossing was tantamount to conversion, their hardships in settling the country were the temptations of Satan, the blossoming New World 'garden' made tangible the *hortus inclusus* of the redeemed soul."[41] When the founders did not use the image of the "errand," they spoke of a "city set on a hill." Its purpose was clearly exemplary, that the world might behold in New England the final and climactic development of the Reformation and imitate it.

As the original ambition to be the model for England to follow failed and faded, the succeeding generations revised their sense of national election, as can be seen in their jeremiads. The paradox was that even in confessing their failure (in comparison with their ancestors) they were celebrating their communal loyalty to God. This millenarianism is as vigorously maintained by Cotton Mather as it is by Jonathan Edwards. There was, it should be noted, no English equivalent to the jeremiads or the extended millenarianism, for the English Puritans settled down to a second-class religious and social status from 1662 onward as mere Nonconformists or Dissenters.

Moreover, the jeremiads and millenarianism were linked, as Sacvan Bercovitch has indicated: "And like the errand into the wilderness, the genetics of salvation is a distinct product of American Puritanism. It blends the heterogeneous covenants of community and grace; and it

---

[41] *The American Puritan Imagination: Essays in Revaluation*, ed. Sacvan Bercovitch (New York: Cambridge University Press, 1974), Introduction, 11.

adapts the rhetoric to new conditions without abandoning the founders' views."[42]

A third American Puritan distinction has already been hinted at. This is that in its function as the "established Church" in New England, Independency or Congregationalism dominated the rites of civil religion for over two centuries, just as the Anglicans did in England, while the English Puritans were persecuted under the Clarendon Code from 1662 to 1688 and thereafter tolerated as inferior religious and social citizens. In consequence, the American Puritan meetinghouses dominated the landscape and the skyscape of New England towns and villages as the centers of religious and civic community life. Furthermore, while English Puritan ministers were disqualified through their Nonconformity from celebrating important civil anniversaries, American Puritan clergy preached with great panache on such civil occasions as election or artillery days. On such days the clergy were interpreters of the national spirit and destiny.

Election day was an occasion in the spring set for the counting of the votes for the governor and his assistants. It was customary in each colony's capital to deliver an election sermon before the assembled magistrates and such citizens as could be packed into the largest meetinghouse. Typical ministerial themes included jeremiads, the flaying of crying sins, and the qualities needed by magistrates.[43] Willard's election-day sermon of 1682 in-

---

[42] *The American Jeremiad* (Madison: University of Wisconsin Press, 1978), 65.

[43] Samuel Eliot Morison, *The Puritan Pronaos: Studies in the Intellectual Life of New England in the Seventeenth Century* (New

dicated how unpopular this task was, since "the fouler the Stomack the more nauseous is the Physick."[44]

The annual artillery sermons were delivered to the company "at an annual muster and drumhead election of officers," and the conventional discourses were, according to Samuel Eliot Morison, the themes of preparedness and duties of a Christian soldier.[45]

A fourth, little-known but important contribution of American to English Puritan worship was architectural. The American meetinghouse appears to have significantly influenced both the structure and the style of English meetinghouses. There was a near sixty-year period when Americans were building their meetinghouses (from 1629 to 1688) when the English Puritans had no need to build any because they took over the Anglican churches during the Commonwealth and Protectorate, and adapted them to their own use. They built their own meetinghouses only from 1688 onward when the accession of William and Mary brought tolerance. What was more natural than to then imitate the original colonial meetinghouses? It is also likely that some of the recent graduates of Harvard, finding better salaries and more openings as ministers in England than New England, re-

---

York: New York University Press, 1938), 170.

[44] Samuel Willard's "The Only Sure Way to Prevent Threatened Calamity," printed in *The Child's Portion* (Boston, 1684), 163–164. See also John Norton's election-day sermon of 1661, analyzed by Babette May Levy, *Preaching in the First Half-Century of New England History* (Hartford, Conn.: The American Society of Church History, 1945), 95f.

[45] *Op. cit.*, 171. Morison refers sarcastically to "the sort of pacifist-preparedness sophistry" of such sermons, and illustrates it from one preached by Urian Oakes in 1672.

called for English builders the shapes of American meetinghouses with the greatest pride and nostalgia.

The distinctive shape and arrangement of the meetinghouses in New England comprised rectangular buildings with the pulpit against one of the long walls (usually on the north side) with the main door on the opposite long wall, with galleries on the three sides from which the congregants using them could easily hear and see the preacher in the pulpit on the fourth wall. Behind the preacher there would often be a large, round-topped Palladian window, and all the windows were of transparent, not stained, glass. Below the pulpit was the seat for the deacons and the central Communion table from which the deacons would carry the consecrated elements to the members of the church. The earliest churches had forms and benches, and as the churches grew in prosperity, pews replaced them; these pews were eventually paneled and curtained, and paid for by the owners. Family pews indicated that the earlier division of men on one side and women on the other side of the meetinghouse had been abandoned.

It is, of course, possible that Sir Christopher Wren's "auditory churches" with their galleries had an impact on both American and English Puritan church buildings, but they were generally much more elegant, and adorned with towers and steeples much earlier than in New England. Furthermore, in Wren's churches the arrangement of the seating, aisles, pulpit, and the Communion table or altar was quite different from the Puritan organization. The architectural historian Marian Cord Donnelly sums up the situation fairly:

> The most dramatic impact of the mid-seventeenth century meetinghouses was on the Nonconformist chapels of England built during the last decade of the century. Here in such chapels as those of Norwich and Ipswich . . . the internal arrangements were clearly derived from New England, with the pulpit on one long wall and galleries facing it on the other three sides.[46]

The only difference was the dual, that is, religious and secular use of the meetinghouses in New England, due to the dominance of Congregationalism.

At the same time, in fairness to English Puritanism, it should be mentioned that during the same period there was a remarkable efflorescence of sacramental meditations and guides that may well have owed much to their authors' persecuted lives "under the Cross" in the second half of the seventeenth century, and the transition from psalmody to hymnody was triumphantly made in the great theological hymns of Isaac Watts, the English Puritan, who alone deserves comparison with the greatest English hymn writer, Charles Wesley.

Analytical Conclusion and Summary Evaluation

It is the unity rather than the significant differences between Puritan worship in England and New England that appears to be more significant. The honorable term "Puritan" was well deserved in both countries, for the enduring aim in worship was to maintain only Christ's pure ordinances as authorized by the Word of God rather than determined by the conventions of ecclesiastical

---

[46] *The New England Meetinghouses of the Seventeenth Century* (Middletown, Conn.: Wesleyan University Press, 1968), 104.

tradition or the willfulness of human invention or fancy. There is at the heart of Puritan worship, both American and English, a profound sense of obedience to God's recorded mandates as having the highest priority. There are two and only two dominical sacraments, and no sacramentalia. Moreover, these sacraments are very carefully "fenced" to prevent pollution by unworthy recipients. Preaching was maintained as the chief means of grace because by it souls were condemned by the judgment of God and converted by the grace of God to repentance and justifying faith, and empowered by the Holy Spirit. This could never be done by the mere repetition of printed homilies. Whole chapters of Scripture seemed to the early settlers of the Puritans to declare the will of God better than mere paragraphs or snippets of lessons. Music was restricted to the metrical psalms because these were as near to the Holy Writ as translations in rhyme could possibly be. Creeds were replaced by the signing and recital of church covenants because they were affirmations of loyalty to God offered from the heart and requiring the obedience of the will, and could not be treated as merely historical rather than contemporary declarations of faith. Instead of a time-hallowed liturgy, the minister, after profound reflection on the Word of God, prayed from a deep knowledge of his flock in the intimate and natural phraseology extemporaneously inspired by the Holy Spirit, as he was directed to do it in St. Paul's example: "For we know not how to pray as we ought; but the Spirit Himself maketh intercession for us . . . and He that searcheth the hearts knoweth what is the mind of the Spirit, because He maketh intercession for the saints according to the will of God."[47] In all these ways, including the excommunication of unworthy church members and extreme care in admission of church members after an examination of their faith, morals, and experience of saving grace, both sets of Puritans tried to maintain the high ideal of making and maintaining their churches as covenanted communities of visible saints through the obedience of faith. This was the steel in the Puritan spirit and ecclesiology.

But if faith in its obedience and trust was dominant, the two other theological virtues of love and hope were cultivated strenuously as well. Who could doubt that Christian love was manifested in the worship when the minister included in his petitionary and intercessory prayers the "bills" or notes handed to him by members of the congregation on behalf of those in anxiety, bereavement, sickness, or danger? Or who could doubt the importance of the hope of life everlasting on those solemn Sabbaths that were filled with the holy exercises of public or private piety and that were believed to be a rehearsal of the life in heaven where the invisible saints adored God?

Classical Puritan worship on both sides of the Atlantic was also marked by a simplicity sometimes amounting to austerity in its ceremonial, as in its architecture. The minister would ascend into the high pulpit like Moses climbing Sinai, clad in a grave black gown whose somberness was relieved only by the white Genevan bands. Apart from the pews, the only furniture would be the high central pulpit on the ledge of which rested a copy of the Bible, which was lit by clear illumi-

---

[47] Romans 8:26, 27.

nation from the Palladian window behind him, and the
central Communion table beneath the pulpit. There
were no stained-glass windows, no carved saints in
niches, no rood screen with the crucified Christ watched
by his mourning Virgin Mother and beloved disciple
John, no brilliantly embossed ceilings, no beguiling organ
music or the soaring trebles of boys' choirs countered by
the tenors and basses of adult male choristers. There
were no processions, bowings, crossings, or other gestures; no responses to keep attention during the longer
prayers. In short, there was hardly any concession made
to human psychology or to the delight of the eye or the
ear. This was the most economical simplicity imaginable.

But it also made for a profound spirituality, not indeed for expert ascetics, but for wayfaring men and
women, in fact the priesthood of all believers. This was
no worship for those who wanted a convenient or com-
placent deity or a lightening of the strictures of the conscience. It led to the strengthening of resolution and
courage. The aim of this worship, as of every kind of
Calvinist cultus, was sanctification, the deeds that prove
dedication and devotion to Christ. It was a highly vertebral worship—the parent of Free Church worship—
which has had a most powerful influence in the English-
speaking world as among citizens of the Third World, and
its impact is very far from being spent.

Unquestionably also, it has had its weaknesses.
Among them, its admirable biblical authority occasionally ran to bibliolatry; its spirituality often became introspective and anxiety-ridden; its fear of idolatry prevented it from making use of other kinds of praise than
psalm singing, and from the harmonies of stringed instruments and organs, and rendered it almost colorblind.

Such beauty as a meetinghouse had was that of an etching, like Rembrandt's, but there was not a hint in the interior that the seventeenth century was also the time of El Greco and Rubens, with their vivid reds, yellows, purples, and greens, used to the glory of God. The extemporaneous prayers were often full of biblical cadences, resonances, and rhythms, but they could often deteriorate into copious and conventional repetitiousness, so opposed to the concentrated devotion of a collect. Puritanism's anxiety to be spiritual often made it forgetful that humans are not discarnate spirits but embodied souls needing the avenues of all the senses through which God and human beings approach us. In the repudiation of a printed and formal liturgy, Puritanism missed the control and balance of the prayerful experience and tried spiritual techniques of many centuries, and was forced to accept a shorter tradition largely of its own restricted interpretation.

Yet all in all, Puritan worship in both Englands, old and New, was ideally constructed to train and express a resistance movement of the Holy Spirit and to promote the heroic virtues in men and women of faith.

Index

Figure 1

The "Ship Meeting House" or Old Ship Church in Hingham, MA. The original structure was erected in 1681. It is the only surviving Puritan meetinghouse.

Figure 2

A detail of the loft timbers that give the Old Ship Church its name.

Figure 3

The pulpit from the main aisle.

Figure 4

The Pastor's chair.

Figure 5

The pews as seen from the pulpit.

Figures 6 & 7

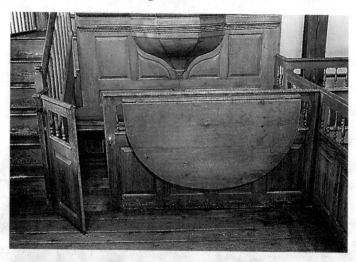

The communion table with the leaf down.
The communion table with the leaf up.